THE REPRESENTATION OF WOM

Selected Papers from the English Institute
New Series

The Representation of Women in Fiction

*Selected Papers
from the English Institute, 1981*

New Series, no. 7

*Edited, with an Introduction, by Carolyn G. Heilbrun and
Margaret R. Higonnet*

THE JOHNS HOPKINS UNIVERSITY PRESS
BALTIMORE AND LONDON

The Johns Hopkins University Press, Baltimore, Maryland 21218
The Johns Hopkins Press Ltd., London

Library of Congress Cataloging in Publication Data
Main entry under title:

The Representation of women in fiction.

   (Selected papers from the English Institute; 1981,
new ser., no. 7)
     1. Fiction—History and criticism.   2. Women in
literature.   I. Heilbrun, Carolyn G., 1926–.
II. Higonnet, Margaret R.   III. Series: Selected papers
from the English Institute; new ser. no. 7.
PN3401.R46   1983   809'.93352042   82–12685
ISBN 0–8018–2928–3
ISBN 0–8018–2929–1 (pbk.)

In Memoriam
Robert C. Elliott and Charles T. Davis

Contents

Introduction

I

The 1981 meeting of the English Institute was both a celebration and an event. We observed the Institute's fortieth meeting with appropriate ceremony, and we witnessed an occurrence of some significance: for the first time an Institute program was devoted to feminist criticism. A fourth of the meeting, that is, explicitly denied the hitherto unquestioned assumption that women in literature were objects either to be contemplated, like daffodils and yew trees, or to be adored or pursued by male ambition and erotic activity. The decision to devote this year's volume of Selected Papers from the English Institute to the program entitled "Representation of Women in Fiction" ratified the significance of the event. Of the six essays here collected, three, those by Elizabeth Ermarth, Susan Gubar, and Nancy Miller, were part of the feminist program; one, that by Jane Marcus, was part of another program; and the essays by J. Hillis Miller and Mary Poovey were especially requested for this volume.

Professor Edward Said, my colleague at Columbia, might accurately assert his own primacy in the presentation of feminist criticism in an English Institute volume of papers. For the 1978 volume, he commissioned an essay from Catharine Stimpson entitled "Ad/d Feminam." In his preface to that volume, *Literature and Society,* Said noted that an important shift had taken place in English Institute papers during the preceding decade. "The simplest way of describing this change," he wrote, "is to say that many people became interested in *criticism,* not as a kind of literate, discriminating gloss on a 'primary' text, but as an activity that, in drawing on such disciplines as linguistics, psychoanalysis, anthropology, and philosophy, made much of itself as a highly specialized, often tendentious theoretical mode of discourse." He concluded by noting that in Stimpson's essay "sexual differentiation is released from its bondage to what she calls 'powerful, discriminatory ideologies.'" Stimpson herself enunciated the degree to which women writers "have confronted a trivialization of their textual ambitions." Their work has always been marginalized, while fields and endeavors that are highly esteemed have been populated by men.

That the English Institute has been in its forty-year history both an esteemed endeavor and chiefly populated by men is a fact made clear by Cleanth Brooks, who recalled the early years of the Institute in opening remarks entitled "Perspective." Indeed, in his very first sentence Professor Brooks denied that he was looking to the future; he offered "a voice from the past, rehearsing a bit of history and summoning up personal reminiscences." He knew well the changes "in the world of scholarship and literary criticism" since the founding of the English Institute. And he referred us, for a history of the beginnings of the Institute, to the introduction W. K. Wimsatt provided to *Literary Criticism: Idea and Act,* a 1974 anthology of Institute papers edited by Wimsatt. In addition to quoting from Wimsatt's account of the Institute's beginnings, Brooks read this passage from a letter sent to him by Rudolf Kirk, "the principal founding father himself": "In the next few months, we talked to officials of Columbia University [where the meetings were held until Columbia changed its academic calendar] to arrange for classrooms and other matters. But we overlooked the social side of our meetings, and at the first getting together we realized that we ought to have tea every afternoon. My wife, Clara Marburg Kirk, stepped in at this point. She went out to buy the necessities and to arrange everything. She acted as hostess every afternoon." Brooks did not pause over this passage in any way, but the head of every woman in the Institute's audience came up. (What these women did not hear was another passage from Rudolf Kirk's letter, now a part of the Institute's archives:

"Clara had a wonderful story to tell about how George Sherburn wouldn't read her dissertation because he had to play tennis. She wrote her dissertation under R. S. Crane, and George was second reader. And there is more if I could dig it out of my memory. Clara made a brilliant record at the U. of Chicago.") Two other women mentioned in Cleanth Brooks's "Perspective" provided a veritable history of women in literary criticism, a sort of subtext to the overt history. The first of these, the wife of Gordon Haight, Mary, produced croissants on a trip back to Yale from New York when Haight, René Wellek, and Brooks had to cope with a flat tire; her thoughtfulness allowed them to "arrive home in the greatest of good humors."

Humors were a trifle less good at the appearance of a third woman mentioned by Brooks. "Trilling," Brooks recounted, "had given a brilliant lecture in which he had described the cultural situation as the contemporary American intellectual had to view it. 'We' had had to give up this or that belief; 'we' were forced to take into account that altered fact; and so on through a whole series of 'we's.' But a tenacious little lady in the audience spoke up to deny that she was included in Mr. Trilling's 'we.' He had a right to speak for the New York Intellectual, but he did not speak to her condition, or to that of her friends. The contrast was interesting: Trilling, as always, gracious, polite and accomplished, trying to smooth her ruffled feathers, and the not fully coherent but manifestly sincere voice from the back row."

I suspect that the voice from the back row would sound a little more coherent now. Trilling's use of *we* in the essay included in the Wimsatt volume is, today, obtrusive to a remarkable degree, even if the essay is compared only with those by his peers from the Institute that were published with it. The "tenacious little lady's" feathers were, indeed, prophetically ruffled.

It is no accident that the first program in feminist criticism at the Institute should concern itself with fiction. For it is in the novel, and in the novel's shorter forms, that, as Bakhtin has argued, true diversity is possible. The novel is, he knows, the one genre that will not cease to develop, that will not purge itself of impropriety and questioning, but will continue to insist on the inappropriate and the "dialogic imagination." Shortly after the Institute meeting, I heard from someone who had attended a conference in Chicago that Wayne Booth had spoken of Bakhtin's failure to consider one discourse among the many he did consider, that would challenge the set world of other genres: feminism. Booth, I was told, had offered a feminist reading of Rabelais.

This suggests that the program devoted to feminist criticism at the 1981 meeting of the English Institute was not out of step with the times, though it may have ruffled the feathers of some who remembered an earlier day. Soon after the 1981 meeting, *Critical Inquiry* would devote an issue to "Writing and Sexual Difference"; *Yale French Studies* would devote an issue to "Feminist Perspectives: French Texts/American Contexts"; and a book by Robert Scholes, published by Yale University Press, would contain a chapter entitled "Uncoding Mama: The Female Body as Text." Scholes tells us that he might have called that chapter "The Adventures of an Organ in Language and Literature," an adventure to which he was led, he assures us, not as a feminist but as a semiotician. The organ is the clitoris. Patricia Spacks of Yale, who directed the program "Representation of Women in Fiction," mentioned in her opening remarks that this was the first Institute meeting at which sanitary napkins would be mentioned *twice*. Feminism has so far refused to be genteel, recognizing all too well what lies hidden behind such gentility.

The group of women scholars at Dartmouth who edited the feminist issue of *Yale French Studies* remarked that their working together was observed with a degree of amazement by their male colleagues. This selection of papers from the English Institute has also been edited by a group, if two may be called a group, though the only amazement may be that of the telephone company. Margaret Higonnet and I, she in Cambridge and I in New York, have consulted on the essays and the tedious details of editorship. We have decided, in the introduction, to let our individual voices be heard, mine on the "event," hers on the essays themselves.

W. K. Wimsatt concluded his introduction to the 1974 anthology of Institute papers with these words: "It is easy to contend with the fathers, to revolt against them, easy to reshape, to recolor, to contaminate received materials, easy to make our own mistakes and to reverse them, to change our minds and even to incorporate changes in our works. But not easy to execute any of these commonplaces with the kind of special reason and authority that turns them into wit and imagination." Those, indeed, are the things feminist critics must now do. Which of them, if any, are easily done I leave to others to judge. But at least the work has now begun.

CAROLYN G. HEILBRUN
Columbia University

II

A new literary history is being written today, shaped in part by feminist studies of the representation of women. The power of this feminist work to change the discussion of literature may be attributed to three distinct but mutually reinforcing phenomena: a rapid accumulation of evidence, both literary and historical; a shift in focus from discrete images to structural and semiotic analysis; and finally, the growth of a body of criticism that challenges our categories of analysis as well as the literary systems we have been analyzing.

Women's studies have altered our perception of literature by retrieving a past that had no status. One premise of this scholarship has been that our ignorance of women's past has been the product of our categories and our indifference; women's studies have therefore emphasized empirical studies yielding evidence about the historical status of women, about their daily lives, their views, and their accomplishments, including their writing. When explored from a feminist perspective, political, social, and literary history have revealed the unsuspected depths and riches of women's achievements. Women's studies have brought to light forgotten texts and drawn attention to marginal forms like diaries, in which women have inscribed their experience. The effect of this scholarship is not simply to move the textual furniture about in some version of literary spring-cleaning. The canon is changing: it is becoming more inclusive, and different, feminine strands of literary tradition can now be discerned. A sense of freshness and discovery can be felt in the best contemporary feminist writing.

By contrast, other, more established modes of literary criticism have had both the advantages and the disadvantages that attend inherited materials. Most scholarship on literary representation deals with known and accepted texts and presumes that we know the historical phenomena represented—or that those phenomena are irrelevant to the representational system. One can understand the arrogance this implies toward admittedly dated forms of positivist and empiricist scholarship: indeed, feminist critics have also indicted as unscientific and false some older, ostensibly objective scholarship. But the frequent corollary of the antipositivist attitude, an idolatry of the self-generating text, is unacceptable to the feminist. The "text," whether taken as a member of the canon that displaces unacknowledged texts, as an interpretation that selectively filters a narrative, or as the sediment of history, must be questioned.

Whereas the dominant modes of criticism today have tended to sort themselves out into antagonistic camps (Freudian, Marxist, post-structuralist, post–New Critic and so forth), one of the striking characteristics of feminist criticism has been the integration of perspectives. It has combined empirical with theoretical work in exploring ways in which history, ideology, psychology, and sociology can be brought to bear on the question, What is being represented by the characters of women in literature? The split between form and "content" which plagues our critical categories (and has its own contradictory sexual associations) has been undercut by studies of the representation of women. Narrative order implies social order. Gender may define genre. If the social determination of women's roles appears to have dictated one or two inexorable plots for women in fiction, it is also true that the social arts of women when mimed have opened up infinite galleries of rhetorical reflections, whose ironic interplay has been exploited in literature for either tragic or comic effects.

The feminist perspective, with its broad range of new evidence, has led to reinterpretation of literature about women, whether written by men or by women. Overlooked, suppressed, displaced, or incomplete patterns of female behavior have become apparent; the dimensions of women's interior lives expand. We are alerted to presences and absences that restructure works we thought we knew. In this process of reinterpretation, a number of critics, such as Elaine Showalter, have allocated a special function to the study of literature written by women (which Showalter calls "gynocritics"). They turn to works by women to find alternative representations of women, distanced if not free from the tacit assumptions of a dominant culture. Although works by women are, of course, mediated by culture, they also provide different evidence of the routines and phases that pattern women's external lives, the psychological affiliations that shape their sense of identity, and the personal ties that give women their social strength. Today this criticism is shifting from a thematic to a structural mode of analysis, linking it to the second type of criticism I shall discuss.

The labor of retrieval undertaken by feminists can be compared to the rather chic study of "marginal" literary forms. The recent multiplication of scholars and dearth of unoccupied literary territory have created a market in "minor" genres, "occasional" literature, "popular" literature, philosophic and religious literature. Work in these areas has been witty, somber, profound, and patronizing, and the same variety could be observed in studies of our topic. Criticism of sustained importance for the revision of the canon must obviously address not merely the accident of an undeveloped market but the failure of taxonomies to embrace certain types of works or to recognize certain dimensions of texts. This is the challenge raised by another recent volume of English Institute essays, edited by Leslie Fiedler and Houston Baker: *English Literature: Opening Up the Canon.* Retrieval is meaningless unless it is accompanied by revision of our ordering and interpretative processes.

Several of the essays included in this volume can be described as contributions to this ongoing labor of recovery, restitution, and revision in the field of gynocritics. Susan Gubar's essay on the changing reality and image of childbirth for women writers uses both the history of science and artistic biography to assist her in close readings of texts that span a century. She shows how the transformation of a fundamental element in female experience is linked to women's changing images of themselves as artists; she sheds light on the female psychology of literary creation as well as on the distinctive genre of the female *Künstlerroman.* In the process, she reminds us of the special significance of "intertextuality" for any reading of women writers and extends our knowledge both of familiar writers like Virginia Woolf and Dorothy Richardson and of comparably powerful texts long omitted from any canon or publisher's list.

Jane Marcus similarly brings ideological, social, and familial history to bear on the interpretation of chastity, that charged theme in Woolf's work. The wealth of her information about the heritage against which Woolf struggled enables Marcus to integrate political and sexual readings of three polemical essays and *Between the Acts.* Marcus unveils both the contradictions and the power of Woolf's critique of women's conventional familial role, suggesting that Woolf wove a protective garment of fiction for her most radical attacks on the patriarchy. The woman's role is a silent, subversive mode of communication hidden within the manifest uses of discourse, as Marcus's discussion of the myth of Philomela and Procne reveals. Or take Penelope: the truth lies in the unweaving.

The third essay belonging to this category of historical revisionism is that by Mary Poovey, which traces the "subtle ideological trails" left in Jane Austen's *Persuasion*. Poovey explicates the contradictions of bourgeois individualism experienced by women of the period, contradictions which are overtly evoked by the novel and which covertly disturb its conclusion. According to Poovey, the reconciliation for Anne Elliot of feeling and duty, of private and public "plots," can only be accomplished by the sleight of hand of romantic love, which Austen protects from deflation by encapsulating devices but which nevertheless must remain a reminder of the degree to which a woman's power to govern herself or affect society is illusory. Behind the surface of Austen's "ivory miniatures" lies a broad sweep of history-painting, depicting a society that assumes sexual inequality and whose individual women are cast adrift in the transition from *Gemeinschaft* to *Gesellschaft*.

The second type of feminist scholarship that is altering our perception of literature emphasizes structural or semiotic modes of analysis. Even contextuality can be perceived as a reflex of bourgeois individualism, an inadequate premise for the study of significance that is generated by systematic relationships. The theoretical premises of this kind of criticism are in part opposed to those of the first, more empirical type. Epistemology here displaces ontology; the feminine functions as category rather than as (un)knowable *Weib an sich*.

This structurally oriented feminist criticism, while obviously grounded in methods of analysis that have developed out of linguistic theory, also reflects a change in our everyday perception of the relationships between men and women or between individuals and society. Texts need not be interpreted as authorial plots for or against women; critics now stress instead the intersexuality of the forces that operate within the social structures of fiction, a commonsense position corresponding to the political argument that women's liberation is really men's liberation. Social forces are seen to have simultaneously shaping and disintegrating effects, at work both on their subjects and on their objects. The roles men and women play not only are complementary or capable of inversion but are doubled by individuals playing both at once. Women and men function as mutual signifiers and signifieds.

Our reassessment of literary relationships between men and women is also colored by the anthropological thesis that differentiation of genders is an expression of the more fundamental antithesis between nature and culture. Women's links to nature are, of course, rife with contradictions of value and significance. The crux of the matter, however, appears to lie not so much in women's varied, contradictory symbolism as in man's need for such distancing devices in his struggle for survival. Like a Janus-faced boundary marker, woman has faced both directions, towards culture and towards nature. Indeed, the coupling of a heroine and a villainess who represent this polarity is one of the commonplaces of literature. Truth, in fact, and even power are not always aligned with culture. Some of the most interesting writers of the past have projected culturally repressed values onto "outside" female characters in order to criticize the established order. Such writers may represent a woman simultaneously as part of the social code, her position determined by set roles, and as a disrupter of norms who unmasks their teleology and their limits. The sympathetic, even tragic treatment of many fictional heroines testifies to their authors' recognition of the social and personal cost of defying the social order. Yet the "dysphoric" plot traced by Nancy Miller suggests that if certain values can be expressed only through their displacement and ultimate sacrifice in the figure of a tragic heroine, the novelist's intended critique of society may actually turn into a tacit confirmation of the existing order. The social exclusion of rebellious women, their relegation to the margins of society, that we find recorded in such fiction reminds us how central in our lives are the patriarchal, hierarchic values and structures; the silencing and absence of those women bespeaks a presence.

Today the social determinism operating to inscribe women's lives in nineteenth-century fiction may seem an artifact. It may also, however, be reinterpreted in terms of modern concerns. Critics who focus today on the heroine's "text" do so, at least in part, because she is seen as representative of humanity in our *Hingeworfensein*. But one risk inherent in such a reading is that of discounting the human, social agency that has rendered women, like other minorities, invisible.

Women's roles and functions, then, unlock social systems and their evaluative hierarchies; the literary representation of women must be interpreted systematically. Women's figures help define and (dis)integrate the multiple heterogenous structures that we call literary texts. The richness of these relationships is suggested by Nancy Miller's essay deciphering George Sand's *Valentine* and exploiting topological and stylistic analysis along lines that bear comparison to Gaston Bachelard and Mikhail Bakhtin, as well as Michael Riffaterre. Ideology and class structures are seen here from a semiotician's perspective, as encoded in genre and gender, in the "chronotopes" of chateau and pastoral pavilion. Miller analyzes the dislocations through which Sand adapts and questions the "female plot," depicting a heroine who struggles in vain against the economic laws of circulation for women and who enacts a fiction of her own autonomy. Valentine's pastoral world excludes but ironically depends on the viability of the patriarchal society that will in the end destroy her. Similar ironic contradictions characterize Sand's description of the "moment of possession," in which Miller discerns a "feminist" (as opposed to "masculinist" or Rousseauist "feminizing") discourse.

One question raised by defining woman as a function within a system of signs is whether we are dealing with signifier, signified, or both. An evacuation of identity appears to be one consequence of seeing woman as Otherness, *altérité*. She may be given positive value as the mystery of the ineffable and the *néant* that permits affirmation of (masculine) being, or she may retain the negative value of a mere empty void. The ambivalence of woman as signifier can be taken as the basso continuo of our topic.

The problem of representing women is magnified by the way women (and female characters) internalize the specular, reifying attitudes of society. Women cannot be represented as themselves, since we cannot know their identities. They are simply present as a consciousness of being perceived and represented as objects. Hence the duplicitous mystery of women in portraits whose gaze outward is really turned inward on themselves.

This duplicity is fundamental to the study of fictions about women. We may find playful release—or sterility—in representing representations, signs about signs, reinscriptions of codes that start from fictions of reproduction. Feminist critics have recognized an ironic undercutting, a doubling of voices, in women's literature and in the representation of women, corresponding to this situation. The role of irony in the representation of women is developed in several of the papers in this volume. It is particularly evident in Elizabeth Ermarth's study of the discrepancy between women's time and narrative time in realist fiction. While such a gap may be implicit in all narrative representations, Ermarth, like Julia Kristeva, has hypothesized a special "Women's time," and her point gathers force in view of the deliberately ironic focus in the nineteenth-century novel on women misunderstood, distanced, and destroyed. She explores questions raised in *Madame Bovary* and *Tess of the D'Urbervilles* about the primary, temporal assumptions of narrative convention and indeed about our epistemological categories as they are defied and undermined by representations of the experience of women.

Post-structuralist critics like Derrida appear drawn to the problem of the representation of women because the redoubling implicit in the topic suggests a *mise en abîme* effect, like that which they find at work undermining all our efforts at representation. In a sense, therefore, this volume continues the labor of *Allegory and Representation,* whose contributors traced many of the issues raised by the literary project of catching or recapturing an objective reality. (Leo Bersani's critique of Freud, in which he hypothesizes a creative mutual transformation of "paternal" modes of closure and "maternal" modes of oscillating and open-ended suggestion, bears comparison to current feminist reassessments of genres.)

The fragmentation of the self that is the corollary of women's self-identification through others also has far-reaching philosophical implications. J. Hillis Miller draws on both post-structuralism and phenomenology in his essay on Clara Middleton, whose characterization reveals Meredith's challenges to narrative, interpretative, and social conventions. The crisis of Clara's engagement to Willoughby precipitates her own self-questioning and the critic's doubts as to whether there is any prelinguistic self that can be expressed in language. "Character exists only in displacement"; "there is no proper language for the self, none but figurative characters for character." The disintegration and discontinuities Miller discovers in chapter 21 of *The Egoist* result from Meredith's multiplication of "incoherent figures," which veil rather than reveal the heroine's character. Miller's essay reenacts such a veiling, as he closes on the promise of an alternative theory of character implicit in the novel.

Any contemporary must be struck by the distance between present and past social structures organizing the relations between the sexes. The symbolism and values attached to masculinity and feminity have undergone similar profound transformations. Not just women readers but all readers of every persuasion today find themselves confronting inherited texts across a gulf that forces them to pass from repetition to reinterpretation. The mediating tradition is in flux today; we have recovered lost strands that lead us back into another past, as well as new perspectives on myths and paradigms of literary history. Because we have come to recognize that concepts of gender are social constructs which are implicated in all our classificatory schemes, we can use the representation of women to enhance our perception of the alignments and dislocations in literary structures. A focus on this topic of women leads us yet further, beyond texts to questions about our very processes of interpretation and representation.

Ultimately, critics who undertake to study the representation of women confront heterogeneity and irony rather than singleness of voice; liminality and universality as opposed to marginality in the functions of women; and dynamic process, not bipolarity, in the relationships of gender.

MARGARET R. HIGONNET
University of Connecticut

THE REPRESENTATION OF WOMEN IN FICTION

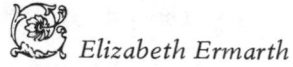 *Elizabeth Ermarth*

Fictional Consensus
and Female Casualties

Plato's dialogue on justice begins with an altercation between Socrates and a friend, Polemarchus, an anecdote that dramatizes an altercation between two contradictory forms of rule. On the one hand is the rule of consensus, or mutual understanding and agreement; on the other hand is the rule of force. At the beginning of *The Republic* Socrates, walking home from the harbor festival with Glaucon, is stopped by the servant of Polemarchus.

> The boy, taking hold of my robe behind, said: Polemarchus desires you to wait. I turned then and asked, where he was. He is coming after you, answered he: but pray wait for him. Yes, we will wait, said Glaucon; and just afterward came Polemarchus and Adimantus, the brother of Glaucon, and Niceratus, son of Nicias, and some others, as from the procession. Then said Polemarchus, Socrates, you seem to me to be hurrying to the city, as on your return. Aye, you do not make a bad guess, said I. See you, then, said he, how many we are? Yes, of course. Well, then said he, you must either prove yourselves stronger than these, or else remain here. One expedient, said I, is still left, namely, to persuade you that you should let us go. How can you possibly persuade such as will not hear? By no means, said Glaucon.[1]

Plato dramatizes here the contradiction between the rule of force and the rule of agreement or consensus. "How can you possibly persuade such as will not hear?" "By no means." The rule of force, with which Polemarchus playfully threatens his friend, is no joke to the patron saint of dialogue and persuasion. Violence forecloses on consensus. You cannot communicate with someone who refuses to listen; also implied here is that those who refuse to listen opt automatically for the rule of force rather than for that of persuasion and agreement. Between the two is an irreconcilable difference.

I shall leave this altercation in place to haunt my discussion while I consider the nature of consensus, its meaning for representation, and the implications of these matters for the treatment of women in realistic fiction. I will begin by arguing that realism is fundamentally a form of consensus, one which characteristically establishes through the narrator the viability of consensus as a perceptual mode. At the level of story individual characters often challenge a social consensus in the name of freedom or humanity, as Maggie Tulliver does in the fictional community of St. Oggs (*The Mill on the Floss*) or as Anna Karenina does in the Russian aristocracy; and these conflicts between force and consent motivate the plot. At the formal level, however, the consensus of realism cannot be challenged successfully without disturbing the effect of verisimilitude because, I will argue, the formal consensus maintains common time.

In the second half I will turn to two examples of fictional representation which illustrate particularly well the altercation between force and agreement as it bears on the experience of some major nineteenth-century heroines.

Two in particular will interest me, Emma Bovary and Tess Durbeyfield. In each case the death of the heroine is not a discrete event but the final stage in a long, generalized suffocation. She is literally cut off from the chief resource available to her community and created by its agreements, the resource of time. In representational fiction, I will argue, consensus *creates* continuous time, the medium of growth and development. The heroine, like everyone, takes seriously this common opportunity. But unlike others, she actually is cut off from that consensus and thus is effectively cut off from the medium of growth and development. Both plots confirm this logic. For the heroine, progress is converted into a slow attrition which kills her. She experiences not time for growth but time running out. Finally, her reserves depleted, a final convulsion ends her existence.

The term "representation" most literally means to represent, that is, to present again what has already been presented once before. Political representation, for example, involves the action of a second, a stand-in, an agent who is elected by individuals to present them again in some forum. But to whom? Here is a most interesting question: not only *by* whom is one represented but also *to* whom is one represented? Here the self-reflexive powers of consensus are most evident. In a system of political representation voters are represented not to God, not to the king, but to *one another,* and eventually to the executive agents of that common will. Political representation is thus a form of consensus, a way of consolidating individual power and of amplifying the individual voice through mutual consent. Representation, or presenting again, makes possible that consensus by which the many can speak as one.

While this much may seem obvious, its extension into art becomes more difficult. Applied to literature, the term "representation" seems to belong to that world on the other side of the looking-glass where words mean whatever you say they mean. My first task, therefore, is to explain why I limit the term "representation" to one kind of aesthetic phenomenon. By "fictional representation" I mean verisimilitude, realism, the art of likeness to individual perception, and this form, for reasons I will explain immediately, is an aesthetic form of consensus. This usage has new precision, rescuing the protean term "representation" from an uneasy obligation to refer to all literature regardless of kind or condition and restricting it to one form so that, like the old man of the sea, it will give us useful information. This usage also broadens the context of fictional representation in a new direction, aligning it with other, homologous forms of consensus such as the political.

In fictional representation or realism (for purposes of this discussion I use the terms interchangeably) the illusion depends on the consensus maintained by the narrator. It is a purely formal agreement, one which does not depend on particular issues of choice and action. The narrator's most important contribution to representational illusion is maintaining continuous time. This common temporal medium, the arena for working out social agreement or consensus, is also, and even more importantly, the product of consensus. In realistic novels each individual awareness appears simultaneously from two viewpoints: one the implied reflex of the character's mind, the other implied by the presence of the narrator re-presenting that reflex from hindsight. The past-tense notation continually gives us the important signal that every now (or present) is also a then (a re-presenting); that what *is* happening at the same time *has* happened already and has taken its place in the emerging pattern of significance. The narrator re-presents a character's viewpoint and, in so doing, makes it public by opening it to the common temporal medium shared by all viewpoints in the novel. This narrator coordinates all private times into one public, common time, thus the narrator is de facto the specifier of a collective result, of a consensus. All points of view in the novel agree in the formal sense that they all belong to the same medium. Despite the manifest limitations of characters' viewpoints, they all can be coordinated by the narrator into one homogeneous medium and so potentially into one single world of concerns. The impersonal, past-tense awareness of the narrator, a presence often felt by readers as a kind of generalized historical awareness, publishes private moments and in thus re-presenting them re-presents them to one another. By making them mutually accessible in time, the narrator gives them the power of mutual confirmation through agreement. The narrator enables the many to speak as one. You might say that the narrator violates even the most private mind and makes it accessible to the gaze and the confirmation of others. The past-tense narration always has that shadow of the future, that arbitrary hindsight which unifies the field.

This consensus in representational fiction has absolute ontologizing power. The agreement between present and past, or present and re-present, is a purely formal agreement that literally objectifies the world. Ordinarily, we may assume, we agree among ourselves about things (to the extent that we do agree) because we all live in the same world. But a close look at the conventions of realism gives rise to a disconcerting reversal: not "it exists, therefore we agree" but the reverse, "we agree, therefore it exists." What is objective in realism is so only because all available viewpoints agree and to the extent that they so agree. Historical continuity itself, then, the common medium of experience, is not a prior condition of consensus but its *product*. The continuity of time in representational fiction, that mutual informativeness between past and present, here and there, now and then which makes realistic novels interesting to read, constitutes a formal consensus that is the realistic novel's most powerful message. This formal consensus is the reader's only means for gaining access to the story; the very act of reading thus entails acceptance of the view that the world is a common world, a "human" world, a world that is the "same" for everyone.

This formal assertion of consensus is an arbitrary act, an artifice, one that depends upon the consent of the governed, but though it is abstract and formal, the power of this consensus in realism is absolute. It must survive all challenges for the picture of a common world to remain stable. Fundamental disagreement among the contributing views would threaten—and in the case of some great heroines does threaten—the implied consensus that sustains the entire fictional system of common agreements. When the common medium is not sustained the represented world develops fissures, cracks in its identity. Everyone probably can recall seeing one of those Renaissance pictures with more than one vanishing point and experiencing a slight, vertiginous sensation at the perception that space does not quite homogenize. The steps of an altar, say, follow one system of converging sight lines, while the canopy of the same altar follows a different system. This schizoid potential in the medium of presentation renders the representational illusion insecure. Even where the vanishing points of these different systems are close neighbors, more or less in the same place on the canvas, they remain different systems. They may seem to cooperate, but they are not one. There are cracks in the common medium, lines of fracture which do not converge and which cannot be recovered according to a common system of visual awareness.

This picture I have just invented is a parable for fiction. What we rather unhappily call the "reliable" narrator maintains the representational illusion because this narrator makes formal contradiction impossible.[2] Where a narrator is *un*reliable, that is, where the narration allows contradictory viewpoints to exist side by side without resolution, the representational illusion falters. The prevailing consensus is not strong enough to stabilize a common, single world. Unreliable Humbert Humbert is a good example of such a narrator, and *The Turn of the Screw* a good example of such a story. Is Humbert Humbert a poet or a madman? How do we know? Such questions as these are not answered in *Lolita* as easily as they are in *Middlemarch* or *Great Expectations*. The éclat and horror of Henry James's story derive from the fact that there is no solution, no single world, and therefore no final rationalization. In such tales Nabokov and James are after other game than representational illusion; more realistic novelists like Dickens or Eliot cannot allow for such contradiction. For the fictional world to be truly objective, the "same" from all viewpoints and not fractured by competing lines of force, the formal consensus must be consistent. Representation thus involves a consensus requiring of those who savor it an act of trust whose power is as breathtaking as its arbitrariness.

Dramatic demonstrations of disagreement among parties in a novel do not threaten this formal consensus any more than dramatic demonstrations of agreement confirm it. Dickens, for example, repeatedly portrays the results of failed consensus. His characters are forever just missing each other in a series of frustrating coincidences that underscore the importance of meeting. *The Old Curiosity Shop,* to take an early example, develops towards the meeting between a stranger and his brother, a meeting that fails in its object owing to narcissism and moral impotence. But although the acknowledgment of brotherhood fails, the novel establishes its critical importance. Had they met sooner, had mutual recognition restored the bond of brotherly trust earlier, the entire story would have been different, the entire definition of the world altered. The reader is left with this uncomfortable knowledge. In a later novel, *Bleak House,* this familiar Dickensian problem shows its influence on psychic life in the history of Lady Dedlock, a woman who in one life loves a man who is nobody and produces an unacknowledged child and who in the other life is the fashionable wife of Sir Leicester Dedlock. During the novel various people turn to Lady Dedlock for recognition, among them her child, Esther Summerson, the lawyer who threatens to expose her, and the diligent inspector on the trail of truth. But these applications fail because the aptly named Lady Dedlock remains split into two identities that refuse to recognize each other. In the end she cannot be found because she cannot find herself, and her dissociated will both feeds and is fed by social fracture. According to her social code, in fact, her personal inclination is illegitimate, distinctly not a consideration in that social consensus which has the power of Providence over her life. In such novels the crucial meeting of minds, the crucial acts of attention, do not take place. Despite local victories, the general syntax of social life seems always to be breaking down. Point of view remains maddeningly private, unavailable to common discourse and thus open to ontological threat.

On the dramatic level, however, so long as the past-tense narrator remains in control, neither failures nor successes affect the formal consensus. Successes themselves do not solve the problem of connection, because each is discrete and thus always partial. Even the social novels preoccupied with recognition, reconciliation, marriage, or any of the gestures that confirm a unified social scene and common medium of exchange fail to generalize absolutely their claims for consensus and common understanding. However, the mutual informativeness, in spite of the meetings of mind that remain unachieved in plot and character, develops triumphantly through the past-tense narrator, who collects all points of view into one continuous mnemonic sequence (such re-collection becomes the central issue in *Bleak House*). Whatever the limitations and failures of particular characters and events, they are outweighed by this unifying presence, shadowing and seconding each discrete moment and providing it with access to all the others through their common temporal medium.[3]

Let me return at this point to Socrates for another look at the contradictory rules of consensus and force. Although Socrates and Polemarchus subscribe to contradictory principles of operation, the contradiction remains implicit. Socrates goes back to Piraeus to conduct the dialogue on justice, and one suspects that he does so gladly. But what if he persisted in refusing? Polemarchus could agree to let him go his own way or, as he points out, could overrule by force of greater numbers. The contradiction remains, threatening the illusion of common agreement, just as in my Renaissance picture of an altar the contradiction between visual systems threatens the illusion of common space. Were the conflict between Socrates and his friend to become explicit and were the rule of consensus to prevail as the alternative to force, consensus would have to demonstrate the inclusiveness which legitimates its power. Plato's anecdote dramatizes not one consensus but two. Socrates and Glaucon agree to hurry home, while Polemarchus and Nicias agree to detain them. The existence of multiple agreements means that each remains a private understanding without absolute credentials. Consensus in realism establishes the homogeneity of the common temporal medium; thus, to be valid, it must be all-inclusive: it must re-present and make available to common discourse all points of view however divergent. Not to do so for whatever reason is automatically to opt for unresolvable competition between two or more different descriptions of how things are. One must find a common denominator between competing systems in order to maintain representational illusion; the alternative is to privilege one of them by force and thus to destroy the consensus.

Representational fiction constantly maintains the all-important mediation that transforms multiple systems into one, multiple private times into one time. This inclusiveness is part of its power, but as some nineteenth-century social novelists were keenly aware, this inclusiveness can be deceiving. So intolerant can a consensus become, so like a rule of force, that it simply makes invisible any view that seriously challenges it. In a realistic novel, correspondingly, any term that challenges the prevailing formal consensus is a contradiction in terms; by definition it can have no ontological status at all. It simply can not be re-presented to perception because to do so would be automatically to include it in the formal consensus. To tell, for example, of "the horror," as Marlow does in *The Heart of Darkness,* is to domesticate it for consumption. If it can be perceived at all, it belongs to the rationalization maintained by the narrator. If it does not belong to that rationalization, it does not exist.

Let me briefly reformulate this crucial point. In the realistic novel anyone who is conscious must be conscious of the same world; consciousness of an alternative world cannot be grounded within the realistic economy. Every viewpoint depends upon the consent of all the others for its access to an objective existence, a "real" existence. Any significant defections—in a novel, say, where even one of the characters successfully challenges the narrator's vision—would leave the narrator powerless to establish the formal consensus. Successfully to disagree with the controlling consensus would be to challenge *its* ontological status, transforming *it* into yet another unconfirmed privacy with no credentials. Although the realistic novel dramatizes conflicts of this kind among characters, it allows no challenge to the narrator or chief administrator of the world.

The conflict between individuals and the prevailing consensus is, as my instances from Dickens suggest, the preoccupation of representational fiction. What chiefly interests me here is the high proportion of important female casualties. The conflict proves fatal to a surprising number of heroines. Their common fate poses a fundamental challenge to the norm of consensus confirmed formally by the novels that destroy them. Among these are some of the great heroines of the nineteenth century — Anna Karenina, Emma Bovary, Maggie Tulliver, Tess Durbeyfield. All these women die of psychic starvation. They die from isolation. Maggie Tulliver and Anna Karenina, two women who could not be more different in terms of education, class, and nationality, both die with practically the same word on their lips. I want to consider more closely two such heroines, Flaubert's Emma Bovary and Hardy's Tess Durbeyfield, and to explore the meaning of their violent deaths for the literary convention of consensus, the convention which asserts that we live in a world of common agreements.[4]

Heroines like Emma and Tess, when they realize how fully they have been dispossessed—how fully their own ideas of themselves have been displaced by ideas thrust upon them by others, and how systematic and inescapable is that invading code—they receive a mortal blow. It is as if the recognition that makes it impossible any longer to play the game is a recognition that entails stepping out of the world altogether. Their histories demonstrate the deep intimacy between psychic and physical existence by showing how, as psychic and physical experience become split, continuance in each is endangered. This problem afflicts many characters in realistic fiction—gentlemen in Dickens, for example—without sending them to the grave; but for a considerable group of heroines there is no way back.

Flaubert follows Emma Bovary to a crisis where she finally confronts her isolation. Her greatest moment is the one when she tells Rodolphe the bitter truth, not only about his comfortable meanness but also about her own abjection. He stands for the series of men from whom she has failed to find corroboration for the illusions she has attempted through the novel to establish. But no more coy lies here. She hurls his paltry offering, a pair of gold cuff-links,

> so hard that the gold chain between them broke as it struck the wall.
>
> "To think that I would have given everything, sold everything, worked with my hands, begging in the streets, just for a smile, for one look, just to hear you say, 'Thank you!' And you sit there peacefully in your armchair, as if you hadn't made me suffer enough already!" . . .
>
> She left. The walls were quaking, the ceiling was about to crush her; she walked back between the rows of trees, stumbling through piles of dead leaves scattered by the wind.[5]

This moment of truth, when she relinquishes her romantic visions, leaves Emma alone in the world. But her solitude is not the healthy romantic solitude of the poet or the artist as a young man; it is not a solitude in the same universe where company exists but something far more radical and astonishing than that. She has turned to one after another of her friends and neighbors to help her avert disaster, and one after another has turned away, not sadly even, but coldly and with mean distrust. Rodolphe is the last. He says (and with more truth than he recognizes) "I have not got it," a refusal that precipitates Emma's clarifying anger and, at the same time, snaps her connection with life. In learning to see herself clearly she has discovered her true isolation, and the unreliability of all her mutual understandings.

The shock of this is felt even in the formal consensus maintained by the narrator. The short, remarkable passage leading from this confrontation just quoted to the fatal poison registers a world distorted, one which like a Van Gogh picture lacks a corroborating vision. "The ground gave way like water beneath her feet. . . . Suddenly it seemed to her that globes of fire were exploding in the air like bullets, spinning, spinning, flattening into sparkling discs, until they finally plunged into the snow between the branches of the trees." These spinning bullets turn out to be the lights of the houses in the village, but the author's treatment subjects the reader to Emma's vision, thus confirming its ontological importance. For her these lights of the community *are* bullets. The world comes unstuck for Emma in this moment. Her final illusion of connection to any living soul snapped, her world develops cracks, billows, distortions too terrible for her solitary mind to control. It is, as Flaubert's narrator calmly says, a form of "madness," but only in the sense that a life of total isolation is a form of madness. In another sense (one that Flaubert also underwrites) her "madness" is the first time she has been "sane" if sane means to act in a way appropriate to her actual situation.

Hardy's Tess also labors as a social exile, and her persecution is tied explicitly to her sexuality. To have been born a woman is the crime for which Tess endures exploitation on her family's behalf and separation from her husband, grimly named Angel Clare. Twice betrayed and abandoned, first by Alec and then by Angel (for Tess the satanic and the angelic in men comes roughly to the same thing), Tess is sustained mainly by a sisterhood of women who can feel their solidarity with her despite their envy. But Hardy does not allow this sisterhood to save Tess from the brutality of one and then another of her male persecutors, as they torture her to a point of numb, mute defeat, her body "dissociated from its living will"[6] and finally given despairingly to Alec in exchange for economic support. This death of the will is a death of self, a death of her own idea, and the continuance of her existence is continuance as a body at other people's disposal. Even the sympathetic intervention of her friends only precipitates the catastrophe because, in sending her husband back to her, they send Tess proof of Alec's betrayal. Having given up her will in dependence upon the man who uses her, it takes an act of violence for her to free herself, and that act, the murder of Alec, is the one that finally costs her what is left of her life.

No one, including Tess's three friends, looks at her as she feels herself to be, a fact in the novel which accounts for the special horror of those moments when, time after time, she finds Alec looking at her from a distance. The intent of mastery only intensifies the sense of Tess's isolation and vulnerability. After years of struggle and neglect, Angel returns, and this reunion momentarily brings her to the center of attention, but only attention of an uncomprehending and dehumanizing kind. She awakens at Stonehenge to find herself for the first time surrounded by spectators, but it is only the cold gaze of the law and one which makes short work of her life. Her healthy act of self-defense and self-assertion is punished swiftly, while the logic of that crucial event—the rationalization of its meaning and hence of her experience—remains for her community an unknown history and, except for the narrator's sympathetic memory, is lost with her. No one in her community knows her experience or learns from it. Even the returned and converted husband does not believe Tess's story of the murder until he sees the sheriff's men. Her story confirms the one in Flaubert's novel. It is not defection on the heroine's part that destroys her but a deeper failure in the entire construction of things achieved by her community through tacit consent. To belong to the community at all, she must belong to the communal idea of her. The gaze of others does little to support her life, but it presides over her death with ritual satisfaction. Perhaps the worst thing about the social engine of destruction is its piety. It executes Tess in the name of Justice.

Both heroines, in trying to shape their lives, move more and more to the margins of social existence represented in their novels, isolating themselves to a point from which, finally, there is no return. The responsibility for the final disaster is spread around in complex ways, but the awesome fact is that in choosing their way they move towards solitude not reconciliation, towards extinction not survival. Their attempts to recover from this solitude with a friend or a lover are fragile and unsupported exercises which only isolate them further and which finally do not secure them. When the last trust fails them they have nowhere to turn, and so they die, with a violence appropriate to their extremity. Though the past-tense narrator maintains the formal consensus in each novel, the heroine's death denies its implied and validating claim of inclusiveness. Like the social agreements of Yonville and Wessex, the formal consensus contains her only at the cost of her life.

Neither Flaubert nor Hardy is unaware of the implications for formal consensus of the social failures they represent. The formal consensus falters when Emma's vision momentarily disrupts narrative control with a competing version of reality; and the uncertainties about explanation in Hardy's narrative can be read as deeply problematic for the idea of a unified world normally maintained by formal consensus. Both authors play ironically with the formal consensus, taking pains to show how its tools are used against their heroines. The gaze of others does not confirm these women by corroborating their own views and linking them with others; and their fictional worlds do not survive them long.

Still, to the extent that the narrator maintains a homogeneous, neutral temporal medium, the formal consensus stands, and the narrator successfully maintains the very norm of consensus that the story belies. The heroine participates in this common system as a sacrifice not a survivor. Her experience challenges the validity of the fictional systems that do not contain her. While the convention of consensus (both in the formal consensus and in the idea of social consensus homologous with it) insists upon its power to objectify a world collectively, at the same time these novels dramatize the denial of this convention's highest claim, that what is objective truly belongs to everyone. Their histories raise the question, What would the re-presentation be like if its objective record fully included a vision of an Emma or a Tess? The plots offer no answer to that question at all, no prefiguration of what, exactly, these women might do, so complete is the contradiction between their common experience and the prevailing agreements. Theirs is an absent voice and, as with victims of violence generally, the absent voice has exquisite importance. The painful thing about Hardy's novel is the sense of injustice unacknowledged, not spoken of, not given the objective existence of public recognition, even though, for the reader, that injustice so clearly exists. The absence of Tess's voice from Hardy's final concord, the absence of Emma's from Flaubert's, casts garish light on the concord itself. [7]

The systems of agreement in which these women try to live require them to commit psychic suicide and to lead lives as automata. The heroine with gumption finds it impossible to sustain this divorce between body and idea. Socrates, too, was invited to renounce his idea and live, and he deliberately refused. But his suicide differs from Emma's and Tess's fatal acts of violence. Where he chooses to confirm a position by dying for it, Emma dies because she has no position. Where Socrates is free to put his body at the disposal of his idea, Tess's body belongs to an idea not her own. For Emma and Tess the rule of agreement is really a rule of force, because it exists without reference to their personal experience. They do not participate in the objectifying consensus but instead are objectified by it—allotted existence according to definitions foreign to their experience.

This conflict between body and idea is something Virginia Woolf finds particularly central to the experience of women. Everyone familiar with *A Room of One's Own* now remembers Shakespeare's sister, Judith, and her difficulty in staying alive long enough to pursue an independent life. "To have lived a free life in London in the sixteenth century," Woolf writes, "would have meant for a woman who was a poet and playwright a nervous stress and dilemma which might well have killed her."[8] My fictional examples suggest that Woolf's metaphor of mortal stress is more than an autobiographical aside. Woolf goes on to claim, in her essay on "Professions for Women," that she, too, struggled with the contradiction between the conventional idea concerning women and her own experience. In her struggle to exist as something more than a figment of other people's ideas, the necessary first step was to kill the idea that most threatened her, the idea of The Angel in the House. "Had I not killed her, she would have killed me." The next step, though, was even harder; it was "telling the truth about my own experiences as a body." By "body" she means her entire passional experience as an individual and not merely romantic attachment or sexual preference. This difficulty—surviving outside a prevailing convention that nevertheless does not allow for her experience—Woolf describes in terms of physical violence. The woman writer who let her imagination "sweep unchecked," rushing on to seek the depth "where the largest fish slumber," eventually found her force shattered against the hard obstacle of convention, in particular the convention that associated her actions with male approval. This violence "roused her from her artist's state of unconsciousness. She could write no more."[9] To write no more does not mean merely putting down a pen, as Woolf's own life and death eloquently testify; it means putting aside the truth of her own experience, the truth of her particular life as a creature with sensation and memory. It means a psychic death, of which physical death is only a final corroboration.

Woolf encourages her audience of women with the thought that "for the first time in history" women have the chance to re-shape the conventions in which both men and women live. In seeking professions women have taken responsibility for their physical and, therefore, their psychic lives—for nourishing and sustaining them; yes, for housing and clothing and feeding them and thus making "a beginning" in shaping the entire social consensus that formerly has shaped them. When women see that "we go alone and that our relation is to the world of reality and not only to the world of men and women, then the opportunity will come and the dead poet who was Shakespeare's sister will put on the body she has so often laid down."[10]

Woolf supposes that there is a world of reality apart from the world of men and women; others have been less sure, finding that the conventions of sexual and domestic relationship everywhere shape this "world of reality." The question now may be whether the convention that sustains the illusion of a common world, the convention of consensus, will validate its claim to inclusiveness by welcoming these contributors or whether it will, by deflecting them, finally prove itself to be just another rule of force.

NOTES

1. *The Works of Plato: A Literal Translation,* vol. 2, trans. Henry Davis (London: Henry Bohn, 1849), p. 2.

2. Calling the narrator "reliable" masks the fact that reliable means "common" not "true."

3. For a fuller discussion of the theory of realism sketched here see Elizabeth Ermarth, "Realism, Perspective, and the Novel," *Critical Inquiry* 7, no. 3 (Spring 1981): 499–520; and idem, *Realism and Consensus in the English Novel* (Princeton: Princeton University Press, forthcoming).

4. The fact that both of these authors are male deserves attention, but that issue is separate from the one I am pursuing here, which has to do with the nature of an entire convention and some characteristic uses to which it is put.

5. Gustave Flaubert, *Madame Bovary,* trans. Merloyd Lawrence (Boston: Houghton Mifflin Riverside Edition, 1969), pp. 265–66.

6. Thomas Hardy, *Tess of the D'Urbervilles* (Boston: Houghton Mifflin Riverside Edition, 1960), p. 338.

7. It can be argued that all we hear of the heroine's voice filters through the voices of various ventriloquist dummies constructed for her—wife, mother, mistress—and that we never hear the voice of an autonomous self which has mystery and depth: the Emma behind the sensuality that men love, for example, the one sitting silently in her father's kitchen with a bead of perspiration on her lip. It could be argued that these constraints apply to male characters as well; but the point is that such men usually find it possible to survive in the roles assigned them (perhaps because their

roles are more capacious than Emma's and Tess's or because their imaginations are weaker), whereas their female counterparts quite often do not.

8. Virginia Woolf, *A Room of One's Own* (New York: Harcourt Brace Jovanovich, 1957), pp. 51–52.

9. Virginia Woolf, "Professions for Women," in *Collected Essays*, 4 vols. (New York: Harcourt Brace and World, 1967), 2: 286–88.

10. Woolf, *A Room of One's Own*, p. 118.

 *Susan Gubar*

The Birth of the Artist as Heroine: (Re)production, the *Künstlerroman* Tradition, and the Fiction of Katherine Mansfield

Vacuum Interlude
I should have been emptied of life
Giving life
For consciousness in crises races
Through the subliminal deposits of evolutionary processes
Have I not
Somewhere
Scrutinized
A dead white feathered moth
Laying eggs?

—Mina Loy, "Parturition"

I'm a riddle in nine syllables,
An elephant, a ponderous house,
A melon strolling on two tendrils.
O red fruit, ivory, fine timbers!
This loaf's big with its yeasty rising.
Money's new-minted in this fat purse.
I'm a means, a stage, a cow in calf.
I've eaten a bag of green apples,
Boarded the train there's no getting off.

—Sylvia Plath, "Metaphors"

On Monday, 3 September 1797, after six days of feverish labor pains, Mary Wollstonecraft lay in bed nursing a litter of puppies that had been administered to draw off her milk. One week later she died of poisoning produced by fragments of the placenta lodged in her womb.[1] She had not completed *Maria; or, The Wrongs of Woman*, a novel in which an imprisoned mother is deserted by her lover during a pregnancy, which leads to a suicide attempt. Such a tragic view of motherhood elucidates the birth myth created by her daughter in *Frankenstein*, where the monster formed in the "workshop of filthy creation" signifies Mary Shelley's horror at female generativity.[2] Shelley's contemporary Jane Austen was just as emphatic about her belief that repeated pregnancies would ruin the health and happiness of young women.[3] And the childbirth bed is literally the deathbed in *Wuthering Heights,* as if forecasting the fatal pregnancy of Charlotte Brontë, who could no more stomach the child within her than Jane Eyre could cope with bearing the burden of the dream-child whose encircling arms seemed so strangling.[4] Even literary women like Elizabeth Gaskell, Elizabeth Barrett Browning, and George Eliot, who were bent on perpetuating an ideology of motherhood, associate birth with the depravity of fallen women or with the death of an artistic career.[5] Yet, in Virginia Woolf's fantastic *Künstlerroman Orlando* (1928), where she uses her plot to represent the shape of literary history, the artist-hero triumphs when he is turned into a woman in the eighteenth century, who marries in the nineteenth century and cheerfully gives birth in the twentieth century.

What could have happened to make such a script possible? Woolf provides some answers in her treatise on women and fiction, *A Room of One's Own* (1929). Contrasting the exuberant experimentation of literary women with the retaliatory rhetoric of defensive male writers, Woolf implies that the Great War changed the relationship between the sexes, as did the suffrage campaign. But she explicitly states that the newborn social and literary productions of women, as well as the reimagining of birth itself, are a direct result of a new-found independence from pregnancy. At her visit to Girton, Woolf decides that Mary Seton's mother could not endow a woman's college because she was busy having children:

> Making a fortune and bearing thirteen children—no human being could stand it. Consider the facts, we said. First there are nine months before the baby is born. Then the baby is born. Then there are three or four months spent feeding the baby. After the baby is fed there are certainly five years spent in playing with the baby.[6]

Because Mary Seton is one of the four Marys from the Child ballad that structures the genealogical syntax of Woolf's essay, she and her mother resemble Mary Beton, the aunt who leaves a legacy of five hundred pounds a year, and Mary Carmichael, the novelist who portrays Chloe's affection for Olivia, all of whom are witness-survivors of the tragic fate of Mary Hamilton, who was put to death for bearing and deserting the King's baby. Paying the price for sexuality with her fertility, Mary Hamilton in turn recalls Shakespeare's mythical sister, who also met death, albeit by her own hand, when she found herself with child. What motivates Woolf's triumphant prophecy at the end of *A Room of One's Own* that this dead poet will put on the body to be born again is a radical change in her sense of the ending of this story, a change dictated by a shift in the sexual division of labor. The striking demographic "flight from maternity" that occurred while Woolf was writing marked a redefinition of women's reproductive function and their reproductive system.[7] Not only Woolf's protest against the cost of women's perpetuation of the species but also her recognition of its intrinsic value reflects the prominence of biological speculations about female physiology in three related areas of discourse, generated by gynecologists, embryologists, and birth-controllers.

Whether or not it was a reaction formation to the decline in marital fertility and the increase in so-called redundant women, the pronounced identification of the female with her womb in the late nineteenth century is well represented by M. L. Holbrook's observation in 1870 that it seemed "as if the Almighty, in creating the female sex, *had taken the uterus and built up a woman around it.*"[8] Most doctors held that "the Uterus is the *controlling* [*italics mine*] organ in the female body, being the most *excitable*,"[9] a view dating back to Plato's theory that the unfruitful womb, "an animal desirous of generation," wanders all over the body causing disease.[10] Wandering-womb therapy survived into the seventeenth century in England; for example, in the case of prolapse of the womb: "Yea, apply stinking things to her matrix, as assafoetida, galbanum, castor and stinking pisse; but to the nose, hold sweet things, as musk, divet, and amber."[11] Even when the womb was not wandering, mid-Victorian doctors believed that "in pregnancy, in the parturient period, in lactation, strange thoughts, extraordinary feelings, unseasonable appetites, criminal impulses, may haunt a mind at other times innocent and pure."[12] Practicing upon greater numbers of patients and publishing greater numbers of papers, the medical establishment effectively erected an ideology of the inconstancy of woman that stressed her abject slavery to the mysteriously wayward rhythms of her internal organs. All the prescribed cauterizing, gouging, leeching, and pessarying caused the president of the New Hampshire Medical Society to protest in 1867 that whereas "our grandmothers" never knew they had a uterus until it was filled with a fetus, young women of his day "have wombs shored up" with so many contraptions that they make the vagina into a veritable "Chinese toy shop."[13] Such an ideology and such practices paradoxically endowed the womb with an agency and urgency of its own. Specialists who claimed that the uterus's sway is "no less whimsical than potent" were driven to exclaim, "It is almost a pity that a woman has a womb."[14]

Consciousness of the centrality of the womb was buttressed, moreover, by medical discoveries pertaining to the primacy of its operations. First, in 1759, Caspar Friedrich Wolff's doctrine of epigenesis destroyed the theory of preformation that had allowed philosophers like Leeuwenhoek and Leibnitz to assert that the soul preexists in the semen.[15] Second, in 1827, van Baer discovered the human egg, and eighteen years later

Raciborski proved that it is ejected spontaneously, not as a result of intercourse.[16] While the egg was believed to descend at menstruation, a theory that had dire effects on the definition of the so-called safe time, by the 1880s and 1890s a number of physicians warned that it descends mid-monthly, denying the analogy of estrus.[17] From this point on, scientific recognition of the importance of the egg in conception diverged radically not only from Aristotle's and Aquinas's supposition that the female supplies only the passive matter fit for shaping by the active seminal fluid but also from Harvey's description of the egg as a place where the fetus is formed which is produced from both the male and the female.[18] By the beginning of the twentieth century, Roux, Driesch, and Bovari were investigating the nucleus of the egg.[19] If, as Haeckel had argued in 1868, ontogeny recapitulates phylogeny, then the valuation of the egg might imply that all of existence proceeds from the female principle, a theory that explains why, as Sandra Gilbert has shown, anthropological theories of the Great Goddess became so influential at this time.[20]

Recognition of the empowering aspects of scientific attitudes towards the female body can serve as a corrective to a number of recent books brilliantly analyzing how women were victimized by the rise of the medical establishment. Pointing to the shift from the midwife to the doctor, from hands of flesh to hands of iron, to use Adrienne Rich's evocative phrase, social historians like Ehrenreich and English, Gordon, and Barker-Benfield have blamed the specialists for treating reproduction as an illness, thereby furnishing a biological rationale for misogyny.[21] Yet the medical establishment, relying on the embryologists, had a twofold effect, on the one hand increasing the dependency of women and on the other hand lending them prestige by emphasizing the importance and the complexity of the birthing process. Even the abuses of individual practitioners—the infamous cliteridectomies and ovariotomies—can can be understood in terms of the anxiety physicians suffered

over their secondariness. The mid-Victorian inventor of the
speculum, for example, expressed his awe at the oracular potential of the "new and important territory" he had seen when he
identified the vagina as a mouth, the womb as a neck or throat,
and the cervix as tonsils. While Marion Sims's metaphors, like
some of the more sadistic surgical/cervical experiments he
performed with his "uterine guillotine," express his hostility
toward the female body, they also reveal his sense of its power,
which was implicitly confirmed by his acceptance of the British
Dr. Curling's discovery in 1864 that sterility is not necessarily a
female problem, as had been supposed, that "sterility in the
male does positively exist."[22]

Through a series of sometimes inexcusably inhumane experiments, surgeons developed five operative procedures of importance to women in the course of the century: the removal of
ovarian cysts, the repair of vesico-vaginal fistula, the hysterec-
tomy for fibroids, and the removal of inflamed adnexa and rup-
tured tubal pregnancies.[23] At least some physicians used their
knowledge to inform women, as Frederick Hollick did when he
lectured to halls of hundreds of American women during the
1860s with life-sized models of the female reproductive organs.[24] From Florence Nightingale and Elizabeth Blackwell,
who spoke widely on "Medicine as a Profession for Ladies,"
to Sophia Jex-Blake, who founded the London School of
Medicine for Women, women successfully infiltrated into the
medical establishment, defending their right to attend the
birthbed against even the most vociferous opponents of the
obstetrical societies.[25] The scientist Mary Putnam-Jacobi and
the dean of the Women's Medical College of Philadelphia, Ann
Preston, agreed that the "special capabilities of women as a
class"—their tact and sympathetic insight—ensured the success
of female physicians.[26]

Furthermore, in spite of the dependency and disease bred by
the hospitalization of childbirth, a number of technological
advances freed women from physical and psychological anguish.

In 1853, when Queen Victoria elected chloroform delivery, she silenced religious objectors who claimed pain as the proper punishment for Eve's sin, as did a new breed of feminist physicians who turned to the rapidly developing technology to relieve female fears: Dr. Aletta Jacobs, for example, dispensed the new spring-form diaphragm in Amsterdam in 1882, and Dr. Eliza Ranbome established the first Twilight Sleep Maternity Hospital in Boston in 1914.[27] In the first decade of the twentieth century, the IUD was invented in Germany, maternity clothes for street wear were advertised in American newspapers, Emma Goldman opened her mouth in Paris about the possibility of women closing their wombs, and the National Congress of Mothers sought to elevate motherhood into a profession.[28] The next decade witnessed the invention of the first disposable sanitary napkin and the establishment of the first birth control clinic in England.[29] Feminists could begin to valorize maternity, precisely because the promise of a declining infant- and maternity-mortality rate relaxed the biological imperative. Harriet Stanton Blatch wrote to Margaret Sanger: "Especially did I appreciate your placing in the hands of the mother of the race control of her life giving principle. If women would listen and act they would be as gods. . . ." Sanger herself called the idea "free motherhood."[30]

The relationship between antisepsis, anaesthetics, and aesthetics can best be understood in the fiction in which women artists play a prominent role as characters, where artistic production and biological reproduction are either contradictory models furnishing alternative scripts or analogous, parallel paradigms. Two polar attitudes toward generativity—revulsion and revision—remain the axis on which female definitions of creativity hinge. The movement from what the Victorians called confinement to twentieth-century delivery is reflected in literature where the biological sequence of impregnation, pregnancy, and labor functions as a kind of ur-story or subtext. From the Victorian anxiety of female authorship, which infects the woman artist with the fear that she is a monstrous contradiction in terms, we move toward a celebration of female artistry that blurs the distinction between life and art so as to privilege neither one, a political act that reevaluates the woman as the exemplary creator, the heroine as the artist. If, as Plato argued, love is a desire for generation and a birth in beauty, then the woman with a womb of her own really could dream about controlling the economy of eros.[31]

The startling centrality of childbearing in the *Künstlerromane* of women represents a response to the hegemonic texts and contexts of our culture that either appropriate the birth metaphor to legitimize the "brain children" of men or, even more destructively, inscribe female creativity in the womb to insult women whose productions then smack of the mere *repetition* of *re*production, its involuntary physicality.[32] For the woman writer who seeks to uncover not only the fiction of male motherhood, but also the factious biological metaphor, the *Künstlerroman* conventions fashioned by male writers are insufficient.[33] Although it may seem audacious to focus here on the stories of Katherine Mansfield, a writer who never wrote a novel about a professional artist, such a choice highlights the reason why women's unique contributions to this tradition may be considered a critique of the genre constituting an anti-tradition of their own. If "women writers do not imagine women characters with even the autonomy they themselves have achieved," as Carolyn Heilbrun persuasively argues,[34] they cannot write in a genre that plots the continuous process by which a male artist progresses towards the transcendence necessary to create art. Certainly nineteenth-century women novelists exploit the artist-character to explain why women cannot sculpt or paint or write. Yet, in the modernist period women did produce recognizable *Künstlerromane*. To understand how they shaped the conventions of this genre to their own purposes, we need to analyze the shift in perspective that salvaged uniquely female images of creativity. As Mary Burgan has already demonstrated, the stories of Katherine Mansfield reveal how one woman artist overcomes her revulsion against generativity.[35] By coming to terms with the centrality of birth without mystifying it, by reconciling her writing with her rearing, Mansfield calls into question the identification of artistry with autonomy.

Precisely because her stories redefine creativity, they provide a model for understanding how feminist modernists accommodated their own freedom to the immanence and discontinuity that traditionally have characterized female culture, without portraying themselves as tokens or aberrations, alone of all their sex. Specifically, Mansfield claimed to write out of two "kickoffs": what she calls a *"cry against corruption,"* or a deep sense of hopelessness, and "real joy," a blissful state when everything seems to open before her eyes "like a flower."[36] Her early stories, cries against corruption, reiterate the painful contradictions of production and reproduction in late nineteenth-century fiction by writers like Rebecca Harding Davis, Olive Schreiner, and Elizabeth Stuart Phelps Ward. It is in "Prelude," the story published by Woolf's Hogarth Press, that Mansfield redefines women's unique creativity inside the gap that separates life and art. Finally Mansfield's later stories, written out of joy, typify the redefinition of women as paradigmatic creators in the artist novels of feminist-modernists like Dorothy Richardson, Willa Cather, and Virginia Woolf herself.

In the earliest of her New Zealand stories, Mansfield creates one of her most revealing portraits of the artist as a young girl. "The Woman at the Store" (1911) is narrated by one of three travelers who arrive, on a hot and dusty day, at a remote country store kept by a woman who is far different from the pretty bride she used to be:

> She was a figure of fun. Looking at her, you felt there was nothing but sticks and wires under that pinafore—her front teeth were knocked

out, she had red pulpy hands, and she wore on her feet a pair of dirty Bluchers.[37]

Living in a room where the walls are plastered with old pages of English periodicals, alone except for her daughter, for whom she "'adn't any milk till a month after she was born and she sickened like a cow,'" she explains that her husband is "'away shearin,'" but the travelers do not quite believe her because she seems to their eyes "mad." Still, one of them decides that "'she'll look better by night light—at any rate, my buck, she's female flesh,'" so he spends the night with her, while his two companions are lodged with the little girl in the store, amid strings of onions, half hams, and ads for camp coffee. To get back at her mother for this confinement, the child draws the one picture she is forbidden to represent, "'of the woman shooting at a man with a rook rifle and then digging a hole to bury him in.'"

This first child artist in Mansfield's work expresses her sense of vulnerability and her rage. The daughter's pictures, which are described as "repulsively vulgar" with a "lunatic's cleverness," are a revenge against the mother which simultaneously marks the daughter as "'the dead spit'" of the mother, for the daughter's "mad excitement" while drawing is a repetition of the mother's violence, a cycle that begins with the man who has situated the woman at the store in the wilderness, or so the woman claims:

> "It's six years since I was married, and four miscarriages. I says to 'im, I says, what do you think I'm doing up 'ere? If you was back at the Coast, I'd 'ave you lynched for child murder. Over and over I tells 'im—you've broken my spirit and spoiled my looks, and wot for!" (P. 131)

Even as it exposes marriage as miscarriage, the story of the woman at the store, who has been driven mad by "'bein' shut up . . . like a broody 'en'" (p. 132), explains what happens to a woman who is used as a store and deprived of any story but this one. In spite of her retribution, her daughter's picture implies that she is left minding the store, still handing out her self and her provisions to the men on the road, who may very well meet the same fate as her husband.

Mansfield's story illustrates the asymmetrical terms "patrimony" and "matrimony," or "patron" and "matron," to uncover the cultural and economic impoverishment of women. This theme, so central in *A Room of One's Own,* also distinguishes one of the earliest artistic novels written by a woman, Rebecca Harding Davis's *Life in the Iron Mills* (1861). While the would-be artist here is male, his name—Hugh Wolfe— links him to the powerful female form he has sculpted, with a "wild, eager face, like that of a starving wolf's."[38] Living a degraded life amid the filthy vapors pregnant with death in the ceaselessly satanic mills, Hugh has a woman's face and the nickname "Molly" because he epitomizes the way in which the artist is feminized when, in an industrial setting, he is an unpaid laborer. The plot that sets out to punish him as a thief demonstrates that the label of class makes even the aspiration to artistry a libelous liability. Working with nothing but scraps of refuse, the korl of the pig-iron, Hugh Wolfe produces a huge figure caught in a wild gesture of warning, a threat of violent retaliation. Ultimately, however, the blunt knife he uses to hack away at this woman of giant proportions is reduced to a bit of tin he sharpens at the bars of a jail to use as a weapon against his own body. The horror of wasted talent, of the ungainly dimensions of untutored art, of thwarted ambition, is epitomized by the hump on the back of the woman who fails in her efforts to give Hugh Wolfe a new life.

Harding Davis analyzes the social and economic deprivation that deforms creativity, as does Tillie Olsen, who was instrumental in recovering this novella, or Olive Schreiner, whose passage on female Shakespeares may have been Woolf's source for her portrait of Judith Shakespeare:

We have Shakespeare; but what of the possible Shakespeares we might
have had, who passed their life from youth upward brewing currant
wine and making pastries for fat country squires to eat, with no glimpse
of the freedom of life and action, . . . stifled out without one line written, simply because, being of the weaker sex, life gave no room for
action and grasp on life?[39]

Elsewhere, specifically in *The Story of an African Farm* (1883),
which was originally subtitled "A Series of Abortions," Schreiner explores the figure of the dead baby to articulate the competition between artistic production and biological reproduction,
for her artist-heroine Lyndall dies after giving birth to a dead
baby, who represents the end of her creative ambitions, as well
as the high infant-mortality rate that kept women in a life-
endangering state of perpetual pregnancy. Many of Mansfield's
stories also locate the inhibition and violence with which wom-
en practice art in the violent conflicts of self-interest between
women and children, as if to recall the first woman-artist,
Lilith.[40] From "The Advanced Lady" (1911), a story in which
a lady novelist finds time to write by ignoring her husband and
neglecting her daughter, to "The Child Who Was Tired" (1911),
in which a child exhausted by the incessant demands of four
younger children can only dream her escape by killing one of
them, Mansfield identifies physical labor with the murderous
rage that results from the fall into shattering division. Both
Schreiner and Mansfield agree that the solitary female soul is
caught between the isolated artist-woman like Madame Reisz
of *The Awakening* (1899) ("the artist must possess the cou-
rageous soul . . . that dares and defies") and the mother-woman
like Madame Ratignolle ("Think of the children").[41] Because
there is "no division of labor possible" in a woman's economy,
"to the attainment of any end worth living for, a symmetrical
sacrifice of her nature is compulsory upon her."[42]
    This last is a quotation from Elizabeth Stuart Phelps Ward's
The Story of Avis (1877), a novel about the "civil war" (p. 192)
within Avis Dobell, who, like Edna Pontellier, is torn between

the artistic impulse to eternalize and the repetition of domestic labor that sustains life. Dramatizing Florence Nightingale's complaint that woman has no time to call her own,[43] Avis is condemned to part-time sketching that results in what Katherine Anne Porter and May Sarton identify as the dispersion of the self into fragmentary bits.[44] When Ward describes Avis's life as a "succession of expectancies" (p. 272), she calls attention to the way in which a woman expecting a baby admits the future into her present in an interruption that the child will continue to effect:

> Women understand—only women altogether—what a dreary will-o-the-wisp is this old . . . experience, "When the fall sewing is done," "When the baby can walk," "When the house cleaning is over," . . . then I will write the poem, or learn the language, . . . or master the symphony; then I will act, dare, dream, become. Merciful is the fate that hides from any soul the prophecy of its still-born aspirations. (Pp. 272–73)

Avis is physically exhausted by the sleepless nights, the nursing, the noisy crying. Yet, even as childbearing reduces her to a weakened, childlike state, the physical symbiosis of the mother-child coupling makes the threat of separation as much of a terror as the urgencies of union. To address this riddle in the single portrait undertaken after her marriage, Avis paints a sphinx, whose mutilated face embodies "the mystery of womanhood." While the painting is repeatedly interrupted, the mystery of this creature is clarified when Avis discovers the petty betrayals of her husband and confronts him, silently pointing "to the little Egyptian clock upon the mantelpiece, whose bronze sphinx told the hour" (p. 338). For the sphinx represents the problem of time for women: the rhythmic periodicity of the body, the loss of youth in expecting, the body clock that denies childbearing to the older woman, the domestic interruptions, the part-time nature of women's working careers, women's exclusion from public history. But the fate of the finished portrait further illuminates the riddle: shame causes her to paint in the foreground a child looking at the sphinx with his finger on his lips, swearing her to silence. Striking the sphinx dumb, the child is at one and the same time the subject of the painter's art and the inhibitor of her muse.

Mansfield's sensitivity to the shameful silence enforced by the child who swears the sphinx to silence is dramatized most elliptically in "This Flower" (1917), a sinister story about a consultation between a young woman and a sleazy physician who share a mysterious secret. Prefaced with the epigraph she chose for her own grave, "But I tell you, my lord fool, out of this nettle danger, we pluck this flower, safety" (*Henry IV, Part I*), the story dramatizes the heroine's brief moment of exultation when she ceases to struggle against "the stream of life," and then her complicity with the doctor in keeping her foolish husband, Mr. King, ignorant of what has happened. While he had earlier proclaimed his willingness to "blazen it on the skies," he is terrifically relieved that she is "safe" because "it would have been so—fatal—so fatal!" (p. 408). His ignorance of what safety means—the plucked flower—hints at the guilt Mansfield may have experienced either at her miscarriage or at her abortion. But it also predicts her horror at later dependency on doctors treating her tuberculosis, a disease then associated with abnormal female hormones.[45] In "This Flower" the writer who referred to her stories as "spasms" identifies pregnancy, disease, and the discrete mockery of her own art.[46] Inhabited by a secret presence which they seek to subsume before it can consume them, a number of Mansfield's heroines dread that they are contaminating creatures, neither healthily animal nor fully human, inhabiting a frightening liminal zone where even the boundaries of the body refuse to function predictably. Like Anaïs Nin's fictional surrogate in her short story "Birth" (1938), Mansfield's are carriers of carrion. But Nin's heroine manages to evade the glittering instruments and patronizing commands of her doctor: drumming with her own fingers on her taut belly, she rhythmically evokes the dilating and controls the pushing until the slippery girl-child, glistening with the waters of the womb, is born dead.

Just as Nin's heroine saves herself by establishing her own timing, Elizabeth Stuart Phelps Ward implies that women can solve the riddle of their nature only in a new time ushered in by women's full participation in culture:

> We have been told that it takes three generations to make a gentleman: we may believe that it will take as much, or more, to make A WOMAN. A being of radical physique; the heiress of ancestral health on the maternal side; a creature . . . physically educated by mothers of her own fibre and by physicians of her own sex—such a woman alone is fitted to acquire the drilled brain, the calmed imagination, and sustained aim, which constitute intellectual command. (P. 450)

This same emerging utopian vision of a sustained and sustaining matrilinearity is dramatized in the movement from Charlotte Perkins Gilman's "The Yellow Wallpaper" (1899), a story about post-partum depression at the impossibility of mothering and writing, to Gilman's fantastic *Herland* (1915), where the ascendency of an all-female community is symbolized by the creative womb. The progression from pathogenesis to parthenogenesis is just as important in the development of Schreiner's thinking. While what she calls "the ring" of womanhood confines Lyndall in *The Story of an African Farm,* Elaine Showalter has explained that Schreiner reinvents it in *Woman and Labour* as "the ring" of the "os cervix," which is capable of expanding to admit the intellectual capacity and physical vigor of each successive generation of the human race.[47] Schreiner's last novel, about a mother-writer, begins with her heroine withdrawing from a dead baby into fantasies of the one born alive whom she imagines sprouting like a seed from the pod of a mimosa. "The Prelude" in *From Man to Man* therefore turns us to Mansfield's "Prelude," which assents to Anaïs Nin's statement that "woman's creation far from being like a man's must be exactly like her creation of children, that is it must come out of her own blood, englobed by her womb, nourished with her own milk."[48] In fact, Mansfield's "Prelude" is a story not only about the move of a family from one house to another but also about the move from imagining the womb as a store, a cavity, a hump, a riddle, or a bleeding wound to imagining the womb as the transformative matrix of primordial change.

What triggered this movement for Mansfield was the death of her brother in World War I. Dead in 1915, Mansfield's brother became a muse for her, not unlike H. D.'s brother-muse, whose death sparked her war epic *Trilogy*. Only when Mansfield is writing does she feel that her brother "is calm," that he is with her. The brother who was lying dead on the fields of France would be transformed by her art into the baby lying on the fertile fields of her memory: the last chapter, she confides in her *Journal*, will be "your birth—your coming in the autumn." In the process of writing this book, then, Mansfield was determined to become her brother's mother: she explains that "in every work I write and every place I visit I carry you with me. Indeed, that might be the motto of my book."[49] Bearing her brother big about, she comes to terms with her dread of mothering. Her brother's death liberates her to celebrate women's capacity to birth as an aspect of the artistry she enacts as a fiction writer. Paradoxically, however, even while she provides her brother a sufficient family into which he will be born, Mansfield erases him, for what Mansfield terms her own and her brother's "undiscovered country" is a nostalgic motherland made up of women who, in spite of their differences, live together in a family that is sustained by their common artistry. "Prelude" (1917) describes in twelve discrete moments forty-eight hours of the Burnell family's move from a house in town to a larger house six miles out in the countryside. Besides tracing the three generations it takes to be A WOMAN, Mansfield's main characters constitute an anatomy of female development. Grandmother, sister, and daughter are related as might be four different versions of the self, each embodying the dramatic biological markers that separate the stages of growth in a woman: menopause, pregnancy, the onset of menstruation, and latency. Each stage is an interruption, yet together they form the development of one creative female self, for the ages of women are shown to be blessed by imaginative vision, filtered through family concerns, in a matriarchy, if that word can refer to a country admittedly not owned by women but governed and graced by women's rituals.

The grandmother of them all is Mrs. Fairfield, whose name alone illustrates Mansfield's return to her origins: she had made herself into Mans-field as a writer in London, but now she returns to the pastoral associations of her grandmother's maiden name, Beau-champ.[50] Whether cutting bread and spreading butter for the little Burnell girls or sustaining their mother with oddments from her reticule, Mrs. Fairfield is the unpretentious artist of cups and cloths that became "part of a series of patterns" (p. 236). Her daughter Linda appreciates the kitchen, which "says 'mother' all over, everything is in pairs" (p. 237), although Linda herself is in retreat from the demands of her children and husband. Even as she lets herself be clasped in bed, she dreams of a tiny fluff of a bird, which (when stroked) swells horribly in her arms, turns into a big naked head with a gaping bird-mouth, and smiles knowingly at her in her apron. The swelling bird that is both phallus and baby motivates Linda's resentment of her husband, who looks "like a big fat turkey" (p. 232). Yet, when Stanley Burnell departs for work, Linda is also an artist of interiors who sees in the tassel fringe a procession of dancers, in the medicine bottles a row of men in brown top hats, and in the wallpaper "a leaf and a stem and a fat bursting bud." Having survived some "three great lumps of children" (p. 258), when things seem "to swell out with some mysterious important content," she fears she cannot escape the consciousness that realizes "everything could come alive, down to the minutest, tiniest particle" (p. 235).

Significantly, the character who actually writes in "Prelude" is the least successful as an artist, for Beryl's caustic letter resembles the disgusted, satiric tone of Mansfield's early stories. An unmarried dependent in Stanley's house, Linda's sister is filled with dissatisfaction, which she escapes through fantasies of a handsome man waiting with a bouquet in the shadows of the garden. Decorating herself before the mirror, Beryl exemplifies the lure of romantic thralldom for the youthfully erotic female imagination and the narcissism at the center of such imaginings. When Beryl momentarily realizes that a false self is in danger of robbing her of an appreciation of the mystery of life, she is interrupted by Kezia, who proceeds to sit at her aunt's dressing table, where she puts the cap of a cold cream jar as a crown on her cat. While Beryl's nickname, "Wig," was Mansfield's signature for her own letters, Kezia's name recalls the nickname Mansfield had as a child, "Kass." As a kind of miniature Mrs. Fairfield, Kezia plays house by laying the cloth on a garden seat, using geranium leaves for plates, pine needles for forks, daisy heads on a laurel leaf for poached eggs. Such a domestic use of nature shows insight on Kezia's part into her grandmother's art, as does her creation of picture matchboxes out of flowers. While Kezia shares her mother's dread of rushing animals whose "heads swell e-enormous" (p. 225), she too is able to transform such commonalities as the bread and drippings in her plate into a "dear little sort of gate" just by taking one small bite.

It is Kezia's fascination with the huge aloe at the front of the new house, with its "thick, grey-green thorny leaves" and its middle, where "there sprang up a tall stem" (p. 240), that causes her to ask Linda about it. The "fat swelling plant with its cruel leaves and fleshy stem" at first seems a terrifying reminder of cruel phallic insistence and the concomitant horror of being forced to flower. But, as if to demonstrate the effect of the communal female imagination presiding in the combined domestic artistry of grandmother, mother, sister, and daughter, when we see the aloe again it has been repossessed by the woman and redeemed. When Mrs. Fairfield and Linda look to see if there are buds on the top of the stalk, the plant seems "to ride upon [the high grassy bank] like a ship with the oars lifted. Bright moonlight hung upon the lifted oars like water, and on the green wave glittered the dew" (p. 257). Speaking to each other "with the special voice that women use at night," Mrs. Fairfield and Linda redefine the plant as a ship of sharp thorns that will row Linda far away from the house: no longer a phallic threat, it is a symbol of female resistance, escape, and ecstasy. But the ancient, scarred leaves of the stationary aloe, testifying to the pain of reproduction, also speak of the resiliency, endurance, and strength of women, teaching Linda that Stanley will go on making money and she will go on making babies, a realization that matches Mrs. Fairfield's seemingly unrelated thoughts about "whether we should be able to make much jam" from the fruit trees in the autumn (p. 259), for both women are committed to preserving the life of the family in spite of its terrible call on their own powers of self-preservation. Therefore Mansfield's primordial plant, which exists in marginal conditions by virtue of its conservative tenacity, symbolizes women's intimation of their own regenerative powers: the aloe grows rapidly upward in its central stem precisely when it flowers.

The imaginative transformation of the aloe epitomizes the process that turns the bread into a gate, the quilt tassel into a dancer, daisy heads into poached eggs, birds into babies, domestic metamorphoses affected by the transformative character of the female imagination and related by Mansfield to the body that is entered, swollen, and scarred in childbearing. All the children participate in another transformation, begun when they witness the decapitation of a duck, which is only momentarily terrifying because "it did not look as if it had ever had a head" when Alice places it, "in beautifully basted resignation," surrounded by wreaths of stuffing, on the table for Stanley to carve (p. 254). Mansfield had once laughed over the "female cannibalism of George Eliot"—"She gloats over the fat of babies"[51]—but here she provides a festive rendering of its comic implications, for the chopping off of the head of this "first of the home products" seems to enact Linda's resentment at being forced to bear Stanley's son. At this ultimate domestic triumph, the First Supper at the Burnell house, Stanley unwittingly presides at a eucharistic celebration of a new Incarnation when the ritualistic eating of the bird-phallus is celebrated by the female community which is not only eating the baby to be born to Linda but becoming pregnant with him as well. As a uniquely female event, moreover, this Incarnation holds out the promise of a new word.[52]

Mansfield's savory duck dinner recalls one of her more important letters, in which she exclaims over "the whole process of becoming the duck ... [which] is so thrilling ... it is really only the 'prelude.' There follows the moment when you are *more* duck, *more* apple, or *more* Natasha than any of these objects could ever possibly be, and so you *create* them anew."[53] While the title "Prelude" refers most explicitly to the characters' prelude to life in a new house,[54] then, it also alludes to the prelude before the birth of the little brother and to the process of composition that allows him to live again. Like a musical prelude, "Prelude" presents us with multiple motifs, multipersonal viewpoints, as if to indicate how dispersion of rhythms and diffusion of identity differentiate not only the timing of women but the time of women. It asks us to reconsider the relationship between women's alienation from history and the privacy of their moments. Writing directly about the Great War in her *Journal*, Mansfield admits that she can give no coherent account of either English history or of the history of English literature: "When I think in *dates* and *times* the wrong people come in—the right people are missing."[55] "Prelude" therefore contributes to a new history of the Great War, as well as a new appreciation of literary modernism. Unlike Wordsworth's *Prelude*, finally, Mansfield's implies that the growth of the poet's mind does not need to alienate her from ecstatic youthful spots of time, if she can muse in her art on the nature of origins, in a sequence of events that serve as a prelude or preface to even the creation of life itself.

Manfield's "Prelude" is also a prelude to her later fiction about the Burnells, especially "At the Bay" (1917) and "The Doll's House" (1921). These stories dramatize the three shifts in perspective that allowed feminist-modernists to reshape the *Künstlerroman* in light of the valuation of their own images of creativity: first, domestic disease or sickness *of* home is imaginatively reconstructed as sickness *for* home in what amounts to a revisionary domestic mythology; second, silent female resistance to or retaliation against the male word transforms itself into fantasies of a woman's language; finally, matrophobia, fear of becoming the mother, turns into matrisexuality, the erotics of mother and child. Exploring the mother-daughter bond as a release from the solipsism of individual consciousness, these redefinitions effect a change not unlike the one implied by the titles of Margaret Sanger's books: *Motherhood in Bondage, The Pivot of Civilization, Woman and the New Race.*

In Mansfield's stories it is the purpose of play to redefine art so that it ceases to exclude women's crafts and instead pays tribute to the domestic mythology of the female community. When Kezia in "Prelude" and all the Burnell children in "At the Bay" play house, the configuration of socialization is less important than the consecration of the house into a sacred space. In "The Doll's House," therefore, the Burnell daughters marvel over the wallpaper, the carpet, the beds with real bedcloths in the play house, but "what Kezia liked more than anything . . . was the lamp" (p. 571). Substituting Kezia's lamp for Beryl's mirror, Mansfield uses the image of the dollhouse to revise Ibsen's famous statement about women's confinement within the home. The miniature interiors, decorated with care, valorize female culture even as they serve as a metaphor for her own art.

As in so much nineteenth-century fiction by women, domesticity competes with the ethos of work as a schema for ordering life.[56] At the same time, the idea of bridging the gap between art and life is an invitation to a utopian project which would create a new world *inside* the old.[57] Recognizing the class privilege that shapes its audience, it nevertheless refuses to distinguish between high and low, elite and popular, even as it allows interruption to structure a creative process that can be started and stopped, picked up and put down, a whole produced out of many fragmented parts.

In 1915 Dorothy Richardson re-shaped the *Künstlerroman* to illuminate the private moments that are added together in a successiveness that suggests the incremental nature of women's experience of time. As May Sinclair explained in her praise of Richardson's creation of "stream of consciousness," "There is no drama, no situation, no set scene" in *Pilgrimage* (1915–67).[58] Instead, what Richardson herself preferred to call "interior monologue" or "feminine prose" illuminates the daily moments of intense, sensuous apprehension whereby Miriam comes to experience her own creativity. Whether she is reading her well-thumbed copy of *Villette* or living on Wimpole Street, Miriam is the pilgrim whose progress is paradigmatically female, as her redefinition of women's artistry illustrates: "whereas a few men here and there are creators, originators, *artists,*" Miriam argues, "women are this all the time." In fact, "their pre-eminence in . . . the art of making atmospheres," which is "as big an art as any other," is so "absolutely life-giving" that it is "like air within the air" that men live in all their lives without seeing.[59] Before she can achieve this readjustment in her assessment of female creativity, however, Miriam has had to work through her resentment at "all the literature of the world" that defines woman as "half-human" or as "undeveloped man," as well as her resistance to the sexual division of labor:

Boys and girls were much the same . . . women stopped being people and went off into hideous processes. What for? What was it all for? Development. The wonders of science for women are nothing but gynaecology—all those frightful operations in the *British Medical Journal.* . . . Sacred functions . . . highest possibilities . . . sacred for what? The hand that rocks the cradle rules the world? The Future of the Race? What race? Men . . . Nothing but men; for ever. (*The Tunnel,* 2:220)

Significantly, while Miriam, like her author, suffers the suicide of her mother (who was one of twenty-two children) and a miscarriage that paradoxically extricates her from the men who would rather she function as their muse than the author of her own story, she begins to detect "the truth behind the image of woman supported by man," that "the strong companion was a child seeking shelter; the woman's share an awful loneliness." A radical critique of culture results from Miriam's recognition of the dependency of men: "It was history, literature, the whole way of stating records, reports, stories, the whole method of statement of things from the beginning that was on a false foundation" (*Deadlock,* 3:212, 218). Specifically, she understands the dependency of even the most eminent men who, "while saying all those things about women, lived on them and their pain, ate their food, enjoyed the comforts they made" (*The Tunnel,* 2:222–23). But she also recognizes the dependency of men on an impoverished monolingualism, for men are "but passing guests never initiated into the house-life, where the real freedom of the women resided. . . . Man's life was bandied to and fro from *word* to *word.* Hemmed in by women, fearing their silence, unable to enter its freedom . . ." (*Revolving Lights,* 3:278). Because "she may understand his [language,]" while "hers he will never speak nor understand" (*The Tunnel,* 2:210), woman is "*alone* in [her] vision of the spaces opening beyond the world of daily life"; her bilingual fluency—"by every word they use men and women mean different things"

(*Oberland*, 4:198, 93)—informs Richardson's efforts to fashion what Virginia Woolf called "the psychological sentence of the female gender."[60] In the last scene of the final volume of *Pilgrimage*, Miriam experiences a "sense of perfect serenity" when folding the sleeping baby of a friend against her own body. This act of adoption seems to imply that one way to allay the anxiety of appropriation that haunts the fragile atmospheric art of women may be a reevaluation of the significance culturally of women's role as nurturers, for it is female silence and speech, the presence and absence of the mother, that inscribes children of both sexes into their distinct languages.

Mansfield's "At the Bay" provides two scenes that explore the blurring of sense and nonsense in a context where women provide the passage for children between nature and culture through their primary role in the acquisition of language. First, Linda Burnell, dreaming on the front lawn about the yellow flowers bruised around her, returns to the central problem of her own existence: "Why, then, flower at all?" (p. 278). Even while she feels "broken, made weak, her courage was gone, through child-bearing," Linda is astonished by the brazen confidence of the newborn baby. Dropping down next to him, she whispers, "Hallo, my funny!" (p. 280). Her words of welcome, effected by the serious indifference of the baby, are matched by Kezia's words of warning when she wants her grandmother to promise that she will not die ("say never . . . say never" [p. 282]). They begin tickling and kissing, Kezia on the old woman's lap, and by the time Mrs. Fairfield regains her knitting, both of them have "forgotten what the 'never' was about." Finally, as if guiding our attention to the freedom conferred by linguistic play, Mansfield portrays the children gathered in the washhouse at the close of the day. Each child is transformed by the game into an animal that reflects his or her own secret sense of self: the spontaneously exuberant sounds of rooster, bull, donkey, and bee are a kind of babbling as the children cleanse themselves of their human identities. Tapping the phatic power of pre-speech, the children's language is vatic; for if the ritual feast at the end of "Prelude" connotes the animal's turning human, this game promises some hope of remission whereby humans can recapture the playfulness of animals.

But the babbling of the children, like the wordplay of the women, also explains why anthropologists like Ashley Montagu have claimed that "ever since the first mother sang her baby to sleep, song and chant have been universally associated with women."[61] Curiously, at precisely the time Mansfield was writing, as noted a linguist as Otto Jesperson was generalizing about the distinguishing characteristics of women's language.[62] While writers from Carroll to Joyce associate men with storytelling, in women's fiction fairy tales and nursery rhymes are frequently identified with the mother's voice, just as the Child ballad in *A Room of One's Own* is related to Woolf's quest for an alternative to what she calls the male style. In a story strikingly similar to Mansfield's New Zealand stories, moreover, Willa Cather describes the three generations it takes to make A WOMAN—nurturing grandmother, anxiously pregnant mother, imaginative daughter—by focusing on old Mrs. Harris's reading aloud of children's books, thereby illuminating the significance of Andrew Lang's remark that it was his wife who translated and adapted the famous fairy tales he published under his own name.[63] In *The Song of the Lark* (1915), Willa Cather actually identifies song itself as an ancient female art, a recoverable mother tongue.

Cather's heroine, Thea, consecrates herself as the Thea or Goddess of Song by visiting a "cleft in the world," Panther Canyon, where the remnants of an ancient civilization still remain intact.[64] Inside "this hollow (like a great fold in the rock)" the Ancient People had worn down the paths which inspire Thea to feel the weight of an Indian baby hanging on her back as she climbs (p. 302). Amid these relics—the grinding stone, the pottery, the needles made of turkey bones—she reimagines her voice in terms of the crafts of a prehistoric matriarchy:

What was any art but an effort to make a sheath, a mold in which to imprison for a moment the shining, elusive element which is life itself,—life hurrying past us and running away, too strong to stop, too sweet to lose? The Indian women had held it in their jars. . . . In singing, one made a vessel of one's throat and nostrils and held it on one's breath, caught the stream in a scale of natural intervals. (P. 304)

The Song of the Lark begins by counterpointing Thea's mother's laboring to give birth to her seventh child and her own illness. Later, she cannot remember her feelings at a concert, "how the violins came in after the horns, just there" (p. 201), when a man interrupts her on the street with his sexual advances. After a succession of masters who teach her technique without addressing this painful contradiction between gender and creativity, it is her visit to the Ancient People that allows Thea to construct a myth of origins through which her voice is reimagined as a metamorphosis of uniquely female instrumentality. Only then is she free to reinvent the operatic role of, say, Wagner's Fricka so as to reclaim the goddess from the shrew or to sing in Moonstone at the funeral of a girl significantly named Maggie Evans.

Thea's discovery of an ancient civilization, unknown yet faintly remembered, is comparable to Mansfield's recovery of her "undiscovered country": "All must be told with a sense of mystery, a radiance, an afterglow," she tells her brother, "because you, my little sun of it, are set."[65] The setting son had freed her to express the rising radiance of the daughters through a myth of origins that celebrates the foreplay of "Prelude," the release from genital sex and biological function through matrisexuality. Therefore, "At the Bay" describes the Burnell family's holiday at Crescent Bay, whose very name recalls the crescent moon worn by Mrs. Fairfield. First hidden under a white sea mist, the bay emerges from the heavy dew all glittery with a web of drops. Where "there was nothing to mark which was beach and where was the sea," everything is smothered in moisture, as if Mansfield were describing a time of immersion when the definitions of things were dissolved away. When all the men depart—"Oh, the relief, the difference it made to have the men out of the house"—what each of the women do in their several ways is to "celebrate the fact that they could do what they liked now. There was no man to disturb them; the whole perfect day was theirs" (p. 470). Even the woman at the store has been transfigured, for the widowed Mrs. Stubbs presides over her cluttered shop in the proud assurance that "Freedom's best!" (p. 287). Situated by the endlessly rocking sea, all the women inhabit the blurred boundaries between shore and water which are, as Freud knew, the perfect setting to represent the blurred demarcations between self and other during the "oceanic" time of infancy when the child thinks of the mother as itself. Mansfield implies that the merging identity experienced by mother and child constitutes an erotic interdependence of the kind that the psychologist Nancy Chodorow claims endows female subjectivity with greater complexity, greater plasticity, and greater empathy.[66] The holiday at the bay is therefore a kind of holy day.

Virginia Woolf learned enough from Mansfield's stories to use them as a model for her own fictional autobiography.[67] To the Lighthouse (1927) evokes a seaside holiday, a conflict between a knitting matriarch and a self-absorbed patriarch, an analysis of the tangential significance of war to women's lives, all washed in an elegiac tone that celebrates the family at home in spite of its limitations. Mrs. Ramsay's passion for putting people in pairs, as well as her grandmother's recipe for Boeuf en Daube, are strongly reminiscent of Mrs. Fairfield's kitchen and Alice's duck dinner, just as Minta Doyle's loss of a brooch on the beach recalls the lost and found gems at the bay. When Mrs. Ramsay converts the rooks into Mary and Joseph through her stories, when she transforms the pig's skull with her shawl into a nest or mountain for Cam and a wild boar for James, when her letter writing at the beach frames for Charles Tansley and Lily Briscoe a permanent moment of friendship which seems "almost like a work of art" (p. 240), she triumphs through precisely the revisionary domesticity that Mansfield celebrates in the female community. By reading aloud even a story like "The Fisherman's Wife," which overtly discourages the willfulness of the woman who would be king, Mrs. Ramsay paradoxically establishes her own primacy in much the same manner as does the old woman who refuses to rescue Hume from a bog until he recites the Lord's Prayer. The same compulsion that animates the fisherman's and the philosopher's female Nemeses impels the groaning and creaking Mrs. McNab, mother of two baseborn children and one who deserted her, when she performs through her heroic housecleaning a "rusty laborious birth" (p. 210) to stay the rot and corruption. But if these Victorian paragons represent the perpetuation of real butter and clean milk, of the red-hot pokers and Waverley novels and tea sets that grace domestic life, then Prue, who dies in "some illness associated with childbirth" (p. 199), and Minta Doyle, who is sacrificed on the altar of Mrs. Ramsay's passion for marriage, are representatives of the generation that uncovers the coercion and cost of the mother's script.

It is, of course, Lily who receives, from the little sprig or leaf pattern on the tablecloth, a revelation that allows her to integrate the experiences of mothers and daughters in a vision that reveals how the stories of both echo and reverberate against and alongside each other. In the first part of the novel, Lily knows the "passage from conception to work [to be] as dreadful as any down a dark passage for a child" (p. 32), because her own inadequacy and insignificance bear down on her. Ten years later, listening to Charles Tansley's refrain—"women can't paint, women can't write" (p. 238)—until it becomes more of a goad or an incentive than an inhibition, she feels first a "moment of nakedness" when she is "like an unborn soul . . . exposed without protection to the blasts of doubt" (p. 287). But then she experiences the permeability of women's interiority as she paints in an effort to recover an image of the dead Mrs. Ramsay.

While Lily is wondering if loving "can make her and Mrs. Ramsay one," like "waters poured into one jar, inextricably the same," what she desires is "not knowledge but unity . . . not inscription on tablets, nothing that could be written in any language known to men, but intimacy itself, which is knowledge" (p. 79). With her mind throwing up ideas and memories "like a fountain spraying over" (p. 238), much as Mrs. Ramsay had poured "erect into the air a rain of energy, a column of spray" (p. 58), with Lily's attention divided between her canvas and Mr. Ramsay's expedition to the lighthouse, which "had stretched her body and mind to the utmost" (p. 308), much as Mrs. Ramsay had stretched her attention out to embrace the isolated people around her dinner table and the foreign girl sobbing in the attic, in the process of painting Lily maintains her singular integrity even as she attains the multipersonal consciousness which distinguishes Mrs. Ramsay. Disentangling a maternal psychology and aesthetics from biological motherhood, Lily can reduce the object of universal veneration—mother and child—to a purple shadow "without irreverence" (p. 81). Solving the problem of distance, "to want and want [the mother] and not to have" (p. 300), she wins through to an elegiac vision of the three generations it takes to make A WOMAN. She sees a procession across white, flower-strewn valleys, composed of Prue, who had "let her flowers fall from her basket"; Mrs. Ramsay, who walked "rather fast in front"; and a mysterious third: "They went, the three of them together," over austere, steep hills (p. 299).

After Lily realizes that she can complete her picture by moving the salt cellar on the tablecloth, after she understands that, unlike Prue, she does not need to be a character in one of Mrs. Ramsay's marital plots ("she would move the tree to the middle, and need never marry anyone"), she paints a "tribute" (p. 262) to the domestic artistry of the mother. The sensual stroking of the canvas, like the third stroke of the lighthouse beam, Mrs. Ramsay's stroke, culminates in a moment of ecstatic union which implies on the one hand that mother-daughter eroticism predates heterosexuality for women and on the other hand that the daughter's celebration of the dead mother serves as recompense for a life that repudiates the strictures that structured the mother's. In her last stroke, therefore, Lily puts "the tree further in the middle" (p. 128); she will bring "the line of the branch across so" to "break the vacancy in the foreground" (p. 83). While Lily imagines Mr. Ramsay as the abstract table hung on the pear tree (p. 38), Mrs. Ramsay as the mother-muse is the tree itself, rising up as "a rosy-flowered fruit tree laid with leaves and dancing boughs" (p. 60) and growing still "like a tree which has been tossing and quivering and now, when the breeze falls, settles, leaf by leaf, into quiet" (p. 177). Mrs. Ramsay has heard her own voice in the words, "And all the lives we ever lived and all the lives to be are full of trees and changing leaves" (p. 166), and she has quite unconsciously used "the branches of the elm trees outside to help her to stabilise her position" (p. 169). Finally, then, the line Lily draws in the center of her canvas is a flowering family tree of life that resembles Mansfield's aloe, as well as Schreiner's mimosa, Gilman's forest for Amazons, H. D.'s flowering rod, and, of course, the poem that would win the literary prize for Orlando, "The Oak Tree." The flower that names the painter, the lily so dear to Mansfield, implies that Lily's Chinese eyes, as well as her sardonic self-protectiveness, constitute if not a fictional portrait of Mansfield then a tribute on Woolf's part to Mansfield's achievement.[68]

The ecstatic female aesthetic that evolved out of the female literary tradition, infused with these empowering symbols of female generation, is tempered by the recognition that female autonomy has a tentative fragility, existing (as it does) within an overarching patriarchal structure. Even the most joyously affirmative of Mansfield's stories dramatize the return of men who reassert their right of possession over the community of women and children, as does the darkening vision of Miss LaTrobe, the last and most isolated of Woolf's fictional artists. Even in her euphoric community of women at the bay,

Mansfield includes a portrait of the new woman—Mrs. Harry Kember—whose reptilian coldness casts a sinister spell on her childlessness, her smoking, her fast talk: playing bridge "every day of her life" (p. 275), Mrs. Kember is willing to be a bridge between her husband and other women, almost like a pimp or panderer. What she seems to embody is Mansfield's horror of sexuality and her fear that women's relationships with women can be tarnished by male modes of relating to women. Just as female modernists only managed to envision a moment of exultant delivery, revisionary female psychoanalyists in this period failed to impede the rapid acceptance of Freudian theory after World War I which coincided with the decline of the feminist movement.[69] Experimentation with play in the analysis of children by Melanie Klein, Anna Freud, and Clara Thompson did not lead to a serious revaluation of the importance of the pre-Oedipal bond until very recently, although Virginia Woolf powerfully redefined the Oedipus complex in *Three Guineas* (1938) as a reflex of the "infantile fixation" of fathers like Mr. Barrett and the Reverend Patrick Brontë, who were fiercely determined to make their daughters mother them. Interestingly, Woolf calls the source of men's possessive fears "an egg," the germ of the fathers' disease.[70]

As tragic a consequence of the refusal of writers like Mansfield and Woolf to represent the professional component of the artistic careers they themselves pursued is its reenactment of women's recurrent anxiety over acknowledging their own exceptional extrication from the historical context of the very women who created them. The generation gap between such childless women writers and their mothers resulted in a sometimes guilty, sometimes tender effort to reconcile radically disparate experiences. In their *Künstlerromane,* therefore, the relationship between the daughter-artist and her mother is far less easily resolved through rejection than it is in the famous *Künstlerromane* of their male counterparts. If their efforts to redefine the struggle of creative transcendence refuse to invoke a binary opposition to biological immanence, by representing the discontinuity and diffusion of female experience they nevertheless attain the distance that makes possible the very same displacement experienced by, say, the artist-heroes of Lawrence and Joyce. But in the process, they reject portraits of the woman-artist supplied by writers like Lawrence, who had imagined Katherine Mansfield as Gudrun in *Women in Love,* a sterile, death-dealing miniaturist with a clocklike face that told of a futile obsession with the passing of time.

Just as the early twentieth-century suffrage movement failed to abstract the value of motherhood and domestic labor from the legal and economic commodity system,[71] feminist-modernists struggled against the conservative consequences of asserting a natural and distinct sphere. When it became clear, moreover, during and after World War II, that the visionary feminist physicians and birth-controllers had failed to wrest power over the female reproductive system from the medical establishment and that a feminine mystique was replacing female self-definition, women's *Künstlerromane* suffered a critical disillusionment. We can see the utopian project dampened, if not extinguished, in Christina Stead's *The Man Who Loved Children* (1940) when the daughter-artist can only respond to her mother's painful cry, "My womb is tearing," with the act of matricide.[72] In *The Bell Jar* (1963), Sylvia Plath's artist-heroine agonizes over the "enormous spider-fat stomach and two little ugly spindly legs propped in the high stirrups" of a woman so drugged during a forced labor that she "would go straight home and start another baby," forgetting "how bad the pain had been, when all the time . . . in some secret part of her, that long, blind, doorless and windowless corridor of pain was waiting to open up and shut her in again."[73] Esther Greenwood's horror at her own flesh and her revulsion against working for *Ladies' Day* haunt Doris Lessing's *The Golden Notebook* (1962), where Anna Wulf's writing block is caused by her disgust at the female body, which is "a sort of spider, all clutching arms and legs around a hairy central devouring mouth," her dread of the medical specialist Dr. Bloodrot, her fear that her diaries will kill or maim the children who read them, and her suspicion that women's language is sentimental or coy, like the insipid magazine *Women at Home*. The Algerian soldier who patrols her desk, implying that serious fiction focuses exclusively on the politics of war, almost succeeds in convincing her that the significance of the battlefield obliterates the importance of women inhabiting what Woolf called "the common sitting-room."[74]

Not until the recent fiction of Alice Walker, Margaret Drabble, and Margaret Atwood do we find a resurgence of the utopian imperative that characterizes the modernist period. In "Everyday Use" (1967), Walker's meditation on revisionary domesticity, two quilts—hand-stitched out of the dresses of a grandmother— are bequeathed by a mother not to the daughter who would misuse them by hanging them up as a sign of her mystification of a heritage she refuses to acknowledge in her own life but to the daughter who would put them to everyday use, much as she puts her memory of her family's past practices to use daily.[75] Drabble's recurrent interest in matrisexuality locates the first scene of *The Waterfall* (1969) in the "close heat" of a home delivery that "would surely generate its own salvation," as Drabble transforms the fatal Victorian childbirth bed into a fertile bed of love.[76] And in *Surfacing* (1972), Atwood's unnamed heroine discovers the transformative power of the female body at the sacred signs of power marked by an earlier culture. An illustrator of expurgated fairy tales, she returns to childhood fantasies of her own devising and earlier illustrations: drawings of ornately decorated Easter eggs, page after page of egg-houses with doors at the top, connected by bridges and surrounded by flowers.[77] But this is an old notebook which needs to be revised in light of her new-found consciousness of complicity in death. When she dives down to decode fictions falsifying an abortion and surfaces in a ritualistic act of intercourse that may or may not issue in the birth of a divine child, Atwood's heroine recapitulates a process that addresses the question Amy Lowell asks in her poem about women poets, "The Sisters," actually the question raised by all writers in this tradition: "Why are we/Already mother-creatures, double-bearing/With matrices in body and brain?"[78] As in a chorus, the sisters of literature pray responsively with the ambivalent intensity of Sylvia Plath brooding over her own motherhood, her biological mother, and her literary foremothers:

> Mother, you are the one mouth
> I would be tongue to. Mother of otherness
> Eat me.[79]

Even as she accepts the pain of being consumed in her labor, Plath announces the sacrament of women quickening with art and life and approaching their own crowning.

NOTES

This paper is dedicated to the education and reclamation of Senators John East of North Carolina, Charles Grassley of Iowa, Jeremiah Denton of Alabama, Orrin Hatch of Utah, and Jesse Helms of North Carolina and to my good friend Anne Hedin.
Epigraphs: "Parturition" (1923) is reprinted in *The World Split Open,* ed. Louise Bernikow (New York: Vintage, 1974), pp. 254–57. "Metaphors" (1960) appears in *Crossing the Water* (New York: Harper & Row, 1971), p. 43.
Throughout this paper, I am indebted to the brilliant insights of Sandra M. Gilbert and to the members of our 1981 NEH Summer Seminar on Feminism and Modernism.

1. Ralph M. Wardle, *Mary Wollstonecraft: A Critical Biography* (Lawrence: University of Kansas Press, 1951), pp. 302–6.
2. Ellen Moers, *Literary Women* (New York: Doubleday, 1976), pp. 90–99.
3. Jane Austen, *Jane Austen's Letters to Her Sister Cassandra and Others,* ed. R. W. Chapman, 2d ed. (London: Oxford University Press, 1952), pp. 210, 483, 488.

4. For an account of Charlotte Brontë's illness during pregnancy, see the last chapter of Helene Moglen's *Charlotte Brontë: The Self Conceived* (New York: Norton, 1976).

5. Consider the abduction and rape of Marion Earle in *Aurora Leigh,* or Hetty Sorrel's infanticide in *Adam Bede* and the Princess Halm-Eberstein's desertion in *Daniel Deronda,* or the childbirth death in *Mary Barton.*

6. Virginia Woolf, *A Room of One's Own* (New York: Harcourt, Brace & World, 1957), p. 22. Subsequent page references appear parenthetically in the text.

7. The phrase "flight from maternity" comes from J. A. Banks and Olive Banks, *Feminism and Family Planning in Victorian England* (Liverpool: Liverpool University Press, 1964). See also Sheila Ryan Johansson's "Sex and Death in Victorian England: An Examination of Age- and Sex-Specific Death Rates, 1840–1910," in *A Widening Sphere: Changing Roles of Victorian Women,* ed. Martha Vicinus (Bloomington: Indiana University Press, 1980), pp. 163–81; and Madeleine Riley, *Brought to Bed* (London: J. M. Denton & Sons, 1968), p. 49. Sheila Rowbotham explains that "around the end of the nineteenth century fewer than 20 per cent of all families had less than three children. By the 1930s only 19 per cent of all families had more than three" (*A New World for Women* [London: Pluto Press, 1977], p. 43).

8. M. L. Holbrook, *Parturition without Pain: A Code of Directions for Escaping from the Primal Curse* (New York: Word and Holbrook, 1875), p. 15.

9. Barbara Ehrenreich and Deirdre English, *Complaints and Disorders* (Old Westbury, N.Y.: The Feminist Press, 1973), p. 29.

10. Shirley Green, *The Curious History of Contraception* (London: Ebury Press, 1971), p. 138.

11. Ibid., p. 138; Harold Speert, *Iconographia Gyniatrica: A Pictorial History of Gynecology and Obstetrics* (Philadelphia: F. A. Davis, 1973), p. 8.

12. Ray's 1866 statement is quoted in G. J. Barker-Benfield, *The Horrors of the Half-Known Life: Male Attitudes toward Women and Sexuality in 19th-Century America* (New York: Harper Colophon, 1976), p. 83.

13. W. H. Buck's comments are discussed in Richard Wertz and Dorothy Wertz, *Lying-In: A History of Childbirth in America* (New York: Schocken, 1979), p. 101.

14. Professor Dewees, who worked on midwifery at the University of Pennsylvania in the early nineteenth century, and Professor Byford, who worked on gynecology at the University of Chicago in the 1860s, are

quoted by Ann Douglas Wood in "'The Fashionable Diseases': Women's Complaints and Their Treatment in Nineteenth-Century America," in *Clio's Consciousness Raised: New Perspectives on the History of Women,* ed. Mary Hartman and Lois W. Banner (New York: Harper Torchbooks, 1974), pp. 3–4.

15. Joseph Needham, *A History of Embryology* (New York: Abelard-Schuman, 1959), pp. 208, 220–22, provides a background for the controversies between ovists and preformationists.

16. Elaine Showalter and English Showalter, "Victorian Women and Menstruation," in *Suffer and Be Still: Women in the Victorian Age,* ed. Martha Vicinus (Bloomington: Indiana University Press, 1972), p. 39; and James V. Ricci, *One Hundred Years of Gynaecology* (Philadelphia: Blackiston Co., 1945), p. 10.

17. Carl N. Degler, *At Odds: Women and the Family in America from the Revolution to the Present* (Oxford: Oxford University Press, 1980), pp. 214–25: "As late as 1910 radical birth-control advocates were still describing the safe period as half way between menstrual periods." However, Doctors George Napheys and Frederick Hollick "did hit upon the right timing."

18. Thomas Aquinas argued in his *Summa Theologica* that "the generative power of the female is imperfect compared to that of the male; for just as in the crafts, the inferior workman prepares the material and the more skilled operator shapes it, so likewise the female generative virtue provides the substance but the active male virtue makes it into the finished product" (quoted in Needham, *History of Embryology,* p. 93). This argument may be related to Aquinas's belief that the male fetus has a soul at forty days, while the female fetus has a soul only at eighty days. Certainly it is related to Aristotle's notion that "the female is . . . a mutilated male" who "provides the material" that "the Male . . . fashions" (*De Generatione Animalium,* excerpted in *History of Ideas,* ed. Rosemary Agonita [New York: A Paragon Book, 1977], pp. 36–37). For a discussion of Harvey see Needham, *History of Embryology,* pp. 133–50.

19. Benjamin H. Willier and Jane M. Oppenheimer, eds., *Foundations of Experimental Embryology* (Englewood Cliffs, N.J.: Prentice-Hall, 1964), pp. 2–51, 74–97.

20. Sandra M. Gilbert, "Potent Griselda: D. H. Lawrence's *Ladybird* and Literary Maternity" (Paper presented at the Conference Commemorating Simone de Beauvoir's *The Second Sex,* New York, Fall 1979).

21. Barbara Ehrenreich and Deirdre English, *For Her Own Good: 150 Years of the Experts' Advice to Women* (New York: Anchor, 1974), pp. 69–140; Linda Gordon, *Woman's Body, Woman's Right: A Social*

History of Birth Control in America (New York: Penguin, 1977), pp. 159–85; Barker-Benfield, *The Horrors of the Half-Known Life,* pp. 61–132; Adrienne Rich, *Of Woman Born* (New York: Bantam, 1977).

22. Barker-Benfield, in *The Horrors of the Half-Known Life,* makes the point that Marion Sims felt "an underlying sense of a gynecologist's dependence on women" (p. 108) and discusses Sims's metaphors (on pp. 112–13, 117).

23. Ricci, *One Hundred Years of Gynaecology,* pp. 46–47.

24. James Reed, *From Private Vice to Public Virtue* (New York: Basic Books, 1978), p. 12.

25. Jean Donnison, *Midwives and Medical Men: A History of Inter-Professional Rivalries and Women's Rights* (New York: Schocken, 1977), pp. 64–77.

26. Regina Morantz quotes Ann Preston and Mary Putnam-Jacobi in "The Lady and Her Physician," in Hartman and Banner, *Clio's Consciousness Raised,* pp. 48–49.

27. Constance Rover, *Love, Morals and the Feminists* (London: Routlege & Kegan Paul, 1970), pp. 110–21; and Norman E. Hines, *Medical History of Contraception* (New York: Schocken, 1970), p. 309.

28. Ehrenreich and English discuss the National Congress of Mothers in *For Her Own Good,* pp. 193–94.

29. Reed, *From Private Vice to Public Virtue,* p. 60.

30. For a general discussion of Margaret Sanger see Gordon, *Woman's Body, Woman's Right,* pp. 211–45; the letter Stanton Blatch wrote to Margaret Sanger is quoted in Reed, *From Private Vice to Public Virtue,* p. 131.

31. Curiously, in 1928, the very year Woolf lectured about the four Marys to the Arts Society at Girton, the birth-controller Marie Stopes published a novel entitled *Love's Creation* under the pseudonym Marie Carmichael.

32. Mary Ellmann, *Thinking About Women* (New York: Harcourt Brace Jovanovich, 1968), p. 63; and Nina Auerbach, "Artists and Mothers: A False Alliance," *Women and Literature* 9 (Spring 1978): 3–5. Also, Terry Castle, "Lab'ring Bards," *Journal of English and Germanic Philology* 78, no. 2 (April 1979): 201; and Elizabeth Sacks, *Shakespeare's Images of Pregnancy* (New York: St. Martins Press, 1980).

33. Grace Stewart has written extensively about the disjunction between women's experience of their own creativity and the male *Künstlerroman* conventions in *A New Mythos: The Novel of the Artist as Heroine, 1877–1977* (St. Albans, Vt.: Eden Press, 1979). Specifically, she calls into question the categories of analysis employed by Maurice Beebe in *Ivory*

Towers and Sacred Founts: The Artist as Hero in Fiction from Goethe to Joyce (New York: New York University Press, 1964).

34. Carolyn Heilbrun, *Reinventing Womanhood* (New York: Norton, 1979), p. 71.

35. Mary Burgan, "Childbirth Trauma in Katherine Mansfield's Early Stories," *Modern Fiction Studies* 24 (Autumn 1978): 395–412.

36. Katherine Mansfield to J. Middleton Murry, 3 February 1918, *The Letters of Katherine Mansfield,* ed. J. Middleton Murry (New York: Alfred A. Knopf, 1932), p. 106.

37. Katherine Mansfield, "The Woman at the Store," in *The Short Stories of Katherine Mansfield* (New York: Alfred A. Knopf, 1976), p. 126. Subsequent citations from stories refer to this edition and appear parenthetically in the text.

38. Rebecca Harding Davis, *Life in the Iron Mills,* ed. Tillie Olsen (Old Westbury, N.Y.: The Feminist Press, 1972), p. 32. See Tillie Olsen's afterword, as well as her *Silences* (New York: Delta, 1979).

39. Olive Schreiner, *From Man to Man* (Chicago: Academy Press Limited, 1977), p. 195.

40. Sandra M. Gilbert and Susan Gubar, *The Madwoman in the Attic: The Woman Writer and the 19th-Century Literary Imagination* (New Haven: Yale University Press, 1979), pp. 35–36, 197–99.

41. Kate Chopin, *The Awakening* (New York: Norton Critical, 1976), pp. 63, 110. The labor scene in this novel, witnessed by Edna, who experiences "an inward agony, with a flaming, outspoken revolt against the ways of Nature," is "a scene [of] torture" which immediately precedes the death of a heroine who has begun to take her painting seriously after leaving her husband and children (see chaps. 37 and 38).

42. Elizabeth Stuart Phelps Ward, *The Story of Avis* (Boston: James R. Osgood and Co., 1877), p. 126. *The Story of Avis* self-consciously locates itself in the tradition of Barrett Browning's *Aurora Leigh* and Eliot's *Armgart.* Subsequent page references appear parenthetically in the text.

43. Florence Nightingale, *Cassandra* (Old Westbury, N.Y.: The Feminist Press, 1979), pp. 32 and 34.

44. Porter's *Writers at Work,* quoted in Olsen, *Silences,* p. 216; May Sarton, *Mrs. Stevens Hears the Mermaids Singing* (New York: Norton, 1974), p. 18.

45. Tuberculosis was associated with hormonal changes in puberty and childbearing, as well as with hypersexuality and prostitution, according to Ehrenreich and English, *Complaints,* pp. 20, 30. See also Susan Sontag, *Illness as Metaphor* (New York: Vintage, 1979), p. 35.

46. *Journal of Katherine Mansfield,* ed. J. Middleton Murry (London: Constable, 1962), p. 313.

47. Elaine Showalter, *A Literature of Their Own* (Princeton: Princeton University Press, 1977), p. 196.

48. *The Diary of Anaïs Nin, Volume Two, 1934–1939,* ed. Gunther Stuhlmann (New York: Harvest, 1967), p. 233; and idem, *Under a Glass Bell* (Chicago: Swallow Press, 1948), pp. 96–101. For a critical response to Nin's view see Ellen Peck Kolloh, "The Woman Writer and the Element of Destruction," *College English* 34, no. 1 (October 1972): 31–38.

49. Mansfield, *Journal,* pp. 95–98.

50. Jeffrey Meyers, *Katherine Mansfield* (New York: New Directions, 1978), pp. 5–6; and Anthony Alpers, *The Life of Katherine Mansfield* (New York: Viking, 1980), pp. 244–46.

51. Mansfield, *Letters,* p. 658.

52. For a discussion of how the Incarnation is a female freedom see Walter J. Ong, *Fighting for Life* (Ithaca: Cornell University Press, 1981), p. 174. Mansfield associates her dead brother with Christ in a poem entitled "L.H.B. (1884–1915)," quoted in Leslie Moore's *Katherine Mansfield* (London: Michael Joseph, 1971), p. 96.

53. Mansfield to the Hon. Dorothy Brett, 11 October 1917, in Mansfield, *Letters,* p. 74.

54. Marvin Magalaner, *The Fiction of Katherine Mansfield* (Carbondale: Southern Illinois University Press, 1971), pp. 29–31.

55. Mansfield, *Journal,* p. 104.

56. Nina Baym, *Woman's Fiction* (Ithaca: Cornell University Press, 1978), p. 27.

57. Holbrook Jackson discusses the utopian element in William Morris's crafts movement in *The Eighteen-Nineties* (London: Grant Richards, 1922), p. 248.

58. May Sinclair, "The Novels of Dorothy Richardson," *The Egoist* 5 (April 1918): 58. May Sinclair's *Künstlerroman* entitled *Mary Oliver: A Life* was influenced by Richardson's.

59. Dorothy Richardson, *Revolving Lights in Pilgrimage,* 4 vols. (New York: Alfred A. Knopf, 1967), 3:256–57; Subsequent page references to *Pilgrimage* appear parenthetically in the text.

60. Virginia Woolf, "Romance and the Heart," *Nation and Athenaeum,* 19 May 1923, p. 229.

61. Ashley Montagu, *The Natural Superiority of Women* (London: Collier-Macmillan, 1968), p. 142.

62. Otto Jesperson, "The Woman," in his *Language* (New York: Macmillan Co., 1949), pp. 237–54.

63. Marion Glastonbury, "Holding the Pens" in *Inspiration and Drudgery,* ed. Sarah Elbert and Marion Glastonbury (London: Women's Research and Resource Centre Publications, 1928), p. 28; Willa Cather, "Old Mrs. Harris," *Obscure Destinies* (New York: Vintage, 1974), pp. 74–190. In her essay "Katherine Mansfield," Willa Cather focuses on family life in Mansfield stories (*On Writing* [New York: Alfred A. Knopf, 1953], p. 108).

64. Willa Cather, *The Song of the Lark* (Lincoln: University of Nebraska Press, 1978), p. 301. Subsequent page references appear parenthetically in the text.

65. Mansfield, *Journal,* p. 94.

66. Nancy Chodorow, *The Reproduction of Mothering* (Berkeley and Los Angeles: University of California Press, 1978), pp. 109–10. See also Elizabeth Abel, "(E)merging Identities: The Dynamics of Female Friendship in Contemporary Fiction by Women," *Signs* 6, no. 3 (Spring 1981): 413–35; and Judith Gardiner's response, "The (US)es of (I)dentity," ibid., pp. 436–42.

67. The essay on Woolf and Mansfield by Ann L. McLaughlin, "The Same Joy," in the special issue of *Modern Fiction Studies* 24, no. 3 (Autumn 1978): 369–82, is devoted to Mansfield's relationship with Woolf. Page citations in the text refer to Virginia Woolf, *To The Lighthouse* (New York: Harcourt, Brace & World, 1955).

68. I am indebted here, as elsewhere, to my colleague Mary Burgan, whose knowledge about Mansfield's place in the modernist tradition has enriched my understanding, and to Jane Lilienfeld's fine reading of *To The Lighthouse:* "'The Deceptiveness of Beauty': Mother Love and Mother Hate in *To The Lighthouse,*" *20th Century Literature* 23 (October 1977): 345–76. Lily's identity is incisively tied to Woolf's sister Vanessa in Gayatri Spivak's essay on *To The Lighthouse* in *Woman and Language in Literature and Society,* ed. Sally McConnell-Ginet, Ruth Borker, and Nelly Furman (New York: Praeger, 1980), pp. 310–27. I am not arguing here that Lily represents Mansfield, but rather that the book situates itself in a tradition Mansfield helped to create.

69. Shulamith Firestone, *The Dialectic of Sex* (New York: Bantam, 1971), pp. 61–71.

70. Virginia Woolf, *Three Guineas* (New York: Harcourt, Brace & World, 1966), p. 127.

71. Rowbotham, *A New World for Women,* p. 21.

72. Christina Stead, *The Man Who Loved Children* (New York: Avon, 1966), p. 471.

73. Sylvia Plath, *The Bell Jar* (New York: Bantam, 1975), p. 53. A nice

example of the devaluation of domestic artistry is the description here of what happens to the rug made by Buddy's mother.

74. Doris Lessing, *The Golden Notebook* (New York: Bantam, 1979), p. 612. I am indebted to the excellent unpublished work of Anne Hedin on Doris Lessing's fiction.

75. Alice Walker, "Everyday Use," in *Love and Trouble: Stories of Black Women* (New York: Harcourt Brace Jovanovich, 1973), pp. 47–59.

76. Margaret Drabble, *The Waterfall* (New York: Popular Library, 1977), p. 10.

77. Margaret Atwood, *Surfacing* (New York: Popular Library, 1972), p. 109.

78. Amy Lowell, "The Sisters," reprinted in *No More Masks!,* ed. Florence Howe and Ellen Bass (Garden City, N.Y.: Anchor Press, 1973), p. 40.

79. Sylvia Plath, "Who," in *Crossing the Water* (London: Faber and Faber, 1971), p. 49.

 *Jane Marcus*

Liberty, Sorority, Misogyny

In *A Room of One's Own* Virginia Woolf explicates a Marxist-feminist theory of literary criticism. "Masterpieces are not single and solitary births," she wrote, "they are the outcome of thinking in common, of thinking by the body of the people, so that the experience of the mass is behind the single voice."[1] She was discussing Shakespeare as the product of history and imagined that Shakespeare's sister, the great woman artist, would arrive when women had had intellectual freedom for several generations. In *Moments of Being* she went even further: "there is no Shakespeare, there is no Beethoven; certainly and emphatically there is no God; we are the words; we are the music; we are the thing itself."[2]

Behind these fierce assertions is the hostile and threatening assertion made by men to feminists of Woolf's generation that women have produced no geniuses, no Shakespeares, no Beethovens, no Rembrandts. Woolf always looks at the writer in historical context, at the conditions of women's lives: "intellectual freedom depends on material things" (*Room,* pp. 162–63). We are bound to follow her example when we look at her work. It is in the history of her family that we may find the source of her philosophy. The Stephen men and the men of her circle were shaped by institutions, Cambridge University and the secret society, the Apostles, which affirmed their being as the "intellectual aristocracy" of England.[3]

In order to catapult women into history Woolf analyzed the notions of liberty, equality, and fraternity of her forefathers and her friends. Female liberty, equality, and sorority were her goals. In imagination and in action she met misogyny full-face. Her birth image in the passage from *A Room of One's Own* is only one of many vaginal creative spaces (a room of one's own is the most famous) which she asserted as a response to

birth image

Vaginal creative spaces → a room of one's own

phallocentric culture. The virginal vagina was the place and the space for the production of female culture. Women could not be the producers of culture while reproducing humankind, she felt, and history bore her out. Her task was further complicated by the fact that the misogynists were of two types. The old bullies like James Fitzjames Stephen who thundered about separate spheres and angels in the house were replaced in her own generation and the one before it by a homosexual hegemony over British culture.[4] Woolf did not attack homosexuality itself, nor do I.

But male superiority and the valorization of homosexual over heterosexual love, learned at Cambridge in the study of Greek and reinforced by the philosophy debated in the meetings of the Apostles, resulted in a subtler and more dangerous kind of woman-hating. These men had class and cultural power, an old-boy network with connections in government, diplomacy, education, publishing, and the literary journals. They were not, like homosexuals of more vulnerable classes, the natural allies of women, fellow outsiders. It was working-class men Woolf called upon to be the allies of women in their struggle against patriarchal imperialism and capitalism in *Three Guineas*. By then it was clear to her that "outsiders" needed not only rooms of their own but institutions of their own—buildings, universities, libraries.

In "A Society" Woolf made the most radical assertion of the idea that the production of culture and the reproduction of children were incompatible. Her sorority determines that the only way for women to take control over the production of culture is to find some way for men to bear children. If they are occupied with producing children, then women may produce books. One way that phallocentric culture imprisons women is to enforce guilt.

In *Between the Acts* Woolf rejects Swinburne's recasting of the swallow and the nightingale myth from its original claim of the power of sisterhood over the patriarchal family to a misogynist nagging whine intended to produce guilt. Weighted with this male-imposed guilt, Woolf shows, the married woman cannot begin to bond with her sisters. Into the mouth of the nightingale Swinburne puts a seductive threat: "Thou hast forgotten, O summer swallow/but the world will end when I forget."[5] The nightingale forecasts universal doom if the killing of a male child in revenge for his rapist father's action is forgotten. But the speaker is the rape victim. She has forgotten her own rape and the cutting out of her tongue by her brother-in-law. Her sorrows are not to be sung, the male poet tells us. Woolf rewrites the poem in order to straighten out priorities. *Between the Acts* tells us that "what we must remember" is the rape; "what we must forget" is the male rewriting of women's history.

representation of ♀ :

1) values spinsterhood ie ♀ without ♂

Woolf's feminism marks the representation of women throughout her fiction. Spinsterhood, for her, is the measure of success. Her artists and reformers, from Lily Briscoe to Eleanor Pargiter, Mary Datchet to Lucy Swithin, are women without men. The virgin mothers, Mrs. Ramsay and Clarissa Dalloway, are women who refuse men, even their husbands. Betty Flanders, widow, recalls in *Jacob's Room* gelding her cat with relish, in memory of her former suitor. Miss Kilman and Miss La Trobe represent varieties of lesbian existence. Rachel Vinrace experiences male sexuality as rape and dies. In Woolf's most traditional novel, Katherine Hilbery marries an outsider for intellectual freedom and escape from her class and family. She is not sexually attracted to Ralph, and they acknowledge that their companionate marriage will be made possible by the single women who will shoulder their burdens of both family and social responsibility.

2) female heterosexuality represented as victimization or colonization

Female heterosexuality is most often represented in Woolf's fiction as victimization or colonization. Those women who accept the ideology of female submission in patriarchal marriage are silently condemned. Mrs. Ramsay's insistence on marriage and traditional roles results in the death of her son in battle and of her daughter in childbirth; we see the unhappy results of the marriages she arranged. The patriarchal family is violently assaulted as the source of fascism in *The Years*. Marriage is a primitive form of private property, North thinks. We will never be civilized as long as we wallow in the "primeval swamp" of marriage; if it is a question of *my* children, *my* property, "it would be one rip down the belly; or teeth in the soft fur of the throat."[6] Sara's relationship with Nicholas the homosexual is presented as eccentric but ethical. If the historian had only Woolf's novels from which to deduce the position of women in England, she would be forced to conclude that marriage was a primitive institution in decline; that many women perceived male sexuality as rape; that lesbianism and homosexuality were widespread; that spinsterhood, aunthood, sisterhood, and female friendship were women's most important roles; that motherhood and wifehood were Victorian relics. Peggy, exhausted from sitting up late with a woman in childbirth, is a new woman professional. "All her patients said that, she thought. Rest— rest—let me rest. How to deaden; how to cease to feel; that was the cry of the woman bearing children; to rest, to cease to be. In the Middle Ages, she thought, it was the cell; the monastery; now it's the laboratory, the professions" (*The Years*, p. 335).

The Years asks the question, Is there a pattern? and *Between the Acts* gives a sociobiological answer. The origin of aggression, war, and oppression is in the origin of the species, in the drama of the battle of the sexes. Isa and Giles fight like the dog fox and the vixen before they make love. Giles is a male animal. He kills the snake with the toad in its mouth. With blood on his shoes, he fornicates with Mrs. Manresa like an ape attracted to a female in heat. Is there another plot? Will the author come out of the bushes and invent a new story not enacted in the village pageant or in the lives of the audience? The question is whether Miss La Trobe can imagine the beginning of the human drama without a violent power struggle. So far it is clear that the survival of the fittest is in conflict with the survival of the creative woman. She can only refuse to reproduce, refuse wifehood and *chastity = power* (margin note)

motherhood. Chastity is power. Chastity is liberty.[7] Marriage, to take a phrase from Woolf's contemporary socialist feminist Cecily Hamilton, is a trade.[8] And since women have no control over the means of production in their trade or the means of reproduction, their only access to dignity is the sexual strike.

political implications of female sexuality + male violence against g (margin note)

In three essays published roughly a decade apart and in her last novel Woolf dealt both directly and indirectly with the political implications of female sexuality and male violence against women. The reception of these texts is a corollary of their thesis. "A Society" was published in *Monday or Tuesday* in 1921 and never reprinted because of the hostility of male critics. In *A Room of One's Own* (1928) the author tries to hide her feminist impulses behind the skirts of several narrators and plants her darts at the patriarchy in between passages of fine writing, meant to seduce and solace the male reader. E. M. Forster and his ilk could then, by avoiding her ideas, praise passages of description and create Virginia Woolf the lyrical formalist, minor mandarin, for generations of critics to analyze. *Three Guineas* (1938) plays no games and lost her what was left of her audience. It was met and is still met by male abuse. Finally, I would like to discuss these issues as they appear in *Between the Acts,* published after Woolf's death. All four works are formally experimental, suggesting her unease with tradition and her radical feminist need to overthrow patriarchal forms. "A Society"

?? .. (margin note)

radical fem. need to overthrow patriarchal forms (margin note)

is a propagandistic and personal essay much like the papers delivered by young men at the meetings of the Cambridge University secret society, the Apostles, where a serious philosophical or moral issue was debated with humor in simple language but according to G. E. Moore's rigorous philosophy of truth-telling. "A Society" pretends to be a short story, but the message drowns the characters and the plot, and it is more like Wollstonecraft's *Maria; or, The Wrongs of Woman* than Katherine Mansfield's *Bliss.*

A *Room of One's Own* appears to be a set of lectures given

at Newnham and Girton. Nonacademic and nonscholarly, they revive as characters Mary Beeton, Mary Seton, and Mary Carmichael from the old ballad in a shockingly feminist rhetorical strategy which excludes the male reader and directly addresses the female reader.[9] But to capture the uniqueness of Woolf's form in *A Room of One's Own*, one may say that it is an elegy written in a college courtyard for the last traditions of women's culture, a plea for women writers to "think back through our mothers" encased in a litany of the names of those mother-writers. As Woolf tells her beads to the tune of the ballad of the victims, she names the survivors and heroines. As she lays and slays the ghost of Milton, she captures and revives the ghost of Jane Ellen Harrison, the great classical scholar, in "the voice of some terrible reality leaping."[10]

Three Guineas is even more complex in form. Disguised as an anti-fascist pamphlet in an age of pamphlets, propaganda, and thirties protest literature, it is written in the form of replies to three letters asking for money to support good causes. The author replies as "the daughter of an educated man" in an address which confronts the writers of the letters with the narrowness of their individual demands for social change. But the essay also demonstrates the revolutionary dictum to organize one's own class in that it addresses only other daughters of educated men. Contemporary readers expected a radical protest against the atrocities in Spain and got instead a harsh, angry polemic denouncing capitalism, imperialism, anti-feminism, and patriarchal culture in general.

Three Guineas is a classic in the form of epistolary polemic. Like letters written in exile or in prison, it is in style and content part of the literature of the oppressed. One may certainly argue that the daughters of educated men were not as oppressed as blacks or the working class. But Woolf defines this oppression and seeks an alliance with them. Though we have been unable to convince Woolf's publishers to include her original photographs in reprints of the book, they are an important part of the propagandistic effect. For the reader expecting more photographs of atrocities in Spain, Woolf's photographs of the patriarchs of England in their professional garb were a shock. *Three Guineas* (its title defining the class of her audience as *Three Pounds* might appeal to another class) is, of course, a play on Brecht's *Threepenny Opera*. Besides naming the exact amounts sought by those who want to salve the consciences of intellectuals, the title is an economic metaphor for her arguments. Unlike *A Room of One's Own,* with its supposed lecture form, *Three Guineas* is buttressed by forty-three pages of formidable footnotes. This rhetorical strategy infuriated academic readers like Queenie Leavis, who called *Three Guineas* "Nazi dialectic without Nazi conviction."[11]

The book is more than a work of art. It is a major contribution to political science. Woolf's argument that the origin of fascism was in the patriarchal family (not in Italian, German, or Spanish nationalism or class) is a thesis still too bold for any but the most radical of feminists to take seriously. Recently, however, the same argument has been made in Lina Wertmuller's revolutionary film *Seven Beauties* and in Maria-Antonietta Macciocchi's brilliant essay "Female Sexuality in Fascist Ideology." I suggest that Woolf's pamphlet was influenced by Brecht and his definition of the relationship between women and fascism, which he described as that between prostitutes and a pimp. Woolf's language is much the same. Macciocchi argues that "the body of fascist discourse is rigorously chaste, pure, virginal. Its central aim is the death of sexuality: women are always called to the cemetery to honor the war dead, to come bearing them crowns, and they are exhorted to offer their sons to the fatherland." She quotes Eleanor Marx: "That is why we, for the most part socialists, affirm that chastity, although sacred, is unhealthy . . . we consider chastity a crime."[12]

The thesis made explicit in *Three Guineas* provides the plot and tensions of all four works under discussion here. Woolf came from a culture and a family obsessed with female chastity,

[margin, handwritten: origin of fascism in patriarchal family]

and she was obsessed with their obsession. While she consistently attacked this idea and recognized the fascist component in the repression of sexuality, it is a poignant and ironic measure of how one's politics can be more radical than one's life to note that she seems to have lived most of her life in physical chastity, and the powerful and moving images for her own creative processes are of the chaste imagination retreating to a nunnery. Macciocchi claims that "the Nazi community is made by homosexual brothers who exclude the woman and valorize the Mother."[13]

one's politics can be more radical than one's life //

The Cambridge Apostles' notions of fraternity surely appeared to Woolf analogous to certain fascist notions of fraternity. And Woolf's model of sorority as a parallel concept to the Apostles' model of fraternity had to confront male concepts of female chastity and brutality and violence against women, as well as its own lack of an institutional power base.

In *Between the Acts,* Woolf again follows Brecht in a classical Marxist dialectic expressed in the pageant of British history set near Roman ruins in wartime Britain and insisting on the participation of the audience. As Evelyn Haller argues, there is an underlying feminist appropriation of Egyptian mythology to counter the Anglo-Saxon myths of war and aggression.[14] But the form of *Between the Acts* is dramatic. I believe that what Woolf was trying to do in the novel was to write the modern version of a lost Greek play—Sophocles' play on the myth of Procne and Philomela. This story of rape and sisterly revenge set in wartime is the theme which structures *Between the Acts* with its recurrent images of the swallow and the nightingale.

I said earlier that these four formally innovative and explicitly feminist works of Virginia Woolf's were written in response to the misogyny of her family and her culture. Macciocchi identifies the elements of homosexual brotherhood, brutality, and violence against women, the adoration of motherhood and the simultaneous repression of sexuality. The Brechtian political thesis that women consent to play angel in the house and encourage war, which Woolf attacks in *Three Guineas*, suggests the underpinning for certain ideological components in the work of the Stephen family in nineteenth-century England.

Victorian violence against women and the institutionalization of that violence in fraternal organizations like the Cambridge Apostles stirred Woolf's imagination. Her declaration to Dame Ethel Smyth that "women alone stir my imagination" was only half the truth. For women were dispossessed of culture, and it was Woolf's revolutionary goal to storm the gates of Cambridge to steal the secret of what sociologists call "same-sex bonding," that brotherhood which appeared to own the means of production of culture—in law, politics, literature, and life. The men of the Stephen family were dependent on the consent and support of their women in this enterprise.

Woolf was working against the work of her grandfather, James Stephen, Permanent Under Secretary for the Colonies and architect of imperialism under seven changes of government, and professor of modern history at Cambridge; her uncle Fitzjames Stephen, codifier of English law and Indian law, judge of the High Court, and conservative political philosopher; Fitzjames's son, J. K. Stephen, Virginia's first cousin, "bard of Eton and of boyhood," misogynist poet and famous parodist, thought by some to be a likely candidate for the role of Jack the Ripper; her father, Leslie Stephen, compiler of the *Dictionary of National Biography*, a powerful political tool in the Victorian definition of English history as the biographies of England's great men. (Woolf wryly remarked that there were no lives of maids in the DNB.)

But she had also to exorcise the work of her female family as collaborators in the making of nineteenth-century British patriarchal ideology. Virginia Woolf's aunt Caroline Emelia Stephen was the author of a monumental history of sisterhoods, an anti-feminist piece of propaganda which perceived and argued forcefully that all separate organizations of nuns and nurses (even women's colleges) were a dangerous threat to the patriarchal family.[15] Woolf scholars have known of Julia Stephen's signing of Mrs. Humphrey Ward's anti-suffrage petition and Meredith's warning to her of the dangers to her daughters of a self-chosen role as "princess to a patriarch." But Martine Stemerick has recently documented and discussed Julia's neglected and unpublished manuscripts, essays on women and agnosticism and on the servant question which clarify her unswerving conservatism and anti-feminism.[16]

Julia Stephen's *Notes From Sick Rooms* valorizes nusing as woman's highest role.[17] Caroline Stephen, on the other hand, rejected and severely criticized district visiting and the charity of ladies bountiful like Mrs. Ramsay in *To the Lighthouse* as unprofessional and productive of an unwholesome sense of moral superiority in women.[18] But Caroline's role in her history of sisterhoods was exactly like her brother Fitzjames's in the codification and clarification of whole fields of English law. She argued for professionalization of nursing and social work as efficient occupations with clear duties, training, and paid workers. Like her father, James who built a huge bureaucracy in the Colonial Office (supposedly satirized by Dicken in *Little Dorrit* as the Circumlocution Office),[19] and like Fitzjames, who synthesized centuries of contradictory laws, Caroline Stephen was part of the unacknowledged family plot to take over the institutions of England. There is no more perfect example of the rise of the middle class and its imposition of Clapham Sect morality and the work ethic in place of a lazy, indifferent aristocracy. The Stephens were a progressive force in the interest of the power of the rising middle class.

But Julia Stephen's idealization of nursing derives from a different and more traditional upper-class culture. She was a doctor's daughter and nurse to her mother, family, and friends. She trained her daughter Stella in the same role, but Virginia abhorred these trips to the sickrooms of the slums, complained bitterly, and rejected the role for herself, with the exception of caring for her dying father. Her observations were keen, however, in her comments on Florence Nightingale and in the portraits of Mrs. Ramsay and of Eleanor Pargiter in *The Years,* whose devotion to the poor has the same mystical visionary aspect as Caroline Stephen's Quaker philosophy. But Woolf's most telling comment is Peggy's remark in *The Years* that the statue of Nurse Cavell reminds her of an advertisement for sanitary napkins. Cavell, the nurse-martyr, was executed by the Germans in Belgium. She was in no sense a nationalistic female self-sacrificer and claimed, "Patriotism is not enough!" But when her statue was erected in London, her death was used as propaganda against the Germans, and the slogan "For God, King and Country" was added in large letters.[20] The linking of menstrual blood and the blood of the wounded soldier, sanitary napkins and bandages, supports the anti-war theme of the novel and suggests how difficult it is for women to dissociate themselves from war. Macciocchi, who agrees with Woolf's argument in *Three Guineas* that fascism is inseparable from patriarchy, describes as distinctly fascist the male enforcement of woman as the ideal nurse, which encourages a sadistic passion in the nurse like the mystical desire for blood in a Saint Theresa. She notes that the Italian fascists created this role for women in the image of the Red Cross nurse which reached its peak in Rosselini's film *The White Ship,* "a filmscript of pure repressive fascist mystique."[21]

There is one other woman in her family against whom Virginia rebelled: her first cousin, Katherine Stephen (1856–1924), principal of Newnham. Woolf associated her cousins, the two Stephen sisters, with the most frightening aspects of evangelical patriarchal Christianity. She told Ethel Smyth that Hyde Park Gate preachers made her shudder with horror in memory of her cousins' brutal attempts to convert her in her youth. She thinks of their God as a rapist: "He's got a finger in my mind." How, we may ask, did the daughter of the man who ferociously attacked John Stewart Mill, who made it his business as a judge to hang women suspected of murdering their husbands, who railed against the emancipation of women, mocking Millicent Garrett Fawcett, and who was hounded out of office as the "mad judge" for prejudicing the jury in the case of Mrs. Maybrick—how did she become principal of a woman's college?[22] Whatever the answer, we may assume that it was at Katherine's invitation that Virginia Woolf gave her lectures at Cambridge; she became one of the Marys of *A Room of One's Own.*

The Stephen women were collaborators in their own oppression, but they also found ways to assert their independence, Katherine in a career in women's education, her sister Dorothea in the study of Eastern religions, and Caroline Emelia Stephen — aunt in her break with the evangelicals, her conversion to Quakerism, and her Quaker books *The Vision of Faith* and *The Light Arising: Thoughts on the Central Radiance.* According to Quaker historians, she single-handedly revived the moribund English Society of Friends and found a personal solution to the patriarchal and authoritarian philosophy she had found at home, especially in espousing pacifism.[23] Caroline's Quaker pacifism, which is the source of the pacifism of Virginia Woolf which rankles so many readers of *Three Guineas,* is a form of bourgeois feminist withdrawal from the struggle against patriarchy. The mysticism which characterizes Woolf's fiction and Caroline Stephen's religious essays is an imaginatively fulfilling substitute for mounting the barricades, a passive-aggressive protest against the violence of the men in their families, which violence they then describe as a characteristic of the male sex.

But women are even more crippled by madonna-worship than men, as the lives of women artists tell us. In the case of Woolf, this, coupled with the public and private misogyny of the men in her family, led to her definition of herself as an outsider and to her repeated equations of both freedom and creativity with chastity. Though she did relent in her pacifism enough towards the end of the Second World War to advocate defense from the enemy, she could not bring herself to the brink of actual

fighting, for that would be tantamount to changing her sex.
Suicide, in some sense, is perhaps the only solution masochistic
enough to satisfy the pacifist when the politics and violence of
war become too much to bear.

The legacy of Stephen misogyny went back to James Stephen
of the Colonial Office. His son Leslie described him as a "living
categorical imperative." And one of his colleagues said he was
"a transcendental Quaker with a tendency to Popery."[24] But
Catholicism offended a "patriarch of his standing" (to use his
own words) because of its worship of the Virgin Mary. When he
saw the Pope in Rome, he wrote that his face had a "benevo-
lence and mental feebleness as becomes a promulgator of the
Immaculate Conception." And in Brussels in 1852 he was dis-
dainful of a Saint Nicholas procession with "the goddess and
her child turned into two deplorable dolls" as "the old heathen
worship in a new dress." He certainly idealized motherhood,
but not in any form from which the father was excluded. James
Stephen was the chief ideologue of British "benevolent" imperialism, described by Henry Taylor as the most powerful
man in England, yet his public behavior was "profoundly sub-
ordinate." Stephen was a tyrant at home, and Leslie remembers
him dictating to his mother and sisters with a Miltonic tread.
But to the feminist imagination Virginia Woolf's grandfather
was more than a petty patriarchal tyrant over his family. He
was actually the architect of an ideology of oppression which
used the model of patriarchal domestic tyranny as a basis for
colonial imperialism. His concepts and metaphors have become
embedded in our language and thought, and his policies as hal-
lowed as Biblical precept. The press called him "Mr. Mother-
Country Stephen," for it was he who coined the phrase "the
mother country." It was he who made the policies which bound
the British colonies in a domestic metaphor which was to determine their relations for more than hundred years, to yoke
whole nations in a position from which to rebel was to insult
sacred motherhood itself. The rebel was then a moral outcast,

a bad son. It took a brilliant patriarchal mind to conceive of such a notion for maintaining social control, enforcing dependency, and demanding unquestioning obedience from subjects whose role was defined as that of children.

"No reasonable man would ever affirm broadly and generally," he wrote in 1850, "that a mother country ought at some time or other to part with her colonies. . . . England ought never to give up a single colony." The Canadian course (which he had directed) was the right one, "cheerfully relaxing the bonds of authority." The rest of the colonies were "wretched burdens to this country, which in an evil hour we assumed, but which we have no right to lay down again. We emancipate our grown-up sons, but keep our unmarried daughters, and our children who may chance to be ricketty, in domestic bonds. The analogy is a very close one."[25] Mr. Mother-Country Stephen was one of the patriarchy's geniuses. He despised Catholics for pagan mother-goddess worship but tapped the same human impulses for political ends with enormous success. Queen Victoria herself seems to have grown in girth throughout the century to meet the demands of Stephen's majestic mother-image.[26] The matriarch, the maternal embodiment of the mother-country (we see her in Woolf's obituary of Lady Strachey and in her portraits of Lady Bruton and Dr. Bradshaw's wife in *Mrs. Dalloway*), seems to have been the invention of a patriarch. We must never underestimate the power of a man and his metaphor. How clever it was to invest the philosophy of imperialism with the theology of the patriarchal family. Women were burdened with guilt and implicated in exploitation at the most fundamental psychic levels. The master-servant relation, even more clearly defined by James's son, James Fitzjames Stephen, as the relation of a father to his wife and children, was then enforced by their women in relation to colonial subjects and servants. This ideology of imperialism, based on the structure of the patriarchal family, needed woman's consent to dependency and rewarded her with power over her servants.[27]

It should come as no surprise then that both Julia Stephen and Caroline Emelia Stephen were eloquent explicators in print of the necessity of a woman's power over her servants, that she rule autocratically and with a very firm hand. Virginia Woolf's lifelong struggle with the rejection of the matriarchal role and her savage attacks on the patriarchal family in her novels and essays is also not surprising. The letters and diaries reveal a socialist feminist in agonies over the servant problem, for she had none of the matriarchal confidence of her Aunt Caroline and her mother in a benevolently powerful role. Figures of sympathetic charwomen appear in her novels, and they are related to the middle-class reformers like Eleanor in *The Years* (a figure much like Caroline Emelia Stephen), who cleans up the slums and is a mystical figure of the artist as charwoman to the world. But Woolf's rebellion against the matriarchal subjection of servants of her mother and her aunt did not, interestingly enough, result in the idealization and romanticizing of servants. In fact, Crosby in *The Years* is portrayed as an example of that cultural gap we discussed earlier. Long after her masters and mistresses have abandoned the patriarchal family, she remembers and tries to enforce the old roles.

Perhaps the best example may be found in Louise De Salvo's edition of *Melymbrosia,* one of the earlier versions of *The Voyage Out.*[28] On board ship, Mrs. Chailley comes to Rachel to complain that all the sheets are worn and torn and that she has been put in a tiny, noisy cubicle next to the boiler. Rachel says she'll try to get new sheets and have the servant moved to better quarters. But Mrs. Chailley is not pleased by this response. She wishes Rachel's mother were still alive to put her in her place and demand that she mend the sheets and stay near the boiler room where she belongs.

It should now be clear that under the influence of James Stephen's philosophy, the model of the patriarchal family was used in dominion over the colonies and then by upper- and middle-class women to define relations with servants. At home unmarried women like Caroline Stephen nursed their aging parents, their own broken health an exact counterpart to the broken spirits of colonials under the yoke of the mother country, where love and obedience were expected. Caroline's struggle for freedom and self-reliance paralleled the struggles of the colonies. Rejecting the matriarchal role of denigrator of sisterhoods and definer of mistress-servant relations, she chose a single life in a Quaker community as an alternative to life in the patriarchal family. This was a great achievement given the dependency and self-hatred born of her position in the family.

If we accept the notion that women were the largest colony under Victorian British imperial domain, we can understand the metaphor of enforced infantilization and how it oppressed women and colonial Africans and Indians. The unpaid labor of such women was as necessary to the functioning of the patriarchal family as was the slave labor of the colonies to the expansion of the British empire. Mr. Mother-Country Stephen put it exactly when he said that they kept their unmarried daughters in domestic bondage. Modern feminists are often frustrated in their attempts to understand why Victorian middle-class women so often failed in their rebellions. I suggest that the master-slave relationship, enhanced by a domestic metaphor unassailable in its demands for loyalty and love, is at the root of the problem. A way out for Virginia Woolf was to define herself not only as the "daughter of an educated man" but also as the niece of a nun. Caroline managed not to offend her father's memory by joining the sisterhood which captured her youthful imagination, but she found community among the Quakers.

She is directly responsible for Woolf's vision of sisterhood and is duly thanked in *A Room of One's Own* for her legacy of £2,500 (the others received only £100 apiece): "Indeed my aunt's legacy unveiled the sky to me, and substituted for the large and imposing figure of a gentleman, which Milton recommended for my perpetual adoration, a view of the open sky" (p. 59). The ghost of "Milton's bogey" is laid for Woolf by the visionary example of a maiden aunt and her money. Caroline is transformed in *A Room of One's Own* from a nun wrapped in her shawl in religious retreat in Cambridge to a horsewoman as mythical as Percival in *The Waves:* "My aunt, Mary Beton, I must tell you, died by a fall from her horse when she was riding out to take the night air in Bombay." The narrator claims that she got her legacy at the same time as women got the vote: "Of the two—the vote and the money—the money, I own, seemed infinitely more important" (*Room,* p. 56).

Even the title of *A Room of One's Own* derives from Caroline. Katherine Stephen boasted that she had converted her aunt to the cause of women's education by showing her the students' private rooms at Newnham.[29] Privacy, for women like Caroline and Virginia, who had lived in Victorian patriarchal families (and those of us who live in them now), was a holy state akin to the state of grace for Christians, a goal to be fought for. On one of her visits to Cambridge in 1904 Caroline had introduced her niece to the great classical scholar Jane Ellen Harrison. It was an event of great importance for Woolf's fiction; she was a role model in scholarship and life, proving that women could master and understand Greek (even if, like Woolf, they struggled alone with their texts and with a tutor like Janet Case instead of in a university class with their peers). The narrator sees on the terrace at Fernham a vision of the woman genius: "as if popping out to breathe the air, to glance at the garden, came a bent figure, formidable yet humble, with her great forehead and her shabby dress—could it be the famous scholar, could it be J— H— herself? All was dim, yet intense too, as if the scarf which the dusk had flung over the garden were torn asunder by star or sword—the flash of some terrible reality leaping, as its way is, out of the heart of the spring" (*Room,* p. 26).

Was "the terrible reality leaping" the idea that chastity, outsidership, and poverty were the conditions of life for the woman of genius? Famous as Jane Harrison was in her field, she never held a professorship at Cambridge, was harrassed in print and in person by some classics professors, and died in poverty in Paris. The sky was unveiled for Woolf by the lives of these women. The star or sword which broke through the veil was a sense of continuity, that women are responsible for passing on freedom to the next generation.

A Room of One's Own does just that. Like most of Woolf's fiction, it is an elegy. As I said earlier, it is an elegy written in a college courtyard for all our female dead, the reformers, the pioneers, the artists, buried like Shakespeare's sister, in unmarked graves at places like "the Elephant and Castle." The essayist begins by trying to place herself in the patriarchal tradition, with a prayer to "Saint Charles" Lamb. Lamb had come to the college a hundred years before to read the manuscript of Milton's "Lycidas." She, too, longs to see the revisions, and also those in another of the library's manuscripts, Thackeray's great fictional elegy, *Henry Esmond*. She may not enter the library (the library of her brothers, cousins, father, uncles, grandfather) because she is a woman. "That a famous library has been cursed by a woman is a matter of complete indifference to a famous library." Woolf's curse joined the chorus of curses, perhaps, from working-class men and women and all the "ordinary people" and common readers also excluded from the library. Woolf vows to reject male literary tradition as she descends the steps of the library in anger: "Never will I wake those echoes, never will I ask for that hospitality again" (*Room,* p. 12). If she rejects Milton's elegy as a model, and even the "memento mori" mood of Thackeray's elegiac novel, self-described as "grave and sad," the *Bildungsroman* of youth at Trinity College, with its appealing, almost Proustian remembrances, how then will she proceed?

Obviously she will have to invent the female elegy. Woolf mourns the death of Judith Shakespeare in the voice of the anonymous female balladeers. She may have stolen Thackeray's digressive elegiac form, but it is molded anew. The lugubrious mourning of the agnostic Leslie Stephen and her uncle Fitzjames's fixation on hellfire and eternal punishment are rejected in her memorial service for Judith Shakespeare. And she rejects too that Victorian "Women Must Weep" of Kingsley (used, incidentally, as the title of *Three Guineas* when it was published as an anti-war essay in the *Atlantic Monthly* in a more receptive America) for a position much like Caroline Stephen's Quaker rejection of mourning as unbecoming to those who have real faith. Woolf predicts Judith's resurrection:

> Now my belief is that this poet who never wrote a word and was buried at the crossroads still lives. She lives in you and me, and in many other women who are not here tonight, for they are washing up the dishes and putting the children to bed. But she lives; for great poets do not die; they are continuing presences. . . . (*Room*, p. 171)

origins of Judith Shakespeare

The origins of Woolf's character are obscure but may be detected in her half-serious "Acknowledgments" prefacing *Orlando,* where one finds the name of William Black, the now-forgotten popular Victorian Scottish novelist, known as the successor to Sir Walter Scott for his romantic historical fictions. In 1883, the year after Virginia's birth, he published a delightful novel, obviously aimed at young women readers, called *Judith Shakespeare,* in which he said "the awful figure of Billy" was well in the background. Center stage is Shakespeare's daughter, Judith, the disinherited rebellious younger daughter, who rejects marriage to a proper suitor and is attracted by a stranger from London to whom she gives her father's manuscript of *The Tempest.* It is then published in an unauthorized edition and brings down her father's wrath. The novel has a father-daughter plot which is a form of homage to Shakespeare himself. Black's Judith cannot read or write and is forbidden to enter her father's workroom. She steals the keys and sits in the barn with her best friend, Prudence, laboriously trying to read the great plays. When *The Tempest* appears, Shakespeare is furious, and Judith is struck down by an incapacitating illness in guilt and fear at his wrath. One can see how the daughter of Leslie

Stephen may have responded to such a story, and one may guess why Woolf's Judith Shakespeare became Shakespeare's *sister*, not his daughter. Judith's ignorance of reading and writing and her passion to be an artist express Virginia Woolf's own ironic definitions of reading and writing as radical acts and of the "daughter of an educated man" as one who is dispossessed of culture.[30]

Louise De Salvo's analysis of Virginia Stephen's 1897 diary has documented what feminist readers had already suspected.[31] Reading, writing, and studying *were* radical acts for the young woman. When she fell ill they were precisely the activities forbidden her by her family and the doctors, the activities she had found were a way to keep her sanity. She identified the liberty of intellectual endeavor with men, and no wonder. She often fell ill from the stress of what we might call the "theft" of her father's manuscripts. In 1897 Leslie wrote to her brother Thoby that he would not come up to Cambridge to vote on women's membership in the university, despite many pleas from women to do so. Virginia had been forbidden to read and write, and her request to attend classes at King's College denied. Leslie said that he had bought her a spade and set her to making a garden in the shaded stony soil in back of Hyde Park Gate. The subject of degrees for women was a topic on which Thoby might make his name in his debating society, Leslie suggested—while his daughters were digging.[32] The reader as a radical (the disobedient daughter), the writer as a feminist revolutionary (usurping her father's job) came to birth that year and kept a journal. She then imagined "the common reader" as her audience and her ally against patriarchal academics and institutions, from the early story "A Society" to "Anon and the Reader," the manuscript she was working on when she died. *The Voyage Out*, in which Rachel learns to read, like many first novels, is a reading list of the author's influences. Rachel dies from such knowledge as she gains from books, of woman's plight. St. John Hirst reads Sappho in chapel. It is Swinburne's Sappho that he reads, a violent and bloody male fantasy about lesbianism, and his reading is linked to the sinister figure of a nurse.

Sappho, however, is the woman reader's heroine, and the object of her search in "A Society." One of the sisterhood (a group of young women set out to explore why men have destroyed civilization, written bad books, and made war and weapons while insisting that women simply reproduce) goes to Oxbridge to find Sappho. Castalia (named for her purity) is disguised as a charwoman and compares the Sappho expert, Professor Hobkin, to her aunt's cactuses. His life's work is a book six or seven inches thick, most of which is not by Sappho but is his defense of her chastity, which has been denied by a German professor. The dispute about Sappho's chastity centers on "the use of some implement which looked to me for all the world like a hairpin."[33] Sue declares that Professor Hobkin cannot possibly be a real scholar if he is only concerned with such a silly issue. "Probably" she says, "Professor Hobkin was a gynaecologist" ("Society," p. 21). Castalia is sent back to Oxbridge to investigate further and returns pregnant. She is triumphant at the loss of her chastity. Unlike Judith Shakespeare in *A Room of One's Own,* she does not contemplate suicide but produces a daughter to inherit the society's concerns. And unlike the professor's book on Sappho, the debate on whether to expel Castalia for impurity is short and sweet. "What is chastity, then?" they ask, and Poll answers that "chastity is nothing but ignorance—a most discreditable state of mind. We should then admit only the unchaste to our society" ("Society," p. 25). They move on to Judith's scientific study of two other aspects of female sexuality, artificial insemination and the elimination of the need for prostitutes. Both could be used to deprive men of their power over women.

There are ways in which Woolf's women's club resembles meetings of NOW, Redstockings, the Women's Caucus of the MLA; or, considering its political goals, it best reminds us of the socialist caucus of the Women's Studies Association, where women share the radical aims of Woolf's 1917 club. When they question the capitalist system, they learn how much men despise them. And they are told that not since Sappho has there been a first-rate woman artist. Woolf's explanation was socialist, for since Sappho women have never enjoyed the social conditions necessary for the freedom of the artist. But she shared with many members of her sex in the late nineteenth and early twentieth centuries the desire to find the real Sappho, not Professor Hobkin's Sappho and certainly not the Sappho of his German colleague.

Some feminists actually sat down with the German professor, von Wilamowitz-Moellendorff, who was probably the man Woolf meant. Her friend Ethel Smyth, the composer, tells a delightful story in her memoir, *Streaks of Life,* which appeared in the same year as "A Society," reviewed with high praise by Woolf herself. Dame Ethel tells of meeting the Sappho scholar, a treat for women like herself, who had little Greek and had been dependent on Swinburne and Gilbert Murray for a glimpse of the great poet. Wilamowitz-Moellendorff showed her an unknown poem of Sappho's which he had just deciphered. "Incidentally, he informed me that in his opinion Sappho was the most maligned of women, that she was really a sort of High School Mistress, and the famous passions merely innocent 'Schwärmerei' between her and her pupils. Luckily it is open to those who have no Greek to reject this depressing reading of 'burning Sappho.'"[34]

The modern cult of Sappho for daughters of educated men, women artists, feminists, and lesbians began with their reading of Swinburne and was followed by a rejection of his version and a search for the real Sappho which reached its peak in Paris before the First World War. Ethel Smyth had made a "Three-Legged Tour of Greece"; Natalie Barney and many lesbian artists had also gone to Greece to find their heroine and to recreate Sappho's school. The modern inhabitants of the isle of Lesbos were not sympathetic to their aims, and the amazons returned to make a new Mitylene in the French republic's green and pleasant land. It was in these salons that women artists began to flower and islands of sorority began to surface in the cities of the patriarchy. The isle of Lesbos stirred their imagination, and Virginia Woolf's "Friendships Gallery" was only one of many lesbian utopias.[35] Compton Mackenzie's 1928 novel *Extraordinary Women* is a comic satire on the cult of Sappho and the new women's island utopias. The chapters are headed with quotations from the poet, and Olimpia Leigh, the composer, who sounds suspiciously like Ethel Smyth, has set all of Sappho's poetry to music.

Radclyffe Hall was a member of these same circles. Woolf did not think *The Well of Loneliness* was a great book, but urged by Vita Sackville-West, she joined in support of the lesbian artist during the obscenity trial for the novel. Woolf's creation of Shakespeare's sister in *A Room of One's Own* derives not only from William Black's popular novel but also from the intellectual cause célèbre surrounding Radclyffe Hall, who was known to be the descendant of Shakespeare's other daughter, Susanna Hall. The homosexuality of Shakespeare's sonnets was of course a major part of the defense in the obscenity trial. Stephen Gordon in *The Well* is christened Mary Olivia, a "man's soul trapped in a woman's body," like Shakespeare's Olivia. Is it this Olivia whom Chloe likes in *A Room of One's Own?* In her draft Woolf wrote, "Chloe liked Olivia. They shared a ——." Then she wrote that she was afraid to turn the page to see what they shared, and she thought of the obscenity trial for a novel.[36] The blank is filled in in the published version. What the two women share is a laboratory. But the lecturer makes her point by engaging her student audience to make sure there are no men eavesdropping.

In the official biography of Virginia Woolf, Quentin Bell described his aunt as a "sexless Sappho." Feminist readers objected at the time, but we have come to think he might be right. When the women return to their society much later, one of them remarks, "It is now well-known that Sappho was the somewhat lewd invention of Professor Hobkin" ("Society," p. 31). If the classics professors are merely gynaecologists *manqué,* the women of the society have gained enough education to outstrip them, and after the war they can laugh together over "old Hobkin and the hairpin." But they have lost their innocence. Reading has radicalized them. When the story opens, Poll, who has been left a fortune provided she will read all the books in the London Library, bemoans her fate: "Why, why, did my father teach me to read?" ("Society," p. 12). After the war Castalia complains bitterly that if they hadn't learnt to read

> "We might still have been bearing children in ignorance and that I believe was the happiest life after all. I know what you're going to say about war," she checked me, "and the horror of bearing children to see them killed, but our mothers did it, and their mothers, and their mothers before them. And *they* didn't complain. They couldn't read. I've done my best," she sighed, "to prevent my little girl from learning to read, but what's the use? I caught Ann only yesterday with a newspaper in her hand and she was beginning to ask me if it was 'true.' Next she'll ask me whether Mr. Lloyd George is a good man, then whether Mr. Arnold Bennett is a good novelist, and finally, whether I believe in God." ("Society," p. 36)

It is significant that Woolf's sorority, unlike our modern counterparts, does not study the history of women. Its object is to understand why men have not produced good people and good books, why the male sex has made war and capitalism and imperialism. The sisterhood is very sorry to conclude after years of study and the presentation of many papers that "our belief in man's intellect is the greatest fallacy of them all" ("Society," p. 37). Like generations of men, they have defined a good member of the opposite sex as "honest, passionate and unworldly" ("Society," p. 35). "What could be more charming than a boy before he has begun to cultivate his intellect?" ("Society," p. 38). But the daughter of those great nineteenth-century

Stephen professionalizers puts the blame for man's mistreat-
ment of women squarely on the shoulders of the professions.
Leslie Stephen had made the profession of journalism respect-
able and powerful in its "higher" forms and left behind "those
68 black books," the *DNB*, as a monument to the fathers. His
brother Fitzjames had done the same for the legal profession
with his digests, his manual for the conservative politician,
Liberty, Equality, Fraternity, and his role as judge. Caroline
Emelia Stephen had spearheaded the professionalization of
nursing and social work. Virginia Woolf identified this process
of professionalization with the subjugation of others. Her
grandfather had built a bureaucracy in the Colonial Office
which kept down the natives. Fitzjames made it very clear that
physical force was necessary to control the working class. In
Liberty, Equality, Fraternity, he declares that women and the
working class must be kept down forcefully in order to show
the colonies how rebellion will be treated. Those seemingly
outrageous demands Woolf makes on professional women to
transform their professions were the result of a political analysis
of the rise of the middle class in her own family and the corruptions of power which go with professionalization:

> They teach him to cultivate his intellect. He becomes a barrister, a
> civil servant, a general, an author, a professor. Every day he goes to
> an office. Every year he produces a book. He maintains a whole family
> by the products of his brain—poor devil! Soon he cannot come into a
> room without making us all feel uncomfortable; he condescends to
> every woman he meets, and dares not tell the truth even to his own
> wife; instead of rejoicing our eyes we have to shut them if we are to
> take him in our arms. True, they console themselves with stars of all
> shapes, ribbons of all shades, and incomes of all sizes—but what is to
> console us? . . . Oh, Cassandra, for Heaven's sake let us devise a method
> by which men can bear children! It is our only chance. For unless we
> provide them with some innocent occupations, we shall get neither
> good people nor good books. . . . ("Society," pp. 38-39)

"A Society" is even more fundamentally subversive than a
modern version of *Lysistrata,* when read as mockery of the

institutions of the men of her class, Cambridge University, and the secret society of her friends, her husband, her brother, her uncles, and their cousins, the Cambridge Apostles. If the Apostles were the "Cambridge Conversazione Society," Woolf's fictional females formed a London conversazione society. There are no restrictions on the number of members of this sorority. The Apostles limited themselves to twelve. But Woolf is anti-elitist, and fourteen women come and go. Besides Cassandra, Castalia, and Poll, we meet Ruth, Clorinda, Rose, Jane, Fanny, Helen, Sue, Moll, Eleanor, Jill, Elizabeth, and Castalia's daughter, Ann. When Poll, the prototype of Woolf's common reader, complains about the books in the London Library, the remark is significant because the London Library was founded by Apostles in an age when a more radical sense of brotherhood held them together and they also built East End settlement houses for boys and founded workingmen's colleges. Virginia Woolf taught at Morley College and supported the London Library, for public libraries were necessary to educate her "common reader." She developed what her husband called her "London Library complex" when she expected E. M. Forster to invite her to be the token woman on its board. But his effort failed, he said. They wanted no woman, and cited as precedent Leslie Stephen's annoyance with the previous woman, Mrs. Henry Green, the novelist.

"A Society" is Woolf's attempt to penetrate the mysteries of male secret societies like the Apostles and to offer a parallel sisterhood of intellectual inquiry and social conscience. The wrath it provoked is unaccountable unless one takes seriously the British male's paranoid fear that woman's loyalty to her own sex was a real threat to male hegemony and the patriarchal family. The fraternity functioned as primary male bonding and demanded loyalty above a man's loyalty to his family. It allowed attacks on authority but still reinforced the patriarchy. By the late nineteenth century, the Apostles served to find wives and professional jobs for their members, though they still idealized homosexuality and the "Greek view of life."[37]

This old-boy network which Fitzjames Stephen proudly claimed as the backbone of British imperialism and his son J. K. Stephen called "the intellectual aristocracy" in his "Defense of the Compulsory Study of Greek at Cambridge" had no parallel "old-girl" network.[38] There were no girl's schools which taught the superiority of the female sex, no sororal organizations which claimed future loyalty to one's sisters over the claims of family, no power or place to be shared as a reward for loyalty to one's own sex, no woman-designed cult of female chastity or idealization of lesbianism as the highest form of love, no female philosopher of the stature of G. E. Moore to shed sweetness and light on female friendship. If such female friendship networks existed, and they did, they did not bear the hallmarks of an institutional stamp of approval, and they did not serve as exchanges of power, money, and careers. Plato was revered for loving his students. Sappho was reviled for loving hers. To separate the real Sappho from centuries of scholarly calumny, as the feminist Elizabeth Robins wrote, was the goal of women like Woolf. In their London Lesbos the women were hampered by Professor Hobkin and his hairpin.

The knowledge of Greek was the key to power, J. K. Stephen argued when he coined that phrase, since used by historians and biographers to describe his class and family, "the intellectual aristocracy." Woolf felt that not knowing Greek—not knowing Greek in groups of schoolboys, in gangs of Apostles, only knowing Greek alone or with a tutor—meant no female intellectual aristocracy. "The voice of some terrible reality leaping" was Jane Harrison's voice, piercing through the classics back to the matriarchal religious cults.

I believe that the Apostles as a fraternal organization were the descendants of freemasonry and European guilds and youth organizations, that the overt homosexuality and woman-hating of the late Victorian Apostles as inadvertently revealed by Paul Levy in his recent book were corruptions of the revolutionary ideal of fraternity.[39] The cultural gap is evident in Woolf's attempt to articulate a revolutionary ethic of sorority when fraternity had declined into decadence, into being merely a club for jobs and preferment. As a socialist she urged women writers to think back through their mothers. As a feminist she urged them to think sideways through their sisters. It goes without saying that they should know Greek, and they should know Greek in groups. They should recover Sappho from the lewd professors.

Virginia Woolf continued to propose sisterhood, to speak in "a little language unknown to men" which we might call "sapphistry" in *Night and Day, A Room of One's Own,* "Professions for Women," *The Years,* and *Three Guineas.* In *Jacob's Room* and *Mrs. Dalloway* she attacked the notion of fraternity and its collaboration with patriarchy, capitalism, and imperialism. She tried to work out the sororal idea for the last time in *Between the Acts* but admitted its failure at the end of the novel.

"Lempriere will settle it," Lucy Swithin says, as the Olivers try to understand the origin of the phrase "Knock on wood," in Pointz Hall during the Second World War. Lucy needs a classical dictionary, and Woolf and women like Dame Ethel Smyth depended on one as well. What Lempriere settles is the origin of the superstition in the Greek myth of the giant Antaeus. The moral of that myth is that patriarchy, like fascism, functions only with women's consent. Antaeus, the Libyan giant, son of Terra and Neptune, boasts that he will erect a temple to his father with the skulls of his enemies. Hercules tries to kill the killer, but he revives whenever he touches his mother, Earth, and Hercules has to crush him in his arms in midair. If we accept that description of Antaeus building a temple to his father with the skulls of his enemies as a definition of the patriarchal

culture of heroism, war, and violence, we can see how angry
Woolf was about the war and women's inability to stop it.

Both Fitzjames Stephen and his son, J. K. Stephen, were
known as giants and nicknamed "the Giant Grim" and "the
genial giant." Fitzjames made his name by building a patriarchal temple. Simultaneously and anonymously he published
in all the major journals of the day vicious reviews of Dickens's
Little Dorrit because he believed his father was being satirized
in the "Circumlocution Office."[40] In *Liberty, Equality, Fraternity* he denounced Mill's idea of liberty and defended the patriarchy against feminism and egalitarianism. The "genial giant"
advocated violence against women and the working class in his
misogynist poems and essays. Even Leslie Stephen wrote a
"Mausoleum book" for the patriarchy in the *Dictionary of
National Biography*.

But there is another metaphor in the novel which even more
effectively evokes the image of sorority. It is an amazon's war
cry from the supposedly pacifist Virginia Woolf, buried in the
book in all the references to the swallow and the nightingale.
But unless women "know Greek" in a sense, they may miss the
message. In "The Voice of the Shuttle" Geoffrey Hartman joins
the Greek fathers in analyzing the myth of Procne and Philomela
as a story in which "the truth will out." He universalizes the
story as saying that the artist will not be silenced and suggests
that in these universal terms the myth is an archetype.[41] In
Three Guineas Woolf says that in the profession of literature, no
one rules "that metaphors shall only be used by one sex." Let
us see how the other sex sees that story.

Lempriere tells us that, like *Between the Acts*, it was a war
story. Pandion gave away his daughter to Tereus as part of the
spoils of war. Procne wept bitterly at the separation from her
sister, Philomela. Procne bore Tereus a son, Itys. Tereus then
went off again, raped Philomela, cut out her tongue, and left
her on an island. Philomela wove the story of that rape into a
tapestry and sent it to Procne, who rescued her sister and in an

awful rage at the violation of sisterhood attacked the patriarchy itself in revenge: she killed her son and served him to his father to eat. The gods turned the sisters into the swallow and the nightingale and Tereus into the hoopoe, a bird which fouls its own nest.

Geoffrey Hartman is not alone in misreading the tale's message of sorority and revenge for rape. In *Between the Acts* Woolf ironically lets Bart adapt Swinburne to his own concerns: "Oh sister swallow, O sister swallow,/How can thy heart be full of spring?" Swinburne's nightingale in "Itylus" castigates her sister for not feeling guilty about murdering her son; she remembers "the voice of the child's blood crying yet" but not the voice of the shuttle and her own rape. Swinburne's suggestion that both sisterhood and revenge are unnatural reveals his failure to understand the implications of the myth, as Woolf's development of the theme will show.

The "voice of the shuttle" in *Between the Acts* is a newspaper account of the gang-rape of a girl by soldiers. Isa sees herself as the violated girl and her husband as the rapist: "The girl had gone skylarking with the troopers. She had screamed. She had hit him. . . . What then?"[42] Isa struggles towards sisterhood. She gets no vicarious erotic pleasure from thinking about the rape victim. While her husband is in the greenhouse seducing Mrs. Manresa, she stands outside with William Dodge, singing "songs my uncle taught me" (*Between,* p. 64). She rejects the role of the virgin mother and encourages herself: "Hear not the frantic cries of the leaders who in that they seek to lead desert us. . . . Hear rather . . . the brawl in the barrack room when they strip her naked" (*Between,* p. 183). But she is bowed down by the weight of fruit from the family tree and its burden of family injunctions, "what we must remember, what we must forget" (*Between,* p. 182).

Isa is a prisoner in her father-in-law's home. She is Irish and subject, like Ireland to England, to that old colonial tyrant, Bart Oliver. She does not kill her son and serve him to his adulterous father. She does not avenge the girl victim or herself. She goes to bed with the enemy. But we should have known, for Woolf's description of Isa runs, "She never looked like Sappho" (*Between*, p. 22). Isa and the other wives of England are recolonized, resubjugated by war. They lose their liberty and sorority. Misogyny triumphs over the patriarchal family as war triumphs over Europe. The giants are loose again, building temples to their fathers with the skulls of their enemies. Women cannot resist reviving their wounded—and the civilians are knocking on wood.

In 1930 Woolf had imagined that the Working Women's Cooperative Guild and other women's political groups would create international peace and the world would be safe for socialism and feminism in what she called "the sisterhood of nations."[43] By 1941 she saw that fascism had appropriated the ideology of brotherhood. And sorority was suppressed as it always has been during most wars, except in the service of men.

The representation of women in Woolf's last novel makes an inexorable point.[44] The primitive poems of Isa, scribbled in an account book, are a wife's work of art. It is all she can manage as a domestic prisoner, and cannot be compared to the power of Miss LaTrobe's pageant and her ambitious plans for rewriting Genesis. Woolf reaches further back in history than Shakespeare's sister for Miss LaTrobe's character. She is the sister of the anonymous writers of the Bible. And Lucy Swithin imagines herself as a powerful woman, Cleopatra, under the influence of the lesbian artist's vision. Lucy represents Caroline Emelia Stephen's Quaker mystical belief in the oneness of the universe; she heals and mends like an ancient goddess. One wonders at Woolf's point in naming the painted life force Mrs. Manresa, for Manresa is the place in Spain where Saint Ignatius wrote his *Spiritual Exercises,* devoted to the Virgin Mary.

In Miss LaTrobe Woolf has ended the sorority's search for Sappho sketched out in "A Society." She is not a poet but a playwright in her modern incarnation. Her lovers are not

students but actresses. She has left her island home to teach her
audience their own role in history. There are lessons in the novel
for the modern sisterhood of scholarship, for the feminist literary
critic of *A Room of One's Own*, for the Outsiders' Society of
Three Guineas. One lesson is that if we allow male critics to
universalize our stories—as Swinburne retold the myth of
Procne and Philomela, and Geoffrey Hartman claims that
reading the myth as the story of the artist and the truth rather
than as a sister's revenge for the rape of her sister is "higher"
or "deeper" than the story of the power of sisterhood—we will
be domesticated and subjugated into the loss of our own history. After all, J. K. Stephen warned his brothers in the study
of Greek that if they did not retain their knowledge, it was
their own fault if they ceased to be an "intellectual aristocracy."
In *Between the Acts* Englishwomen are even further than they
were in "A Society" from securing sorority as a political principle. The novel makes it impossible to imagine that they could
ever form an intellectual aristocracy, even if they wished to.
Women's consent is necessary for men to go on making war and
making love as if it were war. Isa consents, but Miss LaTrobe
does not. She is a rather shabby Sappho, with no school to sustain her, no daughter to console her. But at least she is not
Professor Hobkin's Sappho. She is the woman artist's honest
portrait of the woman artist.

NOTES

This paper was written in honor of David Erdman. Members of the English
Institute are aware of his encouragement of scholars in his own field. Less
well known is the role he has played as mentor to feminist critics and publisher of their work on Virginia Woolf. See *Bulletin of the New York Public Library* 80, no. 2 (Winter 1977), a revaluation of *The Years; Bulletin
of Research in the Humanities* 82, no. 3 (Autumn 1979), on *The Voyage
Out;* Virginia Woolf's *The Pargiters,* ed. Mitchell Leaska (New York: New
York Public Library and Readex Books, 1977); and *Melymbrosia,* ed.

Louise A. DeSalvo (New York: New York Public Library and Readex Books, 1982).

title of essay The title of this paper is a play on James Fitzjames Stephen's *Liberty, Equality, Fraternity* (1873), ed. R. J. White, 2d ed. (1874; reprint ed., Cambridge: At the University Press, 1967), a monument to misogyny written as a reply to John Stuart Mill.

1. Virginia Woolf, *A Room of One's Own* (New York: Harcourt, Brace & Co., 1929), p. 98. All further references to this work are included in the text.

2. Virginia Woolf, *Moments of Being* (Sussex: University of Sussex Press, 1976), p. 72.

3. In *Moments of Being* Woolf wrote, "All our male relations were adepts at the game. They knew the rules and attached immense importance to them. Father laid enormous stress upon schoolmasters' reports, upon scholarships, triposes and fellowships. . . . What would have been his shape had he not been stamped and moulded by the patriarchal machinery? Every one of our male relations was shot into that machine and came out at the other end, at the age of sixty or so, a Headmaster, an Admiral, a Cabinet Minister, a Judge" (p. 132).

4. Reviewing *A Room of One's Own,* Rebecca West, the "arrant feminist" mentioned in the text (*Room,* p. 53), differentiated between two types of homosexuals: "The men who despised us for our specifically female organs chastised us with whips; but those to whom they are a matter for envy chastise us with scorpions" (*Ending in Earnest* [New York: Doubleday, 1931], pp. 208–13). She praised Woolf for braving this "invisible literary wind" of homosexual anti-feminism in her own circles. For further discussion of this issue see my "Taking the Bull by the Udders" (Paper delivered at the Woolf Centenary Conference, Brown University, February 26–27, 1982).

5. Algernon Swinburne, "Itylus," *Collected Poetical Works* (New York: Harper's, 1924), pp. 54–56. See H.D.'s *HERmione* (New York: Dial Press, 1981) for a contemporary and uncritical feminist use of Swinburne's poem: "Were all the poems no use? Some poems are useful one way, some another . . ." (pp. 158–60).

6. *The Years* (New York: Harcourt, Brace and Co., 1937), p. 380. All further references are included in the text.

7. For further discussion of Woolf's valorization of chastity see my "Virginia Woolf and her Violin" in *Virginia Woolf: Centennial Essays,* ed. Elaine Ginsberg (Troy, N.Y.: Whitston Publishing Co., forthcoming), and "'The Niece of a Nun': Virginia Woolf, Caroline Stephen and the

Cloistered Imagination," in *New Feminist Essays on Virginia Woolf,* ed. Jane Marcus, 2 vols. (Lincoln: University of Nebraska Press, forthcoming), vol. 2.

8. Cicely Hamilton's *Marriage as a Trade* was first published in 1909 and has now been reprinted (London: The Women's Press, 1980) with an introduction by Jane Lewis. Hamilton, like Woolf, celebrates celibacy and the single life. This attitude should be compared with that of other leftwing feminists of the time, Rebecca West, for example, or Emma Goldmann, who advocated free love.

9. Alice's Fox's "Literary Allusion as Feminist Criticism in *A Room of One's Own*" (Paper delivered at the 1981 MLA Virginia Woolf Society Meeting, New York, December 1981) discusses the ballad, and Patricia Meyer Spacks treated it in *The Female Imagination* (New York: Alfred A. Knopf, 1975). I compare the rhetorical strategies of *A Room of One's Own* and *Three Guineas* in "No More Horses: Virginia Woolf on Art and Propaganda," in the Woolf issue of *Women's Studies,* 4, nos. 2 and 3 (1977): 265–90.

10. For the influence of Jane Harrison on Virginia Woolf see my essays "*The Years* as Greek Drama, Domestic Novel, and Götterdämmerung," *Bulletin of the New York Public Library* 80, no. 2 (Winter 1977): 276–301; and "Pargetting *The Pargiters,*" ibid., no. 3 (Spring 1978): 416–35.

11. Queenie Leavis's attack on Woolf is discussed in my "No More Horses."

12. Macciocchi, "Female Sexuality in Fascist Ideology," in *Feminist Review,* no. 1 (London: 1979), p. 75. Compare *A Room of One's Own,* pp. 54, 154–55.

13. "Female Sexuality in Fascist Ideology," p. 62.

14. Evelyn Haller, "Isis Unveiled," in Marcus, *New Feminist Essays on Virginia Woolf,* vol. 2. See also Haller's "The Anti-Madonna in the Work of Virginia Woolf," in Ginsberg, *Virginia Woolf: Centennial Essays.*

15. See my "'The Niece of a Nun.'"

16. Martine Stemerick, "The Madonna's Clay Feet: Julia Stephen's Anti-Egalitarian Ideas," in Marcus, *New Feminist Essays on Virginia Woolf,* vol. 2.

17. On nursing see my "Virginia Woolf and Her Violin."

18. Caroline Emelia Stephen, *The Service of the Poor: Being an inquiry into the reasons for and against the establishment of religious sisterhoods for charitable purposes* (London and New York: Macmillan, 1871).

19. *Letters of Sir James Stephen* (with biographical notes by his daughter Caroline Emelia Stephen) (Gloucester: John Bellows, 1906, private

circulation). For a discussion of Fitzjames's reviews of *Little Dorrit* see Edith Skom, "Fitzjames Stephen and Charles Dickens: A Case Study in Anonymous Reviewing" (Ph.D. diss., Northwestern University, 1978).

20. See my *"The Years* as Greek Drama, Domestic Novel, and Götterdämmerung."

21. Macciocchi, "Female Sexuality in Fascist Ideology," p. 75.

22. James Fitzjames Stephen, *Liberty, Equality, Fraternity,* ed. R. J. White, 2d ed. (1874; reprint ed., Cambridge: At the University Press, 1967). See also Sir Leslie Stephen, *The Life of Sir James Fitzjames Stephen* (London: Smith Elder, 1895). On the Maybrick case, see Mary S. Hartman, *Victorian Murderesses* (New York: Schocken, 1977), pp. 215–55. The most interesting study of Fitzjames Stephen is a Seldon Society lecture by Leon Radzinowicz, *Sir James Fitzjames Stephen, 1829–1894, and His Contribution to the Development of Criminal Law* (London: Quaritch, 1957). Leslie Stephen's *Life of Sir James Fitzjames Stephen* also contains a brief biography of Fitzjames's son, the poet J. K. Stephen. Michael Harrison's *Clarence* (London: W. H. Allen, 1972) discusses the son's candidacy for Jack the Ripper, as does Donald Rumbelow, *The Complete Jack the Ripper* (London and New York: W. H. Allen and New York Graphic Society, 1975). Two volumes of J. K. Stephen's verse, *Lapsus Calami* and *Quo Musa Tendis?,* were published in 1891 (Cambridge: Macmillan and Bowes).

23. See Rufus Jones, *The Later Periods of Quakerism,* vol. 2 (London: Macmillan, 1921) and Dr. T. Hodgkin's memoir in Caroline Stephen's *The Vision of Faith,* ed. Katharine Stephen (Cambridge: Heffer, 1911).

24. This and the following quotations are taken from Caroline Stephen's *Sir James Stephen* (Gloucester: John Bellows, 1906).

25. Ibid., p. 143.

26. See Adrienne Munich, "Katisha's Elbow," a study of the representation of Queen Victoria in Gilbert and Sullivan (Paper given at the Northeast Victorian Studies meeting, Philadelphia, April 1980).

27. On mistresses and servants see Stemerick, "The Madonna's Clay Feet."

28. DeSalvo, *Melymbrosia.*

29. See Katharine Stephen's introduction to Caroline Stephen's *The Vision of Faith.*

30. Virginia Woolf's essay "The Enchanted Organ," about her aunt Anne Thackeray Ritchie, quotes from "Annie"'s letter to her husband: "The sky was like a divine parrot's breast" (*Letters of Anne Thackeray Ritchie,* ed. Hester Ritchie [London: John Murray, 1924], p. 294). This letter also

includes the remark that she was glad to join the William Black Memorial Fund. Black's readers erected a lighthouse in his name on Duart Point in the Sound of Mull in the Hebrides. In *Silences* (New York: Delta, 1979), Tillie Olsen points out that Woolf may well have taken the idea of Shakespeare's sister from Olive Schreiner. Yvonne Kapp lists an 1897 London performance of a play by Eleanor Marx's common-law husband, Edward Aveling, called *Judith Shakespeare* (*Eleanor Marx,* 2 vols. [New York: Pantheon, 1977], 2:678). It is reasonable to suppose that Virginia Woolf or members of her family would have seen or heard of this production, since her half-brother Gerald Duckworth was treasurer of an avant-garde theatre group organized by Elizabeth Robins for the performance of Ibsen, and Aveling was a member of these circles, along with Olive Schreiner, Eleanor Marx, and Shaw.

31. Louise DeSalvo, "1897: Virginia Woolf at Fifteen," in Marcus, *New Feminist Essays on Virginia Woolf,* vol. 2.

32. These points on the Stephens's attitudes toward education are discussed by Martine Stemerick in "The Distaff Side of History" in Ginsberg, *Virginia Woolf: Centennial Essays.*

33. "A Society," *Monday or Tuesday* (New York: Harcourt, Brace and Co., 1921), p. 20. Unlike Woolf's other books, this early collection (with fine woodcuts in the Hogarth Press edition) has not been reprinted. All further references to this essay are included in the text.

34. Ethel Smyth, *Streaks of Life* (London: Longmans Green, 1921), p. 174.

35. "Friendships Gallery," ed. Ellen Hawkes, is now published in *Twentieth Century Literature* 25, nos. 3 and 4 (Fall/Winter 1979), a special issue edited by Lucio Ruotolo on unpublished manuscripts of Virginia Woolf.

36. This information regarding the draft of *A Room of One's Own* was kindly supplied to me by Alice Fox, in her usual generous spirit, from notes taken from the Monks House papers, University of Sussex. Several Woolf scholars had been trying to track down this draft for years when it suddenly appeared at Sussex. Where it was previously is not known.

37. See Paul Levy, *G. E. Moore and the Cambridge Apostles* (New York: Holt, Rinehart and Winston, 1979); and Frances Mary Brookfield, *The Cambridge "Apostles"* (New York: Scribner's, 1906).

38. J. K. Stephen, *The Living Languages: A Defense of the Compulsory Study of Greek at Cambridge* (Cambridge: Macmillan and Bowes, 1891). This essay deserves comparison with Woolf's "On Not Knowing Greek." Stephen takes up the cudgels against the scientists with great rhetorical

power. The study of Greek, he says, will guarantee the "non-survival of the unfittest." Throughout the essay he repeats the phrases "the highly educated man" and "the properly educated man." Virginia Woolf's painfully ironic repetition of the phrase "daughter of an educated man" in *Three Guineas* clearly derives from her cousin's essay. The study of Greek defines the "first flight" of English citizens. Stephen writes: "We are dealing with an *intellectual aristocracy*. Either as a reward for the industry, rapacity or good luck of an ancestor, immediate or remote, or as a reward for their own sterling and unaided qualities, the young men who present themselves at Cambridge to take the first step toward a degree, have obtained entrance into a favoured class: their degree will be a certificate that they have availed themselves of admission to that class . . . and it is for those on whom these benefits have been conferred to show in after life that they are, what they ought to be, the intellectual flower of the nation. If they are not, it is their own fault" (p. 47).

39. See Mary Ann Clawson, "Early Modern Fraternalism and the Patriarchal Family," *Feminist Studies* 6, no. 2 (Summer 1980): "Fraternalism is never a simple egalitarian relationship, even among men. With its patriarchal bias and its origin as a type of kin relation, it always carries with it notions of hierarchy and paternalist authority which appear, because of their roots in kin relations, as categories of 'natural' dominance and subordination." See also John Gillis, *Youth and History: Tradition and Change in European Age Relations 1770–Present* (New York and London: Academic Press, 1974). Walter J. Ong describes Latin as an alien language and secret code of the elite for an exclusive all-male society in "Latin Language Study as a Renaissance Puberty Rite," in *The Presence of the World* (New Haven: Yale University Press, 1967). Unfortunately, Richard Jenkyns's *The Victorians and Ancient Greece* (Cambridge, Mass.: Harvard University Press, 1980) avoids the serious implications of an ideology which provided a homosexual hegemony over British culture in the late nineteenth century, the issues of class, power, and the exclusion of women.

40. See Skom, "Fitzjames Stephen and Charles Dickens." Skom quotes an autobiographical fragment by Fitzjames Stephen on his hatred of the revolution of 1848, his feeling like a "scandalized policeman": "I should have liked first to fire grapeshot down every street in Paris, till the place ran with blood, & next to try Louis Phillipe and those who advised him not to fight by court martial, & to have hanged them all as traitors and cowards."

41. Geoffrey Hartman, "The Voice of the Shuttle," in *Beyond Formalism* (New Haven: Yale University Press, 1970).

42. *Between the Acts* (London: Hogarth Press, 1941), p. 253. All further references are included in the text.

43. See Naomi Black, "Virginia Woolf and the Women's Movement," in Marcus, *New Feminist Essays on Virginia Woolf,* vol. 2.

44. For a fine feminist study of *Between the Acts* see Sallie Sears, "Theater of War," in Marcus, *New Feminist Essays on Virginia Woolf,* vol. 2.

J. Hillis Miller

"Herself Against Herself":
The Clarification of Clara Middleton

Among examples of the presentation of female characters in Victorian fiction, Clara Middleton in George Meredith's *The Egoist* (1877) is one of the most important. Certainly *The Egoist* presents a strong sense of "living characters"—of Willoughby, the egoist himself, of Clara, of Vernon Whitford, of the cranky and garrulous narrator whom the reader first encounters in the celebrated "Prelude." The prelude maps egoism "from the Lizard to the last few pulmonary snips and shreds of leagues dancing on their toes for cold, explorers tell us, and catching breath by good luck, like dogs at bones about a table, on the edge of the Pole."[1] The method of *The Egoist,* the prelude tells the reader, is a form of mapping. It is a presentation of the unimaginable complexity of the geography of egoism in a schematic outline, according to a reductive code, small-scale matching large-scale, part for whole. This is a version of synecdoche which assumes that the structure or grain of the example corresponds cunningly to the structure or grain of the whole from which it is taken. For this reason, "art is the specific," "the inward mirror, the embracing and condensing spirit," which can "give us those interminable mile-post piles of matter . . . in essence, in chosen samples, digestibly," "so that a fair part of a book outstripping thousands of leagues when unrolled [the great Book of Earth or the Book of Egoism, the record of all man's social intelligence over the generations], may be compassed in one comic sitting" (1:2–3).

The reader will note a crucial feature of Meredith's theory of the novel. Meredith recognizes that a novel is necessarily based on a figure of speech. Rather than merely containing "illustrative" figures, it *is* a figure of speech. A novel is not merely in itself, *in toto,* a figure, a vast synecdoche. It is a figure of a figure. It does not represent a nontextual reality in a textual condensation but condenses one enormous book, the Book of Earth, in another compendious, shorter one. The social world is already a written record. The verbal art of comedy is a précis of that record. It is not a mimesis in language of something nonverbal but a synecdochic "specific," a homeopathic cure of language by language.

This image is reinforced within the body of the novel by many uses of the conventional figure of speech whereby one person's understanding of another is his "reading" of him. This metaphor is more than merely conventional in *The Egoist*. It defines another person's character as visible in somewhat enigmatic characters which must be deciphered, for example, when Willoughby seems to Clara "an obelisk lettered all over with hieroglyphics, and [she condemned to] everlastingly [hear] him expound them, relishingly [renew] his lectures on them" (1:116), or when, in a crucial paragraph in the chapter "Clara's Meditations," the narrator generalizes, apropos of Clara's "reading" of Colonel De Craye, about the situation of unmarried women in Victorian society, in their deciphering of the characters of men:

> Maidens are commonly reduced to read the masters of their destinies by their instincts; and when these have been edged by over-activity they must hoodwink their maidenliness to suffer themselves to read: and then they must dupe their minds, else men would soon see they were gifted to discern. Total ignorance being their pledge of purity to men, they have to expunge the writing of their perceptives on the tablets of the brain: they have to know not when they do know. The instinct of seeking to know, crossed by the task of blotting knowledge out, creates that conflict of the natural with the artificial creature to which their ultimately-revealed double-face, complained of by ever-dissatisfied men, is owing. (1:245)

Meredith here reads Clara's reading of De Craye. He takes it as a synecdoche for those pages of the Book of Earth that record all those innumerable maidenly decipherings of men. The discourse of the narrator of *The Egoist* is, so to speak, a marginal commentary on the main text. It is an interpretation of the Book of Social Wisdom, working, as does all interpretation, by way of detailed explication of samples, examples which are taken as fair representations of the whole.

What specific form does Meredith's cure of language by language take in its presentation of character? I have said that *The Egoist* creates a strong sense of the presence of specific characters. Meredith matches any Victorian novelist in conveying to his readers sharply etched configurations for each character. The reader knows each character as the presence of a consciousness to itself. Moreover, each of these characters is presented as defined in its essence by its awareness of itself in relation to other people. I am aware of myself, I *am* myself, to the degree that I am aware of the psychic pressure upon me of the psyches of other people. These other psyches are like breaths disturbing the flame of my self-consciousness. At the same time they feed that flame. They are necessary to its subsistence. I am conscious of myself as conscious of the consciousness of others. This is the general law of selfhood for characters in Victorian novels, but Meredith, especially in his remarkable late novels, beginning with *The Egoist* and continuing through *Diana of the Crossways, One of Our Conquerors, Lord Ormont and His Aminta,* and *The Amazing Marriage,* excels in presenting intimately, from within, the subtle pressures that the presence of the consciousness of another presents to the self-presence of a given character. If art is the specific by being an "inward mirror," Meredith's characters are mirrors within that mirror. Each lives by speculation, by his reflection of the lives of others in himself, or by seeing himself reflected in the mirrors of others, according to that law admirably formulated in Shakespeare's *Troilus and Cressida:*

> The beauty that is borne here in the face
> The bearer knows not, but commends itself

To others' eyes; nor doth the eye itself,
That most pure spirit of sense, behold itself,
Not going from itself; but eye to eye opposed
Salutes each other with each other's form;
For speculation turns not to itself
Till it hath travelled and is married there
Where it may see itself. (3. 3. 103–11)

This need by each mirror of another mirror is extreme in Willoughby; it is the ultimate weakness which makes him the slave of others in spite of his satanic "generalship" in deceiving and dazzling the eyes of others. "The breath of the world, the world's view of him, was partly his vital breath, his view of himself" (2:456).

Equally shrewd is Clara's dependence on others. Her unwitting enslavement of herself to Willoughby and her struggle to free herself honorably make up the main action of the comedy. It is apropos of her exacerbated sensitivity to the effect on her sense of herself of what might be called Willoughby's psychic aura, the magnetic field of the forceful will to appropriation with which he surrounds himself, that many of the admirably subtle notations of the law that self-awareness is awareness of others is made. An example is the scene in which Willoughby tries to embrace his fiancée as they stroll through his estate:

The gulf of a caress hove in view like an enormous billow hollowing under the curled ridge.
She stooped to a buttercup; the monster swept by. (1:153)

The Egoist, so it appears, presupposes and powerfully presents the existence of spiritual entities called selves. Each has its own sharp configuration, different from all others. Each is present to itself and to other such spiritual entities as force, as presence. These are merely mediated, described, or interpreted by language. Such figures as are used in these descriptions are expressions of something other than themselves. Key terms in Meredith's psychology of character are "self," "mind," "feeling," "will," and "nature." All these terms presuppose the notion of a prelinguistic fixed character: "She was to do everything for herself, do and dare everything, decide upon everything. He told her flatly that so would she learn to know her own mind" (1:242); "But decide at once. I wish you to have your free will" (2:326); "It's a dispute between a conventional idea of obligation and an injury to her nature.... [H]er feelings guide her best. It's one of the few cases in which nature may be consulted like an oracle" (2:369); "She was not pure of nature ... : she was pure of will; fire rather than ice" (1:211).

What is Clara's "nature," this fixed, extralinguistic self which she must protect from Willoughby's base invasions and appropriations? Chapter 21, "Clara's Meditations," is an extraordinary moment in *The Egoist,* an extraordinary moment even in the Victorian novel generally. It is the moment of the dissolution, from within, as a "lived experience" (but the notions of "life" and "experience" are transformed in this moment too), of the presupposition that each man or woman has a fixed character with definite hieroglyphic outlines which may be figured truly, for example in his or her physiognomy or in the figures of speech with which he or she may be described in language. Since this presupposition is the one on which *The Egoist* as a whole, with its vivid presentation of the intersubjective battle of character with character, is based, since it is the presupposition on which Victorian fiction or even, *mutatis mutandis,* the European novel as a whole appears to be based, much is at stake in these pages. The whole chapter should be read, but extracts will indicate its main outlines:

> She was in a fever, lying like stone, with her brain burning. Quick natures run out to calamity in any little shadow of it flung before. Terrors of apprehension drive them. They stop not short of the uttermost when they are on the wings of dread. A frown means tempest, a wind wreck; to see fire is to be seized by it. When it is the approach of their loathing that they fear, they are in the tragedy of the embrace at a breath....

The false course she had taken through sophistical cowardice appalled the girl; she was lost. The advantage taken of it by Willoughby put on the form of strength, and made her feel abject, reptilious; she was lost, carried away on the flood of the cataract. . . .

Thank heaven for the chances of a short life! Once in a net, desperation is graceless. . . .

She was now in the luxury of passivity, when we throw our burden on the Powers above, and do not love them. The need to love drew her out of it, that she might strive with the unbearable, and by sheer striving, even though she were graceless, come to love them humbly. It is here that the seed of good teaching supports a soul; for the condition might be mapped, and where kismet whispers us to shut eyes, and instruction bids us look up, is at a well-marked crossroad of the contest.

Quick of sensation, but not courageously resolved, she perceived how blunderingly she had acted. For a punishment, it seemed to her that she who had not known her mind must learn to conquer her nature, and submit. She had accepted Willoughby; therefore she accepted him. . . .

She was almost imagining she might imitate him [Vernon Whitford, who has submitted to Willoughby], when the clash of a sharp physical thought: "The difference! the difference!" told her she was a woman and never could submit. Can a woman have an inner life apart from him she is yoked to? She tried to nestle deep away in herself: in some corner where the abstract view had comforted her, to flee from thinking as her feminine blood directed. It was a vain effort. The difference, the cruel fate, the defencelessness of women, pursued her, strung her to wild horses' backs, tossed her on savage wastes. In her case duty was shame: hence, it could not be broadly duty. That intolerable difference proscribed the word.

But the fire of a brain burning high and kindling everything, lit up herself against herself:—Was one so volatile as she a person with a will? —Were they not a multitude of flitting wishes, that she took for a will?—Was she, feather-headed that she was, a person to make a stand on physical pride?—If she could yield her hand without reflection (as she conceived she had done, from incapacity to conceive herself doing it reflectively), was she much better than purchaseable stuff that has nothing to say to the bargain?

Furthermore, said her incandescent reason, she had not suspected such art of cunning in Willoughby. Then might she not be deceived altogether—might she not have misread him? . . .

She reviewed him. It was all in one flash. . . . An undefined agreement to have the same regard for him as his friends and the world had, provided that he kept the same distance from her, was the termination of this phase, occupying about a minute in time, and reached through a series of intensely vivid pictures. . . .

[For one in her condition] the brain is raging like a pine-torch and the devouring illumination leaves not a spot of our nature covert. The aspect of her weakness was unrelieved, and frightened her back to her loathing. From her loathing, as soon as her sensations had quickened to realize it, she was hurled on her weakness. She was graceless, she was inconsistent, she was volatile, she was unprincipled, she was worse than a prey to wickedness—capable of it; she was only waiting to be misled. Nay, the idea of being misled suffused her with languor; for then the battle would be over and she a happy weed of the sea, no longer suffering those tugs at the roots, but leaving it to the sea to heave and contend. . . .

Issuing out of torture, her young nature eluded the irradiating brain, in search of refreshment, and she luxuriated at a feast in considering him—[Colonel De Craye, who would tempt her to elope]—shower on a parched land that he was! . . .

She would have thought of Vernon, as her instinct of safety prompted, had not his exactions been excessive. He proposed to help her with advice only. She was to do everything for herself, do and dare everything, decide upon everything. He told her flatly that so would she learn to know her own mind. . . .

Her war with Willoughby sprang of a desire to love repelled by distaste. Her cry for freedom was a cry to be free to love: she discovered it, half-shuddering: to love, oh! no—no shape of man, nor impalpable nature either; but to love unselfishness, and helpfulness, and planted strength in something. Then, loving and being loved a little, what strength would be hers! (1:237–44)

This admirable sequence is one of the high-water marks of the Victorian novel, indeed of realistic fiction in Europe generally. Here the procedures of realism dismantle themselves by being systematically exploited, taken to their limits, transported to that hyperbolic point where they reverse themselves and become something else. That something else undermines the conventions of storytelling which at the same time make the passage and the novel of which it is a part possible in the first place. This is according to that law which says conventions and assumptions of any mode of writing contain the seeds of their own destruction if they are carried far enough, not very far, actually.

George Meredith has in this passage accepted the implicit charge made to the realistic novelist: represent in words, among other things, what actually goes on from moment to moment within consciousness. In one sense, the passage succeeds in this magnificently. It creates the vivid illusion that there was a person named Clara who went through this experience. The reader is led to reexperience this experience from within, sharing it again, in the renewal made permanently possible, over and over again, by the words of the narrator as Meredith has invented them. The reader dwells not only within Clara's thoughts and emotions but even within her intimate bodily feelings and sensations. As Ramon Fernandez long ago recognized,[2] Meredith's "realism" is based on an assumption of the overlapping, if not quite coincidence, in inextricable copresence of body, "feelings" (in both senses), mind, external physical world, and the bodies and minds of other people. Things outside are apprehended by things inside, mind and body working together. The "incandescent reason" appropriates, often in spite of itself, in "sharp physical thought," both material objects, such as double-blossomed wild cherry trees, and other persons, such as that Vernon Whitford who lies under the tree for Clara to behold. In this feeling for the inextricable inmixing, though not quite identity, as of wine and water or of oil homogenized in water, of realms kept by some philosophers and by some novelists more strictly separate, Meredith anticipates such a "phenomenological" philosopher of our own day as Maurice Merleau-Ponty. There would be room for a systematic interpretation of Meredith's work both in fiction and in poetry along the lines initiated by Fernandez's brilliant essay.

At the same time, this passage, when it is read more carefully, can be seen to lay bare its own machinery of representation and thereby to put in question the validity, as mimesis, of both its conceptual and its figurative terminology. It even puts in question the validity of the distinction between conceptual and figurative, as well as those "phenomenological" assumptions Fernandez formulates so brilliantly and ascribes to Meredith.

In her sleepless, all-night meditation, in Willoughby's house, on her plight in having solemnly engaged herself to marry him, Clara discovers, under the pressure of that situation, that the structure of assumptions presupposed in that promise to marry was false. Basic to this structure was the presupposition that she had a solid character on the basis of which promises could be made and kept. Clara's "nature," on the contrary, is an anonymous and shapeless energy which cannot be outlined. It must be compared, incoherently, to fire, to liquid, to the formless wind, to a featureless desert, or to unshaped stone. It changes from moment to moment. It has no permanent shape as yet, for "the tempers of the young are liquid fires in isles of quicksand" (1: 145). Vernon Whitford is right in seeing that Clara's "character was yet liquid in the mould, and that she was a creature of only naturally youthful wildness provoked to freakishness by the ordeal of a situation shrewd as any that can happen to her sex in civilized life" (2:365). Of Clara it must be said that "her needs were her nature, her moods her mind" (1:145). Her "nature" is her "currents of feeling" (1:141). "Nature," "character," "mind" are here dissolved, liquified. They cease to be anything solid on which a promise or a commitment might be based. Self becomes evanescent tempers, feelings, needs, moods, currents of water or fire without permanent shape. Currents? Water? Fire? What is the status of these figures if the entities for which they are figures—mind, character, and so on—have no literal existence as persisting things but are themselves figures for the unfigurable? To say that Clara is "liquid fire in isles of quicksand" is in this case the same as to say that Clara is her moods or her mind or her character, since she is no characterable character representable by some fixed hieroglyph or seal. *Character* in this case, if it is to have any meaning, must be distorted from its dictionary meaning as a permanent brand impressed on the psyche and mirrored in doubling characters in features, gestures, physiognomy. The word *character* here becomes a figure for what Clara is, namely, "her whims, variations, inconsistencies, wiles; her tremblings between good and naughty, that might be stamped to noble or to terrible; her sincereness, her duplicity, her courage, cowardice, possibilities for heroism and for treachery" (2:365), in short, for her liquid, fiery, or airy mobility. The words *will, nature, feelings, mind, self,* and *character* are not names, in this case, for a stable entity or for its faculties. When applied to Clara, they are figures drawn from an archaic psychology to be used tropologically to describe what has no proper name, since it flits away from any attempt to pin it down. The enterprise of the "realistic representation" of human psychology here reaches a point where it overreaches itself, goes beyond its own boundary lines, in the attempt to fulfill its project completely. Realism dissolves itself in the multiplicity of its notations and in its recognition of its dependence on a figurative language for which there is no possibility of substituting proper terms. What is there to be named does not have a consistence or permanence compatible with literal names.

The double assumption on which that aspect of realism which involves the mimesis in language of states of mind rests is the following: that there is a prelinguistic self or character and that this in its modes may be expressed, mirrored, or copied without distortion in language. Walter Pater, for example, praises Rossetti for choosing the right "term" "from many competitors, as the just transcript of that peculiar phase of soul which he alone knew, precisely as he knew it."[3] *The Egoist,* especially in the "transcription" of Clara's meditations, puts this double assumption in question. The putting in question is accomplished in part by overt thematic statement ("Was one so volatile as she a person with a will? Were they not a multitude of flitting wishes that she took for a will?"), in part by the manifest role of incoherent figures in the transcription.

The theory of figure implicit in the practice of transcription here is made explicit elsewhere in Meredith, for example in a passage in *One of Our Conquerers:* "It is the excelling merit of similes and metaphors to spring us to vault over gaps and thickets and dreary places. . . . Beware, moreover, of examining them too scrupulously: they have a trick of wearing to vapour if closely scanned";[4] or in the following striking formulation in *Diana of the Crossways:* "The banished of Eden had to put on metaphors."[5] Metaphors, one can see, are peculiar. On the one hand they are an essential covering, a web or integument of language which serves as a bridge over places where the continuity of language would otherwise break and tumble us into a crevasse or into a copse of undergrowth. I take it this means that metaphors name the unnamable, present the unpresentable, and thereby serve simultaneously as decent covering, as revelation or unveiling, and as a making continuous of a cloth of language which otherwise would be rent, would fail to reach from here to there in a sequential narrative. Covering of what? Unveiling of what? The second passage makes explicit what is implicit in the first. The function of metaphors is to cover the pudenda of all the daughters and sons of Eve and Adam. Since the fall literal, naked language has been impossible, shameful. Certain things, the genitalia, in fact, have been namable only indirectly, in names displaced from other less shameful places. These figures are fig leaves to cover the gaps and thickets where proper naming is no longer proper.

This metaphorical naming contains the aporia inherent in all acts of simultaneous unveiling and veiling. Such metaphors when closely scanned have a trick of wearing to vapor. They are not appropriate names for those gaps and thickets in dreary places. Their inappropriateness is appropriate to their function as veils. When they wear to vapor and vanish they then best function as veils, since they have revealed nothing, told no secrets. At the same time, their function as sewing, as darning threads crisscrossed over a gap in the discourse, is no longer fulfilled. The gap is revealed, the abyss which disrupts or breaks the smooth texture of the text, for example, the assumption that the characters in a narrative have characters, are proper selves. The cloth of the veil becomes gauze, transparent and insubstantial as vapor, a weaving of clouds. The phallic thicket becomes a vaginal gap. If the metaphors hold, then they have named that gap, revealed it, and the text is once more broken. Is the thicket, however, unambiguously phallic? An impenetrable underbrush in a dreary place seems more like an interlaced integument, a weaving or a veil once more, pubic hair which may hide something or may hide an absence. Weaving, the psychoanalysts tell us, is said to have been invented by women, to have been devised, according to this myth, in the plaiting of pubic hair to make a mock phallus. This weaving was the hiding of an absence and a phantasmal pseudo revelation. At the same time it was a metaphor claiming the existence of what is not there, so covering the fact that the phallus is not there. Between revealing and hiding, the metaphors vibrate, fleeing one extreme, total opacity, as revealing but revealing nothing, a misleading sham revelation claiming substance where there is none, but finding the other extreme, total transparency, coming to the same thing. Far from springing us to vault over gaps and thickets and dreary places or covering the indecent with decency, the improper with propriety in fallen man or woman, a metaphorical text is made of gaps and thickets. That is to say, it is made of metaphors, which comes to the same thing, since the gaps and thickets are the metaphors. [6]

It is no accident that so many male novelists in the Victorian period—Thackeray, Dickens, Trollope, or Meredith himself—so often project into a female protagonist the dramatization of that question fundamental to the novel, Can we or can we not believe that human beings, male or female, have fixed selves? The female protagonist has a lesson to teach us men. The assumption that ontologically substantial characters do exist cannot be detached from the logocentrism or phallogocentrism which underlies it and of which it is a version. The fixed hieroglyphic of character here plays the role of the logos or phallus, the head meaning which is the source and guarantee of all the derivative meanings and configurations of the self: moods, feelings, wiles. Only if Clara is indeed the reflex and mirror image, the choric echo, of the phallic and upright Willoughby, that obelisk covered all over with hieroglyphs, can she be said to have a self: "In walking with her, in drooping to her, the whole man was made conscious of the female image of himself by her exquisite unlikeness. She completed him, added the softer lines wanting to his portrait before the world" (1:48). Clara's discovery in the chapter of her meditations is that she has no central column of self charactered over with permanent emblems of her character. She therefore cannot reflect back to Willoughby his conception of himself as, in promising to marry him, she has tacitly undertaken to do. Instead, there is a gap there around which flow or burn or blow her evanescent moods, whims, wiles, inconsistencies.

This discovery is also an unsettling revelation for Willoughby. He has depended on Clara to give him a stable female image of himself and finds that he must do without such mirroring. It is a discovery also for the narrator and for the novelist behind the narrator. They have peered into the mirror of an invented female character to seek their own images and to put to the test thereby the phallogocentric assumptions presupposed in the notion of character. The reader, too, male or female, according to my hypothesis about the function of "realistic" fictions, puts his or her own assumptions about character, about his or her own character or self, to the test when he or she reads such a novel. The integument of metaphor in the passage cited above is a thin covering over the sexual issue it more or less directly treats, "the difference! the difference!" Clara is unable to bring herself to fulfill her bargain by consenting to submit herself physically to Willoughby's appropriation of her as a "chalice" (1:50), as an "inanimate overwrought polished pure-metal precious vessel" (1:132). She does not have the solidity or consistency to be such a vessel, the reversed image of the obelisk, glove for his hand. The man—lover, narrator, or reader—who looks into Clara as mirror to find confirmation of his sense of his own character finds only unfixable volatility. This volatility is both revealed and hidden by the network of figures which the novelist must use to name it, in a fluid or vaporous parody of the chalice "overwrought" with designs. The chalice is the obelisk turned inside out, the hollow reflex of the Apollonian sunray turned to stone and carved all over with the secret hieroglyphic speech of the sun fixed in legible characters for those who have the interpretation of them, as Willoughby pretends to read himself. From obelisk to chalice to vaporous integument of metaphors, each model deprives of substantiality the one before, in a movement toward the "truth" that there is no truth except in metaphor.

Though this passage of Clara's meditations conveys, to me at least, an entirely persuasive sense of having lived through the vacillations of Clara's "physical thinking," from moment to moment, this following through is impossible without the figures of fire, ocean, storm, stone, wild horses on savage wastes, mapped crossroads, brain raging like a pine torch, and so on. Clara exists as these figures, both in the sense that the reader's phantasmal illusion of her real existence is created by Meredith only with the aid of these figures and in the sense that if we move through the looking-glass to take her as a real "person" being described in elaborate, temporalized notation by the narrator, she exists, in herself, not as a substantial character but as a sequence of figures, fleeting, evanescent, each succeeded by another which contradicts it, as an image of fire contradicts one of water, an image of wind the other two, and so on. In this flow of figures, the conceptual words, *mind, will, nature,* and so on, and the literal words for parts of the body, *brain, blood, head, hand, face,* are also redefined. They are volatilized, vaporized, and become themselves part of the sequence of figures.

In this volatilization a complex system of presuppositions is simultaneously insubstantiated. The self becomes not something fixed but a multitude of fleeting wishes, feelings, thoughts. The distinction between extralinguistic and linguistic, on which mimetic realism is based, breaks down. The self and any society of selves exist as the signs for them. These signs are governed by no fixed columnar head sense. The distinctions between literal, figurative, and conceptual collapse. They are replaced by different versions of catachresis, words transferred from some other realm to name improperly what has no proper name and comes into existence in the improprieties of that strange figure. The temporal continuity of the self, finally, essential presupposition of the connectedness of storytelling, dissolves into the sequence of these pictorial emblems, noted so carefully by the narrator: "An undefined agreement to have the same regard for him as his friends and the world had, provided that he kept at the same distance from her, was the termination of this phase, occupying about a minute in time, and reached through a series of intensely vivid pictures" (1:240). Internal time consciousness in *The Egoist* is the dimension of discontinuity between one moment and the next, of the noncoincidence of mental image and what it images, and of the absence of identifiable origin or end. The moment of beginning or source of a given thought, conviction, or penchant of the feeling mind can never be certainly identified. On the example of Clara's physical distaste for Willoughby the narrator generalizes: "Sweeping from sensation to sensation, the young, whom sensations impel and distract, can rarely date their disturbance from a particular one" (1:71). Much later, trying to explain to Mrs. Mountstuart how and when she came to find that she did not love Willoughby, Clara can express herself only in what might be called a temporal oxymoron: "By degrees, unknown to myself; suddenly" (2:430). There was a time when she intended to marry Willoughby, in fact when she came on her visit to Patterne Hall she did, and then, later, there was a time when she did not, as Mrs. Mountstuart sardonically observes: "And *gradually* you *suddenly* discovered, since you came here, that you did not intend it, if you could find a means of avoiding it" (2:435). Though the change was a fact of consciousness, it did not occur at a time when consciousness was distinctly conscious of it as a fact different from the previous fact of a different intent. She changed her mind or the intention of her mind both suddenly and gradually, in a fashion not compatible with any image of regular temporal continuity. In any case her change of mind did not take place in her mind, but unknown to herself. Choosing, intending, and promising are performatives which depend on the mind's continuity and on the mind's constant presence to itself for their efficacy, but Clara neither constantly knows her own mind clearly nor is able to keep it constant to itself. The aetiology of her choices, intentions, and promises cannot be identified. Their validity is thereby nullified: "And she could vehemently declare that she had not chosen [when she first promised to marry Willoughby]; she was too young, too ignorant to choose. . . . to call consenting the same in fact as choosing [as Vernon has done], was willfully unjust" (1:181). The chapter "Clara's Meditations" is her most acute experience of this discontinuity, this failure of the mind to be present to itself, either in the moment or in the moment's awareness of its origins, in its connection to some past moment. The moment of Clara's greatest self-clarification is the moment when she is most opaque to herself.

The imagery of the broken line, intersected by crossroads at innumerable junctures, like Ariadne's threaded labyrinth or Arachne's web ("Once in a net, desperation is graceless"; "the condition might be mapped, and where Kismet whispers us to shut eyes, and instruction bids us look up, is at a well-mapped crossroad of the contest" [1:238–39]), is latent through the passage of Clara's meditations as figure for the disrupted series of catachreses following one another in time, hieroglyphs of nothing ("Was one so volatile as she a person with a will?"), into which the self has dissolved. The lines of character, of portraiture, and of realistic temporal continuity, as well as the borders between literal and figurative, are blurred and vanish, leaving only "a series of intensely vivid pictures." These are not pictures *of* anything, since nature, the body, other people have been appropriated as emblems for the evanescent states of the non-self. Such pictures are the only substance of what they picture, like the crudely drawn face in Wittgenstein's "Brown Book." What the pictures show us are themselves.

Take for example Clara's image of herself as "a happy weed of the sea no longer suffering those tugs at the roots, but leaving it to the sea to heave and contend." Is this Clara's image for herself or the narrator's image for her? There is no way to be sure. The firm distinction between the language of the narrator and the language of the character is another boundary line which vanishes, necessarily, in this version of indirect discourse, along with the line between literal and figural, the line between linguistic and nonlinguistic, the lines of character, and the temporal line. If there is no stable "character" for Clara or for the narrator, if "she," "he," "hers," "his" name here the language they use, then there are no grounds for distinguishing between them in a passage in which "the narrator" speaks in figure or picture of one momentary whim or fleeting "state of mind" of the character.

None of the expressions, figures, little pictures which are strung together in "Clara's Meditations" are direct reflections or mimeses of something other than themselves. They appear to be metaphors, or perhaps it would be better to say that they have the apparent structure of synecdoches, since they express by way of a particular, flowing water, devouring fire, or whatever something that always exists as an encompassing totality or activity. These figures are all manifestly false identities. Subjectivity is not flowing water or fire. It may only be figured as like water or fire. These figures, however, are not displacements of any "proper" or "literal" language. There is no language except figurative, that is, improper, language for the movements of the soul. This is as true of the conceptual terms for the faculties of the self and of the words for parts of the body as it is of the terms drawn from inanimate nature to describe the self. Character exists only as displacement, not as the solid ground of its various manifestations. Its "nature" is to have no nature, to be what it is not. This fact makes all the phrases about "Clara's nature" oxymora: "her needs are her nature, her moods her mind." Clara's nature exists as the figures for it. This undermines her search for a solid ground in her "nature" or in her "will" for her decision not to marry Willoughby. It undermines also the attempt by the author or by his delegate, the narrator, to develop and practice a theory of fiction based on the adequacy of synecdoche, so that the totality of man's social life can be condensed and presented in chosen samples, digestibly. The part bears no necessary representative relation to the whole. It is a distorted image in a concave mirror. The fact that there is no proper language for the self, none but figurative characters for character, since there is no character as such, neither in fiction nor in "real life," dismantles, finally, the attempt by the reader to develop an interpretation of the novel of the type proposed by Fernandez, that is, one grounded on a "phenomenological" reading, that version of metaphysics which refers everything back to a solid base in subjectivity.

The implicit discovery of *The Egoist* is therefore of the inherence of language in character. Character exists as the language for it. This is true not in the sense that words create the self, that anonymous (in the etymological sense of "nameless") energy which Meredith's narrator calls Clara's will, her nature, fire, flood, and so on, always in figure, but in the sense that the relation between the two is one of constant displacement. Each is the displacement of the other. Their relation generates a line of language extending itself in a circle not quite ever a circle around two foci of an ellipse, each focus an absence or impropriety: language; consciousness. Neither focus is the basis of the other but the underminer of its solidity, the something missing which hollows it out. Clara's character, since it does not exist as an object exists, keeps any language for it from being other than indirect, inadequate. The incoherence of the narrator's characters for that character shows that it cannot exist as a solid column inscribed in hieroglyphs making a unified story. Clara's "will," her "nature," her "character" is her freedom, her lack of a fixed form either in herself or in what is outside her to give her inward form. She is one those "young" of whom the narrator generalizes: "The tempers of the young are liquid fires in isles of quicksand; the precious metals not yet cooled in a solid earth" (1:145). Such a young person as Clara cannot be one of those "inanimate over-wrought polished pure-metal precious vessels, fresh from the hands of the artificer, for ['the devouring male egoist'] to walk away with hugging, call all his own, drink of, and fill and drink of" (1:132). Clara cannot be possessed as an object because she has no objective form. She cannot properly be compared to a precious vase because her nature is her freedom, her volatility, as she tells Willoughby: "I am unworthy. I am volatile. I love my liberty. I want to be free . . ." (1:126). She has no solidity, neither as container nor as something contained within a constraining mold surrounding her from outside. Her temper is liquid fire, neither fire nor water, but something in-between, in language an oxymoron, physically a contradiction or an absurdity. This liquid fire is contained "in isles of quicksand." This is another oxymoron or palpable absurdity, since islands are not containers but things contained, surrounded, embraced, by the circumambient water. An isle of quicksand is in any case no substantial molding force, like the dead or "unquick" sand used in certain casting processes. If liquid fire is neither fire nor water, quicksand is neither earth nor liquid but something in-between, and so Clara's nature is not only shapeless, fiery-watery energy in itself; it has also not yet encountered, neither within itself nor without, "a solid earth" which might give it definite shape when it cools.

Clara's "nature" is her freedom, her spontaneity. This exists as negativity, as her instinctive rebellion against any form of slavery. It comes into perceptible existence only when she is bound, that is, when she has promised to marry Willoughby. It does not exist as a "thing" in itself, but only as a response, though it should be readable from her features. Willoughby's error is that he rushes past her face to plunge for possession of her soul: "He dived below the surface without studying that index page. . . . Miss Middleton's features were legible as to the mainspring of her character. He could have seen that she had a spirit with a natural love of liberty, and required the next thing to liberty, spaciousness, if she was to own allegiance. Those features, unhappily, instead of serving for an introduction to the within, were treated as the mirror of himself. . . . He desired to shape her character to the feminine of his own" (1:51–52).

Among Clara's "features" the most legible sign of her love of freedom is her hair, especially the hair at "the softly dusky nape of her neck, where this way and that the little lighter-coloured irreclaimable curls running truant from the comb and the knot—curls, half-curls, root-curls, vine-ringlets, wedding-rings, fledgling feathers, tufts of down, blown wisps—waved or fell, waved over or up or involutedly, or strayed, loose and downward, in the form of small silken paws, hardly any of them much thicker than a crayon shading, cunninger than long round locks of gold to trick the heart" (1:101). Passage of an admirable erotic beauty! If the banished of Eden had to cover themselves with metaphors, those metaphors were no doubt woven of thickets of hair, revealing and hiding, nape-curls a covering already covered again in a cascade of further metaphors—roots, vines, wedding-rings, feathers, down, clouds, each another figure for an absence which encircles softly and imprisons. This metamorphosed hair in one place stands for unnamed hair in another. That hair in turn stands for the abyss of an unpossessable freedom, "truant," "irreclaimable," which tricks the male observer, traps him cunningly, locks him in, though with hasps like small silken paws, not even crayon-thick, no thicker than the crayon's shading, and dispossesses him of his own freedom. Willoughby learns from his involvement with Clara what it feels like to be a spider caught in another spider's woof, an Apollonian Theseus lost in the intricate, labyrinthine tangles of Ariadne's thread, a male spider in mortal danger in Arachne's web: "His blind sensitiveness felt as we may suppose a spider to feel when plucked from his own web and set in the centre of another's" (2:355).

As features of the visible Clara, her curls are echoes producing further echoes in a chain or net of displacements. These define Clara as not being what she is, as being her freedom. She is therefore never able to give back to Willoughby the stable and reassuring image of himself which he seeks in her countenance. If Willoughby wants "marriage with a mirror, with an echo; marriage with a shining mirror, a choric echo" (2:464), Clara is, in Vernon's precise image, a "Mountain Echo," that is, an echo which does not return accurately the reflected, auditory image of what is shouted to it but disperses that voice irreclaimably. Laetitia thinks of Clara as "the swift, wild spirit, Clara by name, sent fleeting on a far half-circle by the voice is roused to subserve" (1:37).

Here a myth or myths, shadowily present as oblique echoes dispersed as fragmentary éclats throughout the text of The Egoist, come almost to the surface: the myth of Narcissus in Ovid, that myth distorted then, in Mountain Echo, in the great passage about Eve in book 4 of Paradise Lost, and both myths, the classical and the Christian, echoed again in the distorted or broken mirror of The Egoist. In all these texts a similar complex, asymmetrical structure is present. This structure is in fact "fundamental," in the sense that it both affirms and endangers any fundament, throughout Western thought and literature. The structure involves a pair which becomes subverted by a triangular relation which is still precariously balanced. This is then asymmetrically mirrored in another triangle which parodies it and so undermines it. The image is speculative. It is the speculative as such. Its model of perfection is the perfect mirroring of one male figure by another. The female, that imperfect male, missing one member, introduces the deconstructive absence which means there will always be something left over or something short in this mirror, the perpetual too little or too much which makes it impossible for the balance ever to come right and so keeps the story going.

The image of the mirroring pair oscillates in this tradition between the mirroring of male by male in perfect match and the mirroring of male by female in another form of perfect matching, concave meeting convex, as in the androgynous couple in Aristophanes' speech in Plato's *The Symposium.* The triangle is stable, a sure support of the ontological ground of character, only so long as it remains all male, as in the Trinity: Father, Son, and Holy Ghost, the one, its image, and the relation between them, or God, his perfect image, the Son, and the creation which is fabricated by God in the image of the Son, so that the world as a whole and every part of it separately has the countenance of God, is signed with his signature. The female makes always one too many and potentially opens the triangle beyond any hope of closing it again or of filling the gap. As Narcissus's attempt to merge himself with his mirrored image—or, in another version of the Narcissus myth, as his lovelorn search for his lost twin sister—is broken by the love for him of Echo, who has no voice but that given by Narcissus and yet subverts that voice in her echo of it (*aeternae deceptus imagine vocis* [deceived by the image (Echo) of the alternate voice], *Metamorphoses* 3, 385),[7] or as Eve's Narcissistic admiration of her reflected image, in *Paradise Lost,* endangers the chain of perfect imagings which goes from God the Father to his speculative match, God the Son; to Adam, the man created in God's image by the agency of Christ, the Son, the Logos ("Man/God's latest image" [*Paradise*

Lost 4. 566]); to Eve, who is in turn Adam's softer image ("there I had fixt/Mine eyes till now, and pin'd with vain desire,/Had not a voice thus warnd me, What thou seest,/What there thou seest fair Creature is thy self/With thee it comes and goes: but follow me,/And I will bring thee where no shadow staies/Thy coming, and thy soft imbraces, hee,/Whose image thou art, him thou shall enjoy/Inseparablie thine" [*Paradise Lost* 4:465-73]), so Willoughby's satanic arrogation of divine self-sufficiency is imaged in his desire to be surrounded by a world, in particular a wife, that will everywhere reflect back to him his own image. He seeks his mirrored image in miniature in Clara's eyes: "and once gained, they are your mirrors for life and far more constant than the glass" (1:192). This ideal is demolished by Clara, the Mountain Echo, who closes her eyes to him and so annihilates him: "Clara let her eyes rest on his, and without turning or dropping, shut them" (1:88); "He found himself addressing eyes that regarded him as though he were a small speck, a pin's head, in the circle of their remote contemplation. They were wide; they closed" (1:91). Clara gives back to Willoughby always something other than his own voice or image and so annihilates him, since he exists, satanically, only as image, only as doubled in the outward reflection of himself. That Clara is a Mountain Echo means that her character is her uncharacterizable freedom. She has a negative or nihilating power to turn all things (fire, water, mountains, vases, double-blossomed wild cherry trees, even poor curtailed Willoughby himself) into emblems or images of her own lack of character. She turns them into figures of speech whose fundamental characteristic is to be inadequate, to be false equivalences, catachreses, abusive use of terms to name the nameless. Like Echo in Ovid's Narcissus story, who becomes a disembodied voice, floating and ungraspable, after her death, Clara, as her name suggests, is transparent purity, empty air, a mirror with no image in it when a man looks there. She has no character in herself, no voice, no Logos, and so she returns whatever is cast against her with a difference, distorted, disguised, transformed. When Vernon imposes it on Clara's "free will" to decide her fate, he defines her lack of ground as the ground of the decisive commitments which will determine her character and her destiny.

There are many references to the French Revolution in the novel, for example: "This maenad shriek for freedom would happily entitle her to the Republican cap—the Phrygian—in a revolutionary Parisian procession" (2:420). These indicate Meredith's awareness that Clara's self-discovery of her lack of self, on the night of her meditations, has unsettling social implications. It would overturn any structure of society based on conventions implying the consistency and stability of male or female character, the ability of a man or a woman to make promises and keep them, marriage as an institution in which the husband owns his wife, as he owns his horse or his house. This subversion is analogous to the way Clara's self-discovery breaks down the narrator's enterprise of writing a novel which will be an authentic synecdoche of man's social experience as a whole. It is also analogous to the undermining of the reader's enterprise of understanding *The Egoist* according to traditional aesthetic principles of wholeness, consistency, and the reference of all a text back to a pervasive ground of meaning which gathers it into one. If Clara cannot maintain her continuity with herself, if she does not remain the same person from moment to moment, well enough to be said to have a character or a will, how can the reader be expected to hold together in one coherent interpretation the text which records the discontinuities and intermittences of her heart, always and necessarily faithless to itself?

Nevertheless, *The Egoist* has a "happy ending." Clara frees herself from her "promise" to marry Willoughby and gives herself freely to Vernon Whitford in a meeting which takes place outside the boundaries of the book, "between the Swiss and Tyrol Alps over the Lake of Constance" (2:626). Their meeting occurs on the border between Switzerland and Austria, not quite in one country or the other, and in a landscape which is both rock and water, mountain and lake, "over the Lake of Constance." How can this happy ending be prospectively believed? How can the narrator plausibly promise that such a meeting and such a betrothal will take place, or has already taken place to his retrospective eye? How can he plausibly promise that the marriage of Vernon and Clara will be a happy one, based on unshakable love and fidelity? What constancy can Clara promise Vernon by the Lake of Constance if she has no character to guarantee and underwrite her fulfillment of any promise, no stable signature to allow her to sign her name to a marriage contract, if she exists only as a multitude of fleeting and inconsistent wishes? The answer lies in an alternative theory of character and of promising which emerges in *The Egoist*, out of the wreckage left by the deconstruction, in "Clara's Meditations," of traditional theories of character and of promising. The tracing out of the outlines of this alternative theory of character must, however, be done in another essay and in another place.

NOTES

1. George Meredith, *Works*, memorial ed., 27 vols. (London: Constable, 1909-11), 13:2. Further textual references will be to vols. 1 and 2 of *The Egoist*, which are vols. 13 and 14 of the memorial edition (both 1910).
   2. See his "Le Message de Meredith," *Messages, première série*, 4th ed. (Paris: Gallimard, 1926), pp. 120-46. As an example of the extraordinary phenomenological verve and penetration of Fernandez's criticism, I cite the following paragraph from this essay:

> Le principe d'activité concrète qui commande le jeu des images chez Meredith commande également—et dans une mesure qui le distingue de tous les autres romanciers—l'évolution physique et morale de ses personnages. Le tout-fait, le vécu, le monument sont radicalement bannis de son oeuvre. Point de déductions, de documents, de coordonnées abstraites. Ses personnages sont parce qu'ils sont et ne tirent leur raison

d'être que d'eux-mêmes; mais—et ceci est de la première importance—ils ne sont que parce qu'ils agissent, *leur être dépend de leur activité.* Activité toute extérieure, toute physique, activité de relation; activité interne des sentiments que telles circonstances portent au point d'ébullition; réactions, adaptations, contractions et détentes; épreuve incessante de l'élasticité et de la trempe des ressorts vitaux; palpitations, émanations psychiques et physiques de fluide dramatique, chocs de paroles et de volontés; zig-zags de la pensée qui se cherche, vacillements de la conscience: le monde humain de Meredith est un monde de vibrations, ses créatures sont en perpétuel *déplacement,* elles miroitent comme les vagues au soleil. Mais le centre de leur activité—par conséquent la base de l'équilibre qui assure leur situation, leur existence, leur résistance—est en elles-mêmes, non pas dans la zone de leur action extérieure. Celle-ci, d'abord spontanée, est immédiatement réfléchie par leur sensibilité à la faveur d'un choc qui paralyse ou ralentit l'élan vital.

3. Walter Pater, *Appreciations* (London: Macmillan, 1910), p. 207.

4. Meredith, *Works,* 17:189.

5. Ibid., 16:275.

6. I hope it goes without saying that I do not in this paragraph speak for my own view, nor even for Meredith's view, but for what is implicit in the traditional figures Meredith uses, namely that "phallogocentrism" which Willoughby in *The Egoist* embodies, and which it is Meredith's goal to expose and dismantle.

7. See the admirable interpretation by John Brenkman of Ovid's version of the Narcissus story: "Narcissus in the Text," *Georgia Review* 30, no. 2 (Summer 1976): 293-327.

Nancy K. Miller

Writing (from) the Feminine:
George Sand and the
Novel of Female Pastoral

Valentine, the second of two feminocentric novels George Sand published in 1832, begins, as do many French nineteenth-century novels, with the fiction of a traveler (normally male, inevitably arriving from Paris, and always a stand-in for the reader) who is invited to ponder the semiotics of a provincial topography.[1] But the intertextual power of that ironizing convention fades after this inaugural move, for the fictional world of the Black Valley, unlike Stendhal's Verrières (or Balzac's Saumur), is located not under the sign of history and its agitations but under that of pastoral—"the absolute repose of . . . unknown regions":[2] "Luxury has not found its way thither, nor the arts, nor the mania for scientific investigation, nor the hundred-armed monster called industry. Revolutions are hardly perceptible there. . . . [T]he principal virtue of that race of tillers of the soil is heedlessness in the matter of antiquities" (Chap. 1, p. 4). And yet, despite authorial insistence upon a profound, peasant indifference to revolution and referential event, the story of the novel is not inscribed in timelessness. This "delicious pastoral scene" ("nature suave et pastorale") (Chap. 1, p. 3) is grounded precisely in the history of a domain sold "as national property during the Revolution, and redeemed under the Empire" (Chap. 9, p. 73). Indeed, the *before* of the novel is constructed by a marriage uniting "ancient names"—Raimbault—with "newly made fortunes" (Chap. 9, p. 74), and its *after* is posited on a chiasmatic reinscription of that same formula: "It was worth but little to be a landowner if one were not a noble" (Chap. 39, p. 335). Nor can the lovers whose destiny is plotted in the novel properly be identified outside this space in time: Valentine is the rightful heiress of the Château de Raimbault; Bénédict, who becomes her lover, a peasant whose uncle leases the farm Grangeneuve from the aristocratic owners of the château.

What I want to consider here, then, is the ways in which these places, the château and the farm, are (*a*) originally opposed as materially and symbolically discrete spaces; (*b*) subsequently mediated by an architectural construction—a third real and phantasmatic place—a pavilion; and (*c*) finally collapsed into a single signifying space, the château. At the same time, because the pavilion in *Valentine*, as a place which is meant to fix desire outside possession, penultimately locates the plot of Sand's novel of adultery as a fiction of female sublimation, we will want to see to what extent this particular topographical organization of an erotics can tell us something not only about the representation of female desire in the French novel but also about *what else* that representation figures.[3] If, for example, the pavilion in *Valentine* must be read intertextually with the pavilion in *La Princesse de Clèves*—by way of a detour through Julie's garden in *La Nouvelle Héloïse*—what can these privileged places tell us about the stakes of female plot?

By female plot I mean quite simply that organization of narrative event which delimits a heroine's psychological, moral, and social development within a sexual fate. Female plot thus is both what the culture has always already inscribed for woman and its reinscription in the linear time of fiction. It is generally mapped by the heroine's engagement with the codes of the dominant ideology, her obligatory insertion within the institutions which in society and in fiction name her—marriage, for example.[4] These are the narratologically bare bones of a plot that is most commonly bodied forth in scenarios of courtship leading, theoretically, to marriage in the eighteenth-century novel, or to marriage gone wrong in the nineteenth. It comes to us of course from male as well as from female imaginations—*Pamela*, say, or *Madame Bovary*. But female-authored fiction generally questions the costs and overdetermination of this particular narrative economy with an insistence such that the stories produced provide internal commentary on the status of female plot itself. They thereby solicit a reading of narrativity that takes into account the ideology at work in this genderization of experience.[5] Whether such a reading can in turn reveal the unmistakable traces of a specifically female (re)writing remains of course an open question—or an article of faith.[6]

I take *Valentine* as a case in point. The novel begins with a double-courtship plot. Under the heterogeneous and comedic emblem of a local *fête champêtre*, two entirely appropriate marriages are announced. Both assure homogeneity and the proper transmission of property. Valentine and Bénédict meet at the ball of the first of May within the codes of this familiar anthropology.[7] Bénédict is engaged to marry the heiress to the farm at Grangeneuve; Valentine, whose dowry includes both the Château de Raimbault and eventually the farm, is betrothed to a count. The ritual of the local dance—the *bourrée*—requires and authorizes Bénédict to kiss his partner Valentine under the public eye; but despite the blushing and blanching that come to code the event, what is at stake in this scene is neither the erotic potential of sexual difference nor—as it will emerge—Valentine's denial of the erotic potential of social difference. Rather, Sand displaces the predictable narrative sequence by insisting on the difference separating her heroine from her legendary sisters (Emma Bovary, for example): "Valentine did not dream of passion. . . . She promised herself that she would steer clear of those ardent fantasies which made other women miserable before her eyes" (Chap. 5, p. 41). More like the Princess of Clèves on the eve of her marriage, Valentine fully embraces that female destiny which she does not perceive "as a law" (ibid.) but which falls nevertheless within the law.

In the weeks before the marriages, however, Valentine and Bénédict, while playing innocent rustic games on the banks of the river, become subject to the laws of female plot and the structures of novelistic desire. Valentine gazes at Bénédict gazing at her image in the water with rapt admiration: "Absorbed herself in a reverie . . . she yielded to that hazardous curiosity which analyzes and compares. She discovered that there was a vast difference between Bénédict and Monsieur de Lansac. . . . Bénédict at that moment was a man; a man of the fields and a man of nature" (Chap. 13, p. 111). But the discovery of that difference—the awakening, essentially, to sexual difference and to differentiation *within* what was all the same—does not lead Valentine directly to fiction. She postpones the consequences of her new knowledge and chooses to remain faithful to her vows. Thus, though in the name of true love Bénédict will break his engagement to the farmer's daughter, at the end of part 2 of this novel in four parts two marriages are nevertheless celebrated. Valentine marries Monsieur de Lansac; Bénédict's former betrothed, Athénaïs, despite her very real disappointment, weds another peasant suitor from the village. When the peasant wedding party comes to the grounds of the château for a joint celebration, the novel again flirts with the possibilities of comedic equivalence between (the) brides. But the euphoria of celebration cannot resist the dysphoria which underwrites the two contracts: the proper circulation of women breaks down, revealing the price—or the ideology—of that economy.[8]

Between the public, verbal consecration of the marriages as ceremony and festivity and their silent consecration in the private ritual of sacred defloration, Sand opens a gap. The novel thus breaks with the standard representational model of the masculinist novel, a chronotope coded by what we might call a rhetoric of elision.[9] *Pamela,* for example. Pamela, married in the morning, is still writing in her closet at eleven o'clock that night. She is anxious and asks her husband for permission to continue for another quarter-hour. She writes, "two glasses of champaign, and, afterwards, a glass of sack . . . kindly forced upon [her]": "so sweetly terrible did he appear to my apprehensions";

and in her very last virginal inscription to her parents, trusting herself to God, she invokes "this happy, yet awful moment."[10] The dénouement is announced in the next entry, dated the following evening: "O how this dear excellent man indulges me in every thing!" The evacuation of the negative polarity comes to undo the oxymorons of her feminine anticipation, thus giving rise to the maxim, which Richardson later attempted to refute, that a reformed rake makes the best husband—if his wife, of course, like Pamela, vows to "obey . . . in every thing." (We might want to remember here Terry Eagleton's observation that "ideology is not simply a matter of plenitude but also of elision.")[11]

If we look in the French nineteenth-century novel for an intertext to this rhetoric of elision which figures respect for the sacred unsaid of marriage, we find this silence in Flaubert:

> Charles was humorless; he did not shine during the evening. He replied stolidly to the witty remarks, puns, double entendre jokes, compliments and broad remarks that they seemed to feel called upon to direct at him from the soup course on.
>
> The next day, however, he seemed to be a new man. It was he who could have been taken for the virgin of the night before, rather than the bride, whose self-control gave no opportunity for conjecture. Even the most daring jokesters were silenced, and they looked at her with bewilderment when she passed near them. But Charles hid nothing. He called her "my wife," spoke to her in familiar terms, asked everyone where she was, sought her everywhere, and frequently drew her into the yard, where he could be seen from afar, between the trees, putting his arm around her waist, leaning toward her as he walked, and burying his face in the tucker of her bodice.[12]

Although Flaubert here in the elision that takes us from the soup course to the morning after on the whole respects what I will assume to be an unwritten law of the dominant narratology until the twentieth century (where it reverses itself, at least in popular fiction), that the sacred penetration remains sacred by virtue of its ineffability, he also unsettles it slightly by reversing the gender of the postulate: the transformation implicit in penetration is incarnated in the male; Charles, invaginated, as it were, becomes a new man. Emma, however, remains *no less woman* in that unknowable. Emma's "self-control" lets nothing show: "la mariée ne laissait rien découvrir où l'on pût deviner quelque chose." By showing nothing, Flaubert leaves the enigma intact.[13] Thus it is curious to note that in this novel—and in Emma's body—where the institution of marriage is relentlessly desacralized to the point where even adultery can't save it, this founding physical moment of the social contract which makes two people "man and wife" is left veiled.

What, then, does Sand do with the representation of an event that even in Flaubert turns away from representation? To begin with, the novel insists that we witness the acts of the night, and (technically) through the fictional perspective of the male. In this female plot, the heroine, having been allowed to postpone her husband's enjoyment of the first night, spends it "a lifeless statue" (Chap. 22, p. 191), drugged with opium according to her wishes. She is not, however, alone. Bénédict has managed to lock himself into the room with his beloved in order to deliver her, as he puts it, from "this legitimate degradation . . . the vilest degradation inflicted on woman . . . rape" (Chap. 22, p. 184). The wedding night begins with Bénédict's fascinated contemplation of Valentine, and in this sense simply reinscribes the specular economy of desire whose power we saw in the catalytic event on the banks of the river, where Bénédict had earlier "adored her reflection in the water" ("son image répétée dans l'eau") (Chap. 23, p. 193). Though now in the absence of witnesses the gaze could with impunity become the act of carnal knowledge it wants to be, the desire valorized here is that of permanent deferral. This is the time of stasis (of ecstasy); the moment of sublimated perfection toward which the novel strains and which necessarily it never maintains: "Bénédict imagined that the night would never end, that Valentine would never wake, and that he would live out his eternity of happiness in that room" (Chap. 23, p. 194). This desire for a state of bliss that would defy change and therefore bypass all negotiations with reality is a model, I think typically associated with the female, the heroine for whom happily ever after has no form, no shape in time, only an intensity of affect. We could then ask whether by this inversion—like the one undergone by Charles—Sand renews the cliché in a feminine or feminist manner. Literarily the case is complicated, for this lover's discourse has indeed been written from the masculine. By Rousseau, for example. And for the reader familiar with *La Nouvelle Héloïse* (as the French nineteenth-century reader would have been), it is difficult to enter this staging of hysterical adoration—which depends for its intensity on its scene's being literally circumscribed by the law—without feeling interference from the Rousseauist (inter)text.

Saint-Preux, before Bénédict, writes his fetishistic pleasure from a place whose doors open and close within patriarchal authority. Writing to the moment from within Julie's closet, he records and, as he says, "moderates his ecstasy by describing it."[14] As he awaits Julie's arrival in the flesh (a reunion planned under the sign of danger; the death that might result from the legitimate double penetration of the father from his entrance into the room and the thrust of his sword), he both anticipates the fulfillment of his desires and fulfills them in anticipation. For the privilege of living out an hour—the hour of possession—he willingly "gives up the rest of his life to nature's severity." Now the hour of possession, unlike the hour of anticipation, necessarily can be accounted for only after the fact. (Even Valmont must take a break from writing to perform with the "*femme-pupitre.*")[15] And in the aftermath, a curious reevaluation occurs. Although Saint-Preux, from whose perspective this night of love ("that inconceivable night") is accounted for, begins the next letter in the correspondence with an insistence on the plenitude of the experience, the measure of his anticipation ("Oh let us die, my sweet friend! Let us die, beloved of my heart! What shall we do henceforward with an insipid youth now that we have exhausted all of its delights?"), as he reviews the events of the night, he revises their hierarchy of pleasure. Indeed, what he wants to preserve, what he wants *returned* to him after the fact (of consummation), is that which Julie had earlier claimed in *her* economy to be superior to possession: "Come to swear, even in the midst of pleasures, that from the union of hearts they draw their greatest charm." Saint-Preux now accedes to her language, a discourse which dematerializes possession: "Give me back that intimate union of souls you had told me of and which you have made me enjoy so well [*si bien goûter*]." By revising in this sense, Saint-Preux, we might say, seems to wish to attain to a female position (to invagination): "I wish to enjoy [*jouir*] and you wish to love; I have ecstasies and you have passions." What is superior in the female position is its self-sufficiency, "that charming state which is enough in itself," hence its capacity to resist erasure: "The charm of possession [*jouissance*] was in the soul, no longer momentary but eternal." The key to the valorized temporality thus is this notion of permanence: "il durait toujours." But how to fix *jouissance*? How to make the fleeting monumental? Saint-Preux selects the hour *after* possession as the privileged chronicity: "It is of all the hours of my life the one which is most dear to me, and the only one I should have wished to prolong eternally." This crucial lesson was acquired, however, through the fullness of material possession, as an authorial footnote—an asterisk starring the word *eternally*—underlines: "Too compliant woman, do you wish to know if you are loved? Examine your lover as he leaves your arms. Oh love! If I miss the age at which you are enjoyed [*goûter*] it is not for the hour of possession: it is for the hour which follows it."

This passage permits us, I think, to differentiate among three chronotopic valorizations of desire in a sexual and textual economy: masculinist (in its extreme, libertine) discourse, which valorizes the time of possession (and possession as penetration); feminizing discourse, which seeks a loving negotiation with the feminine (Saint-Preux enamored in the hour after; ultimately, Roland Barthes); and finally a feminine/feminist discourse, which indirectly or directly valorizes the hour that precedes and essentially *precludes* possession (though not enjoyment, which becomes *jouissance* minus penetration). This last figure is the timing of desire achieved in *The Princess of Clèves* and ultimately muffed in *Valentine*.

In Valentine's chamber, Bénédict contemplates his sleeping beauty, who suddenly stirring from a euphoric, opium-induced dream and "hovering between reality and illusion . . . innocently revealed all her secrets to him" (Chap. 23, p. 195). Her secret is a variant of Julie's fantasy before "that inconceivable night": pursued by her husband, "with drawn sword, she threw herself on Bénédict's breast, and exclaimed as she put her arms about his neck: 'Let us both die!'" (ibid.). Bénédict, like Saint-Preux, welcomes such a death but inserts a condition: "'Be mine and let us die!'" But Valentine returns to her dreams, and Bénédict struggles against his desire thus to make Valentine his in the name of what ought to remain the plenitude of the scopic: "He raised her thick tresses and filled his mouth with them to prevent himself from crying out; he wept with love and frenzy. At last in a moment of indescribable anguish, he bit the round, white shoulder which she uncovered before him" (Chap. 23, p. 196). This last has the effect of stimulating Valentine to discourse: she deliriously imagines that Bénédict is her husband and welcomes him as such to her bed. Thus the wedding night becomes a locus of *pleasure* only through the fantasized substitution of the illicit for the licit, the forbidden for the contractual. Bénédict, whose fantasy this also is, in response "threw himself upon her in desperation and, on the point of yielding to the violence of agonizing desires, . . . uttered nervous, heart rending cries" (Chap. 23, p. 197). In this staging of what Ann Snitow describes as romantic representations of a contradictory female "desire to be blindly ravished, to melt, and the desire to be spiritually adored, saved from the humiliation of dependence and sexual passivity through the agency of a protective male who will somehow make reparation to the woman he loves for her powerlessness,"[16] Sand, we might say, is writing mass-market pornography. Penetration, therefore, is thus postponed a *second* time—neither the husband, nor the lover—by a key turning in the lock and an opening of the door, which reconnects the sacred space to the banality of circulation.

Returned to his senses as it were, Bénédict now rethinks his position. He determines to leave and kill himself, but he first leaves a trace of his passage in a letter to Valentine. He explains the contradiction of her position after this unveiling of the veiling of nuptials: on the one hand, she is still, he assures her, "pure and unprofaned"; on the other, and not only by virtue of his timing, Valentine is "more entirely in his power than [she] ever will be in [her] husband's." Bénédict has taken her virginity symbolically and without penetration; he has glued his lips to the "unsubstantial garment which hardly covers [her] and thus *possessed her in his thoughts*'" (Chap. 23, pp. 199–200; italics mine). Thus in a way he has had what he wanted, but not quite, for if the night ends, then there is another and daily economy to be supplied (unless, of course, death provides its promised fulfillment). In her dreams, Valentine has only almost returned his caresses (Chap. 23, p. 199). The novel will struggle with the status of this *almost*—the story of Bénédict's "lack" and Valentine's submerged desire—until the plot finds the terms of its closure.[17]

If we make the banal (also correct) assumption that historically and literarily the wedding night is to be read as the institutionalization of male sexuality as penetration, positive female sexuality as virginity, and marriage as possession through defloration, what does Sand bring to the tradition? She insists despite her own fascination with ideality, despite the textual fact of Valentine's local integrity, that marriage is always irreducibly referential for women. "Woman" is more than a locus of symbolic investment, a playground for the synecdoches of

Otherness. In a female economy of same to same, woman's body is a space of material identity. When Sand fleshes out the elision that respects the ineffability of the transaction, she seeks to desacralize the rites of possession.[18] However, in this rewriting, the rights of possession—hence of fiction as representation—remain intact: Bénédict, we have seen, is persuaded that Valentine belongs to him without penetration; and the husband, according to the law, is guaranteed nonetheless the orderly transfer of property to his name.[19] What thus remains subject to resolution and yet unsettled is the matter of inheritance, of descent. And it is perhaps in this displacement—the husband's courtesy is only punctual—this future blank which is the mark of a *sterile* union, that the key to a female rewriting of marriage in the novel should be sought.

This emphasis in Sand's novel upon the material grounds of marriage takes the form of what we might call deictic elision: a "supplied," or supplemented, ellipsis which calls attention to the plenitude of its own unsaid with such insistence that it turns to periphrasis.[20] A more elegant example of this figure might be the remarkable wedding night scene in *Daniel Deronda:* Gwendolen Grandcourt's fit of "hysterical violence" on the threshold of her wifely career. Ellen Moers comments on the metaphorical power of the diamonds that have come to commemorate this liminal moment: "There is . . . nothing that could remotely be called pornographic in George Eliot's treatment of Gwendolen's deflowering by her husband. . . ; the matter is not even mentioned, directly. But indirectly, by means of the jewel case . . . Eliot conveys all that need be told about Gwendolen's hysterical, virginal frigidity; about Grandcourt's sadistic tastes; and about, in addition, mercenary marriages, wedding night customs, and sexual hypocrisy in the Victorian age."[21]

The wedding night (and its ornaments) is of course not the only locus for the woman novelist's protest against the hegemony of male desire supported by the law. I want to turn now to another topical attempt to erect an alternative to the house of marriage and its grounds in fiction: a concrete space that would be outside the law and outside history.

When the count leaves the château for his embassy appointment in Russia, Valentine becomes, we are told, the "sovereign mistress of her château of Raimbault" (Chap. 26, p. 222). This ostensible freedom and authority, however, are in fact restricted in several important ways, since the objects of her affection—Bénédict and her sister Louise—literally are *out of place* in the château. Louise, the mother of an illegitimate fifteen-year-old adolescent named Valentin, who has been banished from the family grounds as a consequence of her female plot, refuses to enter the château bearing her father's name—which is also to say hers—as an intruder. In response, Valentine takes over the pavilion in the park—originally designed to serve as a guesthouse (indeed Monsieur de Lansac had his room there during their engagement)—and converts it into a space theoretically subject to her authority alone. She brings her books and easel to the pavilion, which is thus legitimized as a "sort of study" (Chap. 26, p. 223). A piano soon follows. Louise brings Bénédict to the pavilion in the evenings. (Louise has been nursing Bénédict—after his suicide attempt—in his hermitage, as it is called, his "hut in the ravine," situated in the space separating the farm from the Château de Raimbault.) They make music: "During the summer evenings Valentine adopted the custom of having no light, so that Bénédict might not detect the violent emotion which often took possession of her" (Chap. 27, p. 231). It is as though Valentine, like the Princess of Clèves before her, likes to imagine that if her desire remains invisible, if her lover remains, precisely, in the dark as to the power of her feeling, the inevitable telos of sexual plot can be eluded indefinitely. But the music melts the lovers, and once Bénédict sees by her tears that Valentine is "yielding to one of the most irresistible fascinations that ever woman faced" (Chap. 27, p. 232), the exchange of (devouring) kisses is no longer elided. (In this odd echo of the *Odyssey,* Valentine tries to hide her face with her hands, when she might have thought to cover her ears. And she succumbs, gradually, to the siren.)[22] The danger of the relation, already in place, plays itself out in the topographical codes of moral disaster inherited from eighteenth-century fiction: "Valentine felt that she was on the brink of the abyss into which her sister had fallen" (Chap. 28, p. 239).

It is at this point in the narrative, as the novel begins to move toward closure, that the plot finally finds its moral and psychological center and identifies its repository of value in and as a space, in much the way that Julie's garden, Elysium, can be said to mark the desire for the end in *La Nouvelle Héloïse.* The relations among the characters are reorganized spatially in relation to the pavilion primarily, and to Bénédict's cottage secondarily. Symbolically, economically, and in the play of signifiers, the cottage should be opposed to the château (*chaumière/château*). But that polarization, like the original one opposing the farm to the château, is mediated and displaced by the pavilion. Though the pavilion claims for itself an identity which supersedes origins and social difference, because it is in fact an aristocratic space, its identity and difference from the château must be located elsewhere:

> Valentine caused a fence to be built around that part of the park where the pavilion stood. That little reservation was very thickly planted and very dark. On its borders they planted clumps of climbing plants, ramparts of wild vine and birthwort, and hedges of young cypresses of the sort that are trimmed like a curtain and form a barrier impenetrable to the eye. Amid all this verdure, and behind those trustworthy barriers of shade, the pavilion stood in a delightful situation, near a spring, from which a bubbling stream escaped among the rocks, maintaining an incessant cool murmur about that mysterious and dreamy retreat. . . .
>
> Thus the pavilion was a place of rest and pleasure to all at the close of day. Valentine admitted no profane interloper to the sanctuary, and allowed no communication with the people of the château. Catherine alone was allowed to enter, to take care of the place. It was Valentine's Elysium, the world of her poetic fancy, her golden life. At the château

all was ennui, slavery, depression; her invalid grandmother, unwelcome visitors, painful reflections, and her oratory with its remorse-laden atmosphere; at the pavilion, happiness, friends, pleasant reveries, fears forgotten, and the pure delights of a chaste love. It was like an enchanted island in the midst of real life, like an oasis in the desert. (Chap. 29, pp. 249-52)

The anaphoric sequence which marks the end of the description—"like an enchanted island in the midst of real life, like an oasis in the desert"—in slipping from metaphor to metonymy underlines the interdependence, the irreducible contiguity, of the two spaces. The pavilion, moreover, is totally dependent upon the financial viability of the château for its right to exist as property—an exclusive property—and this vulnerability is crucial to the status of the fantasy. But if the pavilion in *Valentine,* like the pavilion in Mme de Lafayette's novel and the garden in Rousseau's, is the fantasized space of an u-topic retreat within privilege—and within the sociality of the law—it is also opposed in its desire for ideality and sublimation to the license of privilege and the arbitrariness of the law, the law in Sandian terms of "conventionalities and prejudices" (Chap. 29, p. 249). This desire to figure a place that would guarantee happiness against the penetration of history, the attempt to prohibit the profane from entering, even as a specular trespass, can also be read as a variant of the topographical model Tony Tanner has described as housing the play of desire in the novel of adultery: the polarization of fictional places that maps the split occasioned by the irruption of forbidden desires.

The attempt to exclude the social in the name of the natural (or rather the natural supervised by virtue) is of course at work in the eighteenth-century intertext. And the reader of *La Nouvelle Héloïse* will not wonder long whether Sand's rewriting will also reinscribe the earlier failure to sustain what Tanner calls a "genuine outside."[23] For if in the beginning the Elysian fields derive their tranquil beauty from their intimate relation to death, this is no less true of Rousseau's construction. Julie explains to Saint-Preux: "'In truth, my friend, . . . days spent this way suggest the happiness of the next life, and it is not without reason that in thinking of it I have given the name Elysium to this place.'"[24] The golden life at Valentine's pavilion lasts, we are told, for fifteen months: "Fifteen months of tranquility and happiness in the lives of five persons is almost supernatural. Yet so it was" (Chap. 30, p. 254).

The silence that accounts for these remarkable months not only points to the unsaid of a female pleasure that may or may not take place in the blanks; it codes the paradox of a female pastoral where woman's verbs—predicates of *becoming*—are disguised as states of *being*, the better to pass unnoticed. Indeed, the transformation of an essentially worldly place which then names itself a scene of contemplation and artistic production is an interesting modulation for those who wish to decipher a feminist inflection of the heavily marked pastoral matrix. Thus, Valentine, who has chosen to pursue painting over music—her natural vocation but one that "puts a woman too much in evidence" (Chap. 6, p. 50)—imagines that this talent will help her to "support herself in society" if one day her patrimony again becomes state property. This fantasy, as it is then staged in the pavilion of an asocial (artistic) productivity that would bring an active identity and autonomy to women in society, is no less the anguished alibi of the woman who would justify her passage to writing.[25]

Can the fable—supernatural in the French is *fabuleux*—survive its insertion within fiction? Bénédict and Valentine seem to wish to remain outside literature, though they are perpetually cast into the standard plots of sexual destiny. To Bénédict, who like Saint-Preux before him claims to prefer virtue to beauty, mind to body, Valentine replies that she, like Julie, has learned through his teaching that the "nonmaterial alliance" they have formed is "preferable to all earthly ties" (Chap. 30, p. 258). Can one contract a nonmaterial alliance ("une alliance immatérielle")? The logic of the sociolect is against it. While an "alliance" can be understood in nonmaterial terms (theologically, for example), the more common and more compelling sense of the word, given the context, is that of the legal bonds relating families through marriage. And as Valentine should know but refuses to acknowledge, such an alliance, for example her own with Lansac, is nothing but material: grounded in the quantifiable, the concrete, the real.

The husband's unexpected return—he arrives to sell the very property that makes his wife's fantasy possible—brings Valentine abruptly up against the reality of her relation to Bénédict as well. After (blindly) signing papers that will dispossess her of her property and her fortune, Valentine, on the eve of her husband's departure, determines to implore his assistance in her struggle to avoid the abyss she sees before her: "a sublime and romantic project," the narrator underlines, "which has tempted more than one wife at the moment of committing her first error" (Chap. 33, p. 281). Like the Princess of Clèves before her, Valentine confesses: "'There is still time to save me. Do not let me succumb to my destiny; rescue me from the seduction that environs me and presses me close. . . . I am a poor, weak woman, left alone, abandoned by everybody; help me!'" (Chap. 34, p. 289). Lansac, unlike the Prince of Clèves, remains unmoved by this archaic rhetoric of pathos. And he replies in the worldly language of circulation that condemned the Princess within her fiction: "'All this is sublime, my dear, but it is absolutely ridiculous. You are very wrong; take a friend's advice: a woman should never take her husband for her confessor; that is asking of him more virtue than is consistent with his profession'" (Chap. 34, p. 291). With this failed repetition of heroic female plot, Sand swerves away from the fierce sublimation of Mme de Lafayette's solution and moves toward a dysphoric closure.[26] Unlike the Princess, Valentine will finally succumb to a sexual fate in keeping with the telic logic of Rousseauist (here masculinist) desire. In the face of a Bénédict literally swooning from the struggle to repress his passionate nature, "Valentine, vanquished by pity, by love, and above all, by fear, did not again tear herself from his arms" (Chap. 36, p. 307). Thus, some two years after her marriage, and in the thirty-sixth chapter of thirty-nine, Valentine, who had sworn she would die "rather than belong to any man" (Chap. 32, p. 277), ceases to be a virgin within the very walls of Raimbault, in the room said to be her own.

The timing and the language of the "fatal moment" (Chap. 36, p. 307) both score and underscore the Rousseauist model: Valentine's fall, her capitulation to the laws of "natural" desire, repeats Julie's virginal lapse, the filial transgression which in Rousseau's novel is repaired by a proper marriage docile to paternal authority. But unlike Rousseau, Sand writes the act of adultery only fantasized under the cover of incest in *Julie* into her plot. She thus takes her distance from Rousseau here—and by the same token, from the erotics of the Lafayette text so admired by Rousseau.[27] Her novel *reluctantly* inscribes the rights of the body driven from its own fictions, from Elysium. But this gesture cannot write its own consequences: what is the proper space for adulterous love?

No reader of nineteenth-century fiction would expect to see this union integrated legitimately within the novel. Nor is it. Valentine must leave the château, which has become the property of a usurer (called Grapp), and takes refuge with the Lhéry family at the farm within whose walls the novel opened. With the evacuation of the primary signifying spatial oppositions— the pavilion as the scene of chaste love outside time, the château as the incarnation of the historical confirmation of social difference, how is desire to be figured?

The husband dies, killed according to the hazards of his class, in a duel. And Bénédict renews his claim for pastoral union:

> Do you not remember that one day you regretted that you were not a farmer's daughter, that you could not escape the slavery of a life of opulence, to live like a simple village maiden beneath a thatched roof?

> Well, now your longing is gratified. You shall be *queen in the cottage* in the ravine; you shall raise your own flowers, and sleep without fear or anxiety on a peasant's breast. (Chap. 38, p. 327; italics mine)

In this play on the signifiers of social difference—"queen in the cottage"—Bénédict seeks to will into existence through language the collapse of referential polarities that have structured the novel throughout. But the power of narrative structure overrides the iconography of his poetic representations.

Bénédict is killed by his old rival with the weapons of their class—by the thrust of a pitchfork—and dies on Valentine's breast. Valentine dies a week later. Bénédict's murderer dies exactly one year later, having drunkenly mistaken a river for a road. Athénaïs, the farmer's daughter to whom Bénédict originally was engaged, widowed, buys, through an inheritance, the Château de Raimbault; her father exchanges his land for the remaining estates. And closure?

The final chapter of the novel—two pages that serve as an epilogue to that flurry of events—opens with the return to the Black Valley (from Paris) of Louise and her son Valentin, who has become, with the passage of time, a *man;* also a doctor. They are housed by the Lhérys in the pavilion, returned to its original function as a guesthouse. It was "a sad consolation for them," the narrator comments, "to live in the pavilion."[28] What is at stake in the melancholy of this penultimate destination must be understood, I think, in its relation to the tradition into which Sand inserts herself. To the extent that one can claim that the French novel after the *Princess of Clèves* (which is to say, the French novel) always looks back nostalgically to the universe figured there as one which "reconciles fantasy and reality" for the last time, one can also argue that the dominant desire of that tradition is for an aristocratic universe within which the only destabilizing difference is sexual.[29] The "reality" is a homogeneous aristocracy defined by wars within a national Other—like the Homeric universe; it is a "consoling" universe. By the 1750s the model of an "aristocratic Eden" has become

an ironic point of reference for novelists, the golden age irrevo-
cably past. Rousseau, in 1761, fantasizes a modern rewriting,
relocating Elysium in Switzerland. But the dream cannot resist
the dysphoric closure of bourgeois reality.[30]
In the case of Sand after the Revolution, closure looks back
out of time. The Raimbault name returns to the property.
Valentin—returning without the suffixal e of the feminine to
compensate nevertheless for the feminine loss of the inheritance—through a detour becomes the heir Valentine had always
and earlier wished him to be.[31] And through the descendance
of a second mésalliance, the second alliance of old names and
new money, a second Valentine continues in the image of the
Other. In some sense the child legitimately inscribes the otherwise outlawed love of Bénédict and Valentine. She would thus
be the sign of historical difference come to interrupt the pastoral continuity of the Black Valley. But little Valentine is not
the direct issue of rebellion but, rather, its doubled displacement through docile reproduction. Therefore we must wonder
whether the perpetuation of "the beloved name of Valentine"
(Chap. 39, p. 336) is the mark of social transformation or the
sign of circularity—Valentine/Valentin/Valentine—an empty
repetition that might also be called a "defunct ideological
sign, incapable of constituting an arena for the confrontation
of living social inflections," something like the pavilion.[32]
   Sand's novel takes as the site of its closure the place marked
off for death in the architecture of social life.[33] And the last
sentence of the novel takes up again the perspective of the
traveler with which it began: "The traveler, as he passes the
village cemetery, frequently sees the lovely child playing at
Louise's feet, and plucking the cowslips that grow on the
double grave of Valentine and Bénédict" (ibid.). Here the
traveler observes a scene empty of any local meaning, for the
flowers ("primevère"), which by their name signal youth and
renewal, growing as they do on a tombstone, overcode the

already formulaic conjunction of life and death achieved by placing a beautiful, fair-haired child in a cemetery. The novel thus marks in its closing moves the shift of emphasis away from the natural setting of pastoral "onto the child" that Empson has located in the nineteenth century.[34] But if this shift, like the emergence of the graveyard within the pastoral dominion—following the familiar iconography of the memento mori—confirms in the end the staying power of the pastoral *code,* is there a female inflection or feminist inscripton to be read there as well? Is the little girl Valentine the figure of liminal difference, of a female rewriting to come? Or does her presence at this site reinscribe the power of repetition? It is clear that the fate of the dead heroine's living image is proposed as the figure to the answer, but it is equally clear that the answer is withheld. After unveiling the feminine past, the veil of narrative covers up the tropes of a feminine future.

It is not altogether surprising that Sand proposes no clues to the story to come, no more than does Eliot, say, write a future for Gwendolen Grandcourt on the verge of a new life at the end of *Daniel Deronda.* Sand writes in 1842 in a preface to a new edition of her first novel *Indiana* that for years she had sought to resolve an "insoluble problem": "*to reconcile the happiness and dignity of individuals oppressed by society without modifying the constitution of society itself.*"[35] The Sandian solution in the face of this radical insolubility is to stage a protest against what she describes in this same text as "the injustice and barbarity of laws governing women's existence in marriage, family and society." The protest takes the form of a not so subtle attack on what we have been calling female plot: "'Marriage, society, all existing institutions, I hate you!'" is Bénédict's silent cry (Chap. 22, p. 182). And the narrative of Valentine's wedding night represents that refusal of a mythified female destiny. But is that an end to repetition? It is impossible, I think, to know whether little Valentine will in her turn become the eponymous heroine of a novel about marriage and desire that ends in a graveyard. But if I cannot answer my own questions, it is also the case that this hermeneutic impasse is largely overdetermined. Sand's antiproleptic closure *is* her vision for the future, or at least its metaphor. But I want to move away from the dead end of the cemetery and back to the pavilion for the elements of a conclusion.

When the count returns to Raimbault with his creditor, he asks the man what the pavilion is worth: "'Almost nothing,'" was the reply. "'These luxuries and fancy buildings are worth nothing on a country estate. . . . In a city it's different. But when there's a field . . . around this building, or . . . a meadow, we'll say, what will it be good for? Just to tear down for the stone and lumber that are in it'" (Chap. 31, p. 269). The disparity between the man's marketplace evaluation of the pavilion and Valentine's private one, "the secret hiding-place of pure and modest happiness" (Chap. 31, p. 270), is the measure of the founding incompatibility between a *new* fictional female plot and the "laws governing woman's existence in marriage, family and society," to reinvoke the terms of Sand's analysis. Thus necessarily Valentine's aristocratic fantasy of a female-controlled stasis that could withstand both the telic pressure of male desire and the contiguities of the dominant narratology is written off by the laws of economic circulation (*"non-valeurs"*) and back into an older plot.

Nonetheless, the desire for another temporality—a night that never ends—and another topography in which to live it has been written. That the time of perpetual deferral and its space in the end are subsumed by the necessities of closure does not erase the inscription, just as the narrator's ambiguous injunction at the end of *Villette* to "picture union and a happy succeeding life" does not erase our sense that Monsieur Emmanuel has drowned, nor—more to the point—that Lucy Snowe has found her voice. Although in the end Sand's fiction pulls back before the radical solution put in place by Mme de Lafayette—the refusal of male sexuality as a plot, and a plot destined to repetition—it revises the Rousseauist fascination with feminization and the filial by placing Elysium outside the paternal eye. *Valentine* is female plot in nineteenth-century France: mired in nostalgia for what can never be again, hesitating on the threshold of what might yet be.[36]

NOTES

I would like to thank Peggy Brawer, Carolyn Heilbrun, Sandy Petrey, and Peggy Waller for their critical responses to an earlier version of this essay.

1. *Valentine* is the second of the novels signed by George Sand alone under the pseudonym G. Sand that was to assure her livelihood and eventually her place in literary history. Between the overnight success of *Indiana* (May 1832) and the violent critical response occasioned by the publication of *Lélia* (July 1833), *Valentine* (November 1832) marks what we might think of as a pause—a space of repetition and interrogation—in Sand's elaboration of an identity as a writer and a public figure: "I would like to have lived in seclusion [*obscure*]," she writes in *Histoire de ma vie*, "and since, from the publication of *Indiana* until that of *Valentine* I had succeeded in remaining sufficiently incognito for the newspapers always to refer to me as *monsieur*, I flattered myself that this little success wouldn't change my sedentary habits and an intimate circle composed of people as unknown as myself" (*Oeuvres autobiographiques*, ed. Georges Lubin, 2 vols. [Paris: Gallimard, 1970–71], 2:182; translation mine). By the time *Lélia* was published, *Valentine* was obscured, and Sand's "retreat" and "solitude" (*Oeuvres autobiographiques*, 2:183) were lost, as was the fantasized protection of an ambiguously virile identity. *Valentine*, I will suggest in the margins of my central argument, is the story (Sand's own) of a female coming to writing *in the city*—the actual writing at Nohant notwithstanding. This coming to writing cannot and does not name itself, to the point of being readable only as failed pastoral.

2. Both *Le Rouge et le Noir* (1830) and *Eugénie Grandet* (1833) depend for the economy of their fiction on a figured relation between the local history of the provinces in its intersections with a recognizable event and the story of its (local) characters. The *Vallée-Noire*, which is Sand's invented toponym, derives its importance here from another system of connotation:

that of genre. The Berri, we are told, is *picturesque*. One might also wish to consider the whole matter of female landscape as a coded—and not so coded—expression of sexual identity (the "Red Deeps," and so on) (see, for example, Ellen Moers's all too brief, provocative chapter on the subject, "Metaphors: A Postlude," in *Literary Women: The Great Writers* [New York: Doubleday, 1976], pp. 243–64; see also Annette Kolodny's full-length study of American pastoral writing, *The Lay of the Land* [Chapel Hill: University of North Carolina Press, 1979]). Unlike *Indiana* and *Lélia*, *Valentine* is not available in a Garnier (hence annotated) edition; rather, it is available in an 1869 edition (Paris: Lévy) and a 1976 edition (Paris: Editions d'Aujourd'hui), which is merely a reedition of an 1843 edition. I will be quoting from the English translation by George Burnham Ives (Chicago: Cassandra, 1978), which is a reprint of a 1902 edition. References to chapter and page are noted parenthetically; this first quotation comes from chap. 1, p. 3.

3. In other words, what might women want beyond what can be figured as desire? What story cannot be told?

4. For a different take on this relentlessly patriarchal plot see Janet Todd, *Women's Friendship in Literature* (New York: Columbia University Press, 1980).

5. I think this reading is performed with mastery and great plausibility by Sandra Gilbert and Susan Gubar in *Madwoman in the Attic* (New Haven: Yale University Press, 1979).

6. See my "Emphasis Added: Plots and Plausibilities in Women's Fiction," *PMLA* 96, no. 1 (January 1981): 36–48.

7. I allude to the circulation of daughters at the heart of the social contract as described by Claude Lévi-Strauss.

8. In an episode of no small interest to our case, Blutty, the (jealous) groom, provokes Bénédict, taunting him about his feelings for Valentine, and the fallout of their quarrel has Blutty, in a rage, throw a glass of wine at Bénédict which misses its object and instead covers "the bride's lovely dress with indelible stains" (chap. 21, p. 177). Bénédict catches the glass, however, thereby saving Athénaïs from bodily injury; but the consummation of the marriage is momentarily suspended. (At the end of the novel, Blutty corrects his aim and succeeds for the wrong reasons.)

9. I borrow the term "chronotope" from Mikhail Bakhtin. "We will give the name *chronotope* (literally, "time space") to the intrinsic connectedness of temporal and spatial relationships that are artistically expressed in literature. . . . In the literary artistic chronotope . . . [t]ime, as it were, thickens, takes on flesh, becomes artistically visible; likewise space becomes charged and responsive to moments of time, plot and history. . . . The

chronotope as a formally constitutive category determines to a significant degree the *image of man in literature as well. The image of man is always intrinsically chronotopic"* (in *The Dialogic Imagination,* ed. Michael Holquist [Austin: University of Texas Press, 1980], pp. 84–85; italics mine).

10. Samuel Richardson, *Pamela* (New York: Norton, 1958), pp. 371–72.

11. "Text, Ideology, Realism," in *Literature and Society,* ed. Edward W. Said, Selected Papers from the English Institute, (Baltimore: Johns Hopkins University Press, 1978), pp. 153–54.

12. Gustave Flaubert, *Madame Bovary,* trans. Mildred Marmur (New York: New American Library, Signet, 1964), pp. 51–52.

13. Moreover, Emma is no less constrained by the laws of circulation regulating brides as she leaves her father's house for her husband's. Indeed she is referred to here consistently as the bride, whereas her husband remains narrationally entitled to his Christian name; and he calls Emma—with the newfound intimacy marked by the passage in French from *vous* to *tu*—"ma femme," the play in French allowing of course for *woman* and *wife.*

14. Peggy Kamuf has provided a compelling, psychoanalytic account of this episode, to which I am much indebted, in "Inside *Julie's* Closet," *Romanic Review* 69, no. 4 (November 1978): 296–306. I will be quoting from Jean-Jacques Rousseau, *La Nouvelle Héloïse: Julie, or the New Eloise,* trans. and abr. Judith H. McDowell (University Park: Pennsylvania State University Press, 1968), part 1, letters 54 and 55, pp. 122–24.

15. I'm referring to Valmont's troping of "to the moment" in letters 47 and 48 of Choderlos Laclos's *Les Liaisons dangereuses,* where he writes literally *on* one to another: "But I must leave you for a moment to calm an excitement which mounts with every moment, and which is fast becoming more than I can control" (trans. P.W.K. Stone [New York: Penguin, 1961], p. 111). The confusion of presence and absence whereby one woman's circulating body allows the desire for the Other to be sustained will ultimately confound the libertine—but too late.

16. In "Mass Market Romance: Pornography for Women is Different," *Radical History Review* 20 (Spring–Summer 1979): 159.

17. Tony Tanner identifies a similar construction in Goethe's *Elective Affinities:* "The kiss [between Charlotte and the Captain] is *almost* returned. . . . [I]n that *almost* lies all the felt constraints of the marriage vows, the restraining pauses that law can put on passion" (in *Adultery in the Novel: Contract and Transgression* [Baltimore: Johns Hopkins University Press, 1979], p. 198). I am indebted to Tanner for the etymologies that he brings from Vico: "The second solemnity is the requirement that the woman be veiled in token of that sense of shame that gave rise to the

first marriages in the world. This custom has been preserved by all nations; among the Latins it is reflected in the very name 'nuptials,' for *nuptiae* is from *nubendo,* which means 'to cover'. . . . The third solemnity—also preserved by the Romans—was a certain show of force in taking a wife, recalling the real violence with which the giants dragged the first wives into their caves" (p. 59).

I shall resist the temptation—because what is at stake here is very definitely not undecidability—to do more than invoke Jacques Derrida's analysis of the hymen in "La Double Séance," *La Dissémination* (Paris: Seuil, 1972). On the other hand, some of the definition is acutely relevant: "The hymen is located between the inside and the outside of woman, consequently, between desire and fulfillment. It is neither desire nor pleasure but between the two. The hymen only takes place when it doesn't take place, when nothing really happens" (p. 41; translation mine). Naomi Schor, in an unpublished essay on *Salammbô,* provocatively interrogates the Derridean discussion of the hymen in the course of her analysis of the scene of interrupted defloration in that novel. Although the neither/nor of the hymen allows Flaubert to play with what may or may not be known, Sand insists that we (do) know.

18. This project interests women writers other than Sand and (as we will see) Eliot. Daniel Stern (Marie d'Agoult), George Sand's contemporary, provides an unambiguously dysphoric account of a wedding night (seen from the heroine's perspective) in her novella *Valentia* (1847). The heroine is given bouillon which produces a drugged stupor: "Then he approached me. I wanted to speak but I felt it inconceivably difficult to move my lips. My head suddenly felt very heavy; my mind became jumbled, and my eyelids drooped. In vain I tried to open them. The wall coverings seemed to leap off the walls, come toward me, envelop me. . . . My limbs grew numb. Soon after, I felt nothing at all but my heavy breath in my throat . . . and I fell into a deep sleep." The next morning, the heroine observes the disorder of her hair and the pallor of her complexion and draws the "humiliating" conclusions. Leslie Rabine, who cites this passage (in her translation) in her interesting essay "Feminist Writers in French Romanticism," *Studies in Romanticism* 16, no. 4 (Fall 1974), comments on the disparity between the Gothic code "which evokes supernatural and extraordinary experiences, and, on the other hand, a common, ordinary experience (of the bride on her wedding night), familiar to many readers but which is never talked about and which is extraordinary . . . as the subject of a literary passage" (pp. 499–500). Colette supplies a brief, barely oblique description of a wedding night in *Claudine en ménage* (1902): Claudine bravely claims not to be afraid and insists on undressing herself; then, embarrassed by Renaud's

gaze, she throws herself on the still made bed: "He joins me there. He holds me there so tightly that I can hear his muscles trembling. Completely dressed, he embraces me, keeps me there,—Good Lord, what is he waiting for to get undressed too?—and his mouth and his hands keep me there, without his body touching me, from my quivering rebellion up to my frantic consent, up to the shameful moans of pleasure that I wanted to hold back out of pride." That night, though Renaud ultimately undresses, the bed remains made, and Renaud "asks me for nothing, except for the freedom to give me as many caresses as I need to sleep, at daybreak" ([Paris: Livre de Poche, 1963], pp. 13–14; translation mine). This kind of writing from the feminine only becomes possible in the twentieth century, but it should not be seen as the whole story either. There is also Colette's invocation of the room that awaits the newly married couple in "The Wedding," *La Maison de Claudine* (1922): "the massive shutters, the door, all the exits of this stifling little tomb will be closed upon them" ([Paris: Livre de Poche, 1960], p. 70; translation mine); and Isak Dinesen's story "The Blank Page" tells a tale of silence, of framed virginities.

19. Because the count assures the payment of his considerable debts by taking possession of his wife's property (what she thinks of as her patrimony), the contractual *enjoyment* of her person becomes subject to indefinite deferral. He "insists" no further; his (libertine) pleasure lies elsewhere. On the other hand, when, as a result of the altercation between Bénédict and Blutty, Athénaïs wants to remain with her father, the necessity of possessing a wife's body is made clear. The father exclaims: "'I am still at liberty to shut the door on you and to keep my daughter. The marriage is not consummated yet. Athénaïs, step behind me' . . . And she clung with all her strength to her father's neck. Pierre Blutty, whose title as his father-in-law's heir was not assured as yet by any legal document, was struck by the force of these arguments" (chap. 21, p. 179).

20. In this opposition of ellipsis to periphrasis, I am following the categories of Pierre Fontanier in *Les Figures du discours* (Paris: Flammarion, 1977). Ellipsis is a figure of understatement, periphrasis one of emphasis.

21. Moers, *Literary Women*, p. 253.

22. The sirens, Hélène Cixous claims, were men, just as the Medusa is beautiful ("The Laugh of the Medusa," *Signs* 1, no. 4 [Summer 1976]:885).

23. Tanner, *Adultery in the Novel*, p. 23.

24. Rousseau, *La Nouvelle Héloïse*, pt. 4, letter 11, p. 313. See Tanner's section on Elysium, *Adultery in the Novel*, pp. 143–65. In this same letter, Saint-Preux comments on two hours he spent dreaming in Julie's garden, "two hours *to which I prefer no other time in my life*" (italics mine). And he characterizes these extraordinary feelings as being due to "the enjoyment

of virtue" ("la jouissance de la vertu"). It is interesting to consider the intersection between this privileged moment of pleasure in Julie's *virtuous* space and the hour "after" we discussed above.

25. I want to insist on two notions here: the coding of the pavilion as a scene of work and the justification of artistic activity as economically motivated. I am very taken with Claudine Herrmann's observation that George Sand "sought in every way to convince her readers that she was writing to earn a living." This (alibi) in the context of Stendhal's dictum, as she quotes him: "If a woman under fifty publishes, she places her happiness in the most terrible of lotteries; if she has the luck to have a lover, she will begin by losing him. I see only one exception: a woman who writes books ["fait des livres"] to feed or raise her family" *Les Voleuses de langue* [Paris: des femmes, 1976], pp. 32–33). The scorn heaped upon a woman who merely wishes to think is scored by Sand when she has Lansac comment on the activities in the pavilion: "'Tell me, are you in search of the philosopher's stone, or the most perfect form of government? I see that we are wasting time out in the world cudgelling our brains over the destiny of empires; it is all pondered and arranged in the pavilion in your park'" (chap. 31, p. 268). Colette ends her pastoral novel *Break of Day* on the word *oasis:* a space of production that reshapes the sexual into a book, open and without limits ("livre sans bornes ouvert"). What is the space of the female self who would imagine?

26. It could also be argued, of course, that while the prince is moved by his wife's plea to be saved from the telos of her desire—after all, he was the one who had encouraged her to do so—he no less leaves her to find her own (re)solution. In this sense, the "good" husband can't be distinguished from the "bad"; differences must be located in the wife.

27. "I am not afraid to compare the Fourth Part [of *Julie*] with the *Princesse de Clèves*" (Jean-Jacques Rousseau, *The Confessions,* trans. John M. Cohen [New York: Penguin, 1978], bk. 11, p. 505).

28. For altogether mysterious reasons, this line, "Ce fut une triste consolation pour eux que d'habiter le pavillon," which should be the second line of the second paragraph, is deleted in the English translation.

29. I am quoting here from Jacques Rustin's *Le Vice à la mode: Etude sur le roman français du XVIIIe siècle de Manon Lescaut à l'apparition de la Nouvelle Héloïse (1731-1761)* (Paris: Orphrys, 1979), p. 222. Sylvère Lotringer has brilliantly argued this point in "La structuration romanesque," *Critique* 26 (1970): 498–529.

30. Jacques Rustin concludes his book on that failure, reading in Rousseau "the instinctive refusal of the very future he outlines, the passionate denial of the great bourgeois dream that his dear Robinson had concretized

in his flourishing desert island: the absurd and wonderful, naive and diabolical dream of a *profitable paradise*" *Le Vice,* p. 242; translation mine).

31. To a Bénédict worried—for her—that Valentine will foolishly sign away her wealth, Valentine explains the symbolic project animating her: "'It is true that, for my own part, I would be content with this pavilion and a few acres of land. . . . But this property of which my sister was defrauded, this, at all events, I propose to bequeath to her son after my death: Valentin will be my heir. I propose that he shall be Comte de Raimbault some day. That is the object of my life'" (chap. 32, p. 276).

32. V. I. Voloshinov, *Le Marxisme et la philosophie du langage* (Paris: Minuit, 1977), p. 44; translation mine.

33. The inaugural paragraph of the narrative had already proposed, after a brief tour of the scene, "a cemetery a few rods square, enclosed by a quick-set hedge, five elms arranged in a quincunx and a ruined tower" as the exemplary social space of a *bourg* (chap. 1, p. 3).

34. William Empson, *Some Versions of Pastoral* (London: Chatto and Windus, 1950), p. 254.

35. *Indiana* (Paris: Garnier, 1962), p. 16; translation mine, italics hers.

36. Here in Sand's nostalgia for essentially feudal values we are indeed far from the demystified vision of Charlotte Brontë and the portrait, among other things, of a heroine who works.

Mary Poovey

Persuasion and the Promises of Love

In the last decade, several critics have made significant inroads into the old critical commonplace that Jane Austen's novels occupy a special aesthetic domain, that they constitute unassailable proof not only that their author was serenely oblivious to the French Revolution, Napoleon, and the political and ethical debates of her society but also that art can simply be free of politics and, even more important, of ideology.[1] But despite the eloquent arguments of such critics as Marilyn Butler and Alistair Duckworth, we still need more expeditions into the ideological hinterland of Austen's novels, not least because her artistry *has* so skillfully effaced all but the most subtle ideological trails. In this paper I want to describe some of the ways in which the form of Austen's novels is shaped by the ideological tensions that characterized early-nineteenth-century English society. And in the process, I'll also suggest some of the reasons why generations of Austen admirers have been so anxious to overlook the disturbing implications raised by even her most aesthetically satisfying novels.

For the purposes of clarity, I'll focus my discussion on *Persuasion,* but my observations about Austen's moral premises and aesthetic strategies are based on (and should illuminate) all six of her major novels. My most fundamental assumption here is that each of Austen's novels is a symbolic response to a real social situation, or, more precisely, that each novel attempts to resolve a fundamental contradiction within the ideology that governed English society in the first decades of the nineteenth century.[2] In Austen's novels, as in her society, the most pressing contradictions emerged from the challenge posed to the traditional vertical alliances of patriarchal society by the values and practices associated with bourgeois individualism.

By now it is unnecessary to argue that eighteenth- and

early-nineteenth-century England witnessed the triumph of individualistic values in nearly every sphere of theory and practice. During the eighteenth century philosophers, following John Locke, repeatedly stressed the capacity of human reason to reach "self-evident" truths through empirical observations and logic.[3] Individualism also governed political theory, economic principles and practice, and even, under the influence of Protestantism, religious beliefs and observations. Especially in the first decades of the nineteenth century, individualism acquired concrete form in the scientific achievements that rapidly began to transform society and labor. In an increasingly competitive economy, individual effort became the mark of past accomplishments and the guarantor of future success; this was the era of the "self-made man," when aristocratic privilege could finally be challenged on a wide scale by individuals with talent, opportunity, and the capacity for simple hard work. And finally, some scholars have argued that individualism also began to color the way in which personal happiness was conceptualized and courted.[4] Even among the upper classes, fewer marriages were "arranged" by parents, and even if economic considerations and consciousness of rank continued to play a prominent role in many personal alliances, an increasing number of novels celebrating "sensibility," "romantic love," and the prerogatives of the heart no doubt encouraged young women, in particular, to consider not only compatibility and income but also the affective intensity of romantic love as essential components of courtship and marriage.

But the values of individualism were not heralded everywhere as the harbingers of a new and golden age. Especially in the wake of the French Revolution, as many Englishmen contemplated with horror the political and ethical anarchy unchecked individualism might bring, there were repeated warnings from clergymen and laymen alike about the dangers of unleashing individual desire. Social unrest in England—exacerbated by such factors as crop failures, increasing unemployment, and the combination of rising rents and low wages—seemed to be evidence that the French menace was spreading to the English lower classes. And on the other side of the coin, the increasing agitation of employers and tradesmen for a repeal of restrictive tariffs, more efficient machines, and cheaper labor seemed to expose within the middle classes the specter of rampant acquisitiveness and thus less concern about national honor or paternal responsibilities to the poor than about higher profits. By 1817, the year of Jane Austen's death, William Wordsworth could complain that such stresses had completely altered the make-up of English values and society:

> I see clearly that the principal ties which kept the different classes of society in a vital and harmonious dependence upon each other have, within these 30 years, either been greatly impaired or wholly dissolved. Everything has been put up to market and sold for the highest price it would buy.... All ... moral cement is dissolved, habits and prejudices are broken and rooted up, nothing being substituted in their place but a quickened self-interest.[5]

Middle-class women were involved in this conflict of values in a particularly complex way. Even if they had never heard of Joseph Priestley, Josiah Wedgwood, or John Locke, they mouthed the truisms of individualism every time they read their children *Goody Two-Shoes* or taught them the importance of self-discipline.[6] In fact, the middle-class home—woman's "proper sphere"—was, in a very practical sense, the center of individualistic values, for there children were taught the habits that would help young men become efficient workers, and young women desirable wives. And there, in the domestic circle, in the unquestioning sympathy of familial love, a weary man could relax from his labor and the dehumanizing competition of the marketplace and revitalize himself for yet another day of hard and productive work. But, paradoxically, despite their inevitable participation in these values, middle-class women were not encouraged to think of themselves as members of this nation of individuals. Because their virtue (both their sexual fidelity and their moral exemplariness) was so crucial to the serenity and stability of the home, women were taught to practice propriety instead of displaying their intelligence, to perfect self-denial instead of cultivating self-assertion, and to think of themselves collectively—in terms of the universals of "the sex, the sex"—instead of contemplating individual autonomy, talents, capacities, or rights.

As the daughter of a country clergyman with numerous and strong ties to both the landed upper gentry and the entrepreneurial component of the middle classes, as an unmarried woman and a writer, Jane Austen occupied the very heart of such ideological tensions.[7] For as a dependent woman, Austen relied upon the protection and stability of traditional patriarchal society. But as a woman who wrote novels—for her own amusement, for the moral improvement of her readers, for praise, but for profit too[8]—Jane Austen recognized the imperatives of personal feelings and the rewards of individual effort. In her novels, one expression of her complex ideological position is a persistent ambivalence toward both the irresponsibility of such landed gentry as Lady Catherine de Bourgh and the ethical and epistemological relativity introduced by such individualistic characters as Mary and Henry Crawford. Another expression of these ideological complexities is Austen's tendency to appeal to the very individualistic desires which were potentially subversive to paternalistic society in an attempt to reinforce those traditional proprieties which, in governing woman's "sphere," provided women with a social role and sense of importance. For, given the liabilities of both individualism and paternalistic values, Austen's ideal solution was to use one system of values to correct the abuses of the other. But in doing so, Austen inadvertently exposed tensions inherent in both ideologies, and even in her symbolic resolution of these tensions, she laid bare the ideological configuration that was finally most damaging to women.

The moral ambiguities of individualism and propriety play a central role in all of Jane Austen's major novels. But nowhere are the complexities of these two ideologies more clearly set out than in *Persuasion,* Austen's last completed work. In *Persuasion* the fact that the social and ethical hierarchy superintended by the landed gentry is in a state of total collapse is clear not only from the fiscal and moral bankruptcy of Sir Walter Elliot but also from the epistemological relativity which is emphasized both thematically and formally. On the one hand, this individualism is granted narrative and even moral authority by the very quality of the narration: the centralizing narrative authority taken for granted in Austen's earlier novels has almost completely disappeared from *Persuasion,* [9] and in its place, we find a style inflected at nearly every level by the subjectivity of the heroine. But on the other hand, at the level of the novel's action, we repeatedly see the personal and social consequences of this epistemological relativism. In direct contrast to *Emma,* Austen's previous novel, *Persuasion* is punctuated by dramatic changes of locale, and each time Anne Elliot is forced to move, she experiences the vertiginous realization that "a removal from one set of people to another, though at a distance of only three miles, will often include a total change of conversation, opinion, and idea." [10] For Anne, whose twenty-seven years have been scarred by more losses than just of place, the first lesson of relativity is inescapable and painful, for it involves "knowing our own nothingness beyond our own circle." The second lesson, as the action of *Persuasion* proves, is that no judgment is absolute and that even such "objective" principles as "duty" may be susceptible to personal interpretation and abuse. Finally, the complexities of individualism are duplicated in the character of the hero, for the self-confidence, "ardour," and even "imprudence" that make Frederick Wentworth a "dangerous character" in Lady Russell's terms are the very qualities that make him attractive, facilitate his personal success, and help defend England against Napoleon.[11]

In *Persuasion* Austen uncovers the ideological complexities of this problem by exploring the relationship among "manners," "duty," and feeling. The first implication of their conjunction is obvious—and obviously problematic. Given the subjectivity of perception upon which the novel insists, it is clear that each individual's experience is personal and unique. It follows from this both that ethical judgment will be based at least initially upon appearances and that all moral evaluation will be at least implicitly subjective. The reader is exposed to the moral vertigo which results from these twin facts in the presentation of William Walter Elliot. Anne's early evaluation of Mr. Elliot is based upon the appeal of his "manners": "his manners were so exactly what they ought to be," Anne muses, "so polished, so easy, so particularly agreeable" (p. 143). But it is difficult for the reader to know whether Anne's assessment is morally authoritative or whether her response is simply colored by the admiration with which Mr. Elliot so frankly flatters her. Our judgment is further perplexed when, in the next chapter, Lady Russell's response endorses Anne's.

Every thing united in him; good understanding, correct opinions, knowledge of the world, and a warm heart. He had strong feelings of family-attachment and family-honour, without pride or weakness; he lived with the liberality of a man of fortune, without display; he judged for himself in every thing essential, without defying public opinion in any point of worldly decorum. He was steady, observant, moderate, candid; never run away with by spirits or by selfishness, which fancied itself strong feeling; and yet, with a sensibility to what was amiable and lovely, and a value for all the felicities of domestic life, which characters of fancied enthusiasm and violent agitation seldom really possess. (Pp. 146–47)

The problem for Anne, Lady Russell, and the reader is that Mr. Elliot has completely detached the superficial niceties of manners from any ethical underpinnings.[12] In the absence of both an objective, authoritative standard by which to judge such behavior and access to Mr. Elliot's hidden motivation, how are we to know what to make of such a character?

It is at least partly to avoid the implications of this dilemma that Austen never allows Anne to become seriously interested in Mr. Elliot; indeed, she almost immediately informs the reader why Anne does not succumb: "Mr. Elliot was rational, discreet, polished,—but he was not open. There was never any burst of feeling, any warmth of indignation or delight, at the evil or good of others. This, to Anne, was a decided imperfection" (p. 161). The problem with this narrative ruse, of course, is that it privileges the very subjectivity whose moral relativity we have just been led to identify. Before long, Mr. Elliot will be betrayed by Mrs. Smith, who *can* expose his secret design. But it is important to keep in mind that our first and lasting evaluation of him is influenced not by reference to an objective or absolute assessment of "manners" but simply by Anne's subjective preference for "feeling" and "warmth."

In order to resolve the problems introduced by yoking feeling to judgment, Austen relies upon the fact that by the time Mr. Elliot becomes an issue, the reader will recognize that Anne's intuitions are meant to be morally responsible and hence authoritative. Certainly Anne Elliot comes closer to being educated in both principles and feelings when the novel opens than is any other Austen heroine at that point. Like Elinor and Fanny, Anne has from her youth internalized sound moral principles, but more surely than either of them, she has also experienced and fully acknowledged the demands of her heart. Austen's opening description of Anne Elliot's maturity summarizes her unusual career: "She had been forced into prudence in her youth, she learned romance as she grew older: the natural

sequel of an unnatural beginning" (p. 30). But while this statement effectively suspends our estimation of Lady Russell's
original admonition to "prudence," it does not really explain
how even Anne's belated "romance" has acquired moral authority. Especially given both the vanity with which the desires
of Sir Walter, Elizabeth, and William Elliot are inflected and the
instability typical of the romantic inclinations of Benwick and
Louisa Musgrove, the reader must wonder why Anne's desires
are more reliable.

This question of the authority of Anne's intuitions and inclinations introduces a second facet of the dilemma of propriety.
As in *Mansfield Park,* Austen suggests in *Persuasion* that "proper" behavior may have a psychological dimension which eighteenth-century moralists rarely described. This, she implies, may
be the most significant paradox of propriety: not that manners
can be manipulated to express and accommodate desire but that
fidelity to "objective" principles may actually answer personal
needs, that doing one's "duty" may protect one against both
pain and unreasonable desire, and that virtuous behavior may
even provide rewards to substitute for the gratifications it denies. Because the reader does not directly witness Anne's first—
and, in many ways, most important—conflict, that struggle
between her first love for Wentworth and Lady Russell's "prudence," we are encouraged to accept Anne's decision as one of
the premises of the action and to evaluate it more by its consequences than by the principle it originally involved. Instead of
focusing on the correctness of Anne's first decision, in other
words, we are asked to understand *how,* given that decision,
Anne was able to discipline her desire. Lady Russell's argument—that marriage to Wentworth was "a wrong thing . . . hardly capable of success, and not deserving it"—finally influenced
Anne less than her confidence that in denying Wentworth she
was actually "consulting his good, even more than her own."
"The belief of being prudent and self-denying principally for *his*
advantage, was her chief consolation, under the misery of a

parting—a final parting" (p. 28). Anne has essentially been able to displace her own desire not simply by reference to an objective principle but by convincing herself that her love for Wentworth would be more adequately expressed by denying what they both so badly want.

One practical difficulty with this fundamental Christian truism is that in the world of *Persuasion* no one but Anne adheres to the morality of which it is a part. But a second, closely related problem is that if, in the absence of both an objective standard of moral absolutes and a communal consensus about ethical norms, an individual can identify "duty" only by the personal satisfaction it yields, then "principle" may easily shade over into unrecognized self-interest or self-defense. Austen raises the specter of this ethical chaos when she discusses the psychological function Anne's other exercises of "duty" play. When Mary asks Anne to Uppercross Cottage, for example, Anne leaps at the chance to act in compliance with the wishes of anyone else, to act according to any rule that seems to exist outside herself, and hence to be authoritative and reliable; Anne is simply "glad to be thought of some use, glad to have any thing marked out as a duty" (p. 33).

But as Austen describes Anne's situation, it becomes clear that one reason why Anne is so anxious to be dutiful is that the approbation which ideally attends selflessness is the only recognition which Anne is likely to receive. Repeatedly Austen points out that, except for the compassion of Lady Russell, Anne enjoys almost no domestic encouragement or support. "Excepting one short period of her life," the narrator tells us, "she had never, since the age of fourteen, never since the loss of her dear mother, known the happiness of being listened to, or encouraged by any just appreciation or real taste" (p. 47). Left behind by the Musgroves to nurse their child, Anne experiences "as many sensations of comfort, as were, perhaps, ever likely to be hers. She knew herself to be of the first utility to the child" (p. 58). The problem with this fusion of "duty" and "happiness" is twofold. On the one hand, because the "satisfaction of knowing herself extremely useful" (p. 121) is virtually the only happiness Anne has, she is driven to Christian virtue at least partly out of personal need. On the other hand, because this "satisfaction" is virtually her only assurance that what she does is right, Anne will be prone to identify "duty" primarily by the pleasure it brings. Austen never calls into question the authority of Anne's "satisfaction," but by showing us Mary, who happily tempers "duty" with personal convenience, and Mr. Elliot, for whom "'to do the best for himself' passe[s] as a duty" (p. 202), Austen does provoke us to ask how the selfless definition of duty is to be distinguished from its self-serving twin.

But because these questions simply cannot be answered without calling into question the moral authority of both feeling and duty, Austen substitutes for an examination of feeling a conflict focused on romantic love, for *this* conflict is certain to engage her readers' sympathy instead of arousing their judgment. With consummate narrative skill, Austen completely displaces the problem of the basis and nature of Anne's moral discrimination by foregrounding the difficulty with which she exercises her moral intuition in the service of love. Because Anne's situation and her feelings are both given as premises of the plot, Austen can focus on the inevitable confrontation between repressive social conventions and the desires of an individual heart—a confrontation which, unlike the ideologically charged question of duty, *can* be resolved realistically and in the terms of traditional values. Austen never actually examines the process by which Anne's feelings become moral, but because she does focus briefly on the emotional and psychological complexities of self-denial, she conveys the impression that Anne's first acquiescence to "duty" must have entailed soul-searching and a difficult weighing of alternatives. As in *Mansfield Park,* Austen asks us to sympathize with (although *not* to experience vicariously) the principle of self-denial. But unlike the earlier novel, *Persuasion* takes us beyond the subduing of desire to its struggle against social restraint. In so doing, Austen dramatizes the *power* of principled feeling and thus gives us an idea not only of what ideally should be but of how that triumph might actually come about.

So intent is Austen upon foregrounding the conflict between social conventions and moral desire that she dramatizes it not only at the level of content but also at the level of the narrative development itself. At this formal level Austen provides two narrative strains. The "private" plot of the novel corresponds to—and contains the story of—Anne's love for Wentworth. The "public" plot corresponds to repressive social conventions and contains the accounts of the interactions between the Elliots and Lady Russell, the Musgroves and their friends, Mr. Elliot and his relatives, and so on. Typically, we are imaginatively engaged in the private plot but must repeatedly experience a version of Anne's frustration when the public plot usurps center stage. The overall narrative action of *Persuasion* involves the gradual emergence of the private plot into the public sphere and its eventual triumph, just as the overall content involves the ultimate victory of personal needs and desires over social conventions. Thus the first three chapters of the novel confine the reader to the public plot, that domain of social intercourse which originally stifled Anne's emotions and into which her feelings will soon surface again. Even these chapters contain allusions to the hidden, private plot, but that plot does not emerge into visibility for the reader until the end of chapter 3, when we are suddenly exposed to Anne's turbulent consciousness: "A few months more, and *he,* perhaps, may be walking here" (p. 25). Only at this point do we begin to understand why Anne so intensely dislikes Bath and why she knows not only who Admiral Croft is but where he has seen action. And only at this point do we recognize that Anne is not a secondary character but the heroine and that it is *her* plot—as it is *her* desire—that is being repressed by the bustling vanity of her loquacious relatives.

What we are seeing here is Jane Austen's most sophisticated version of that narrative technique she employed at least as early as the conclusion of *Lady Susan*. Essentially, it consists of a shifting of different levels or planes of the fiction so that problems or contradictions raised at one level can be symbolically "resolved" by foregrounding another, nonproblematic level. In *Lady Susan* this "resolution," which is actually only a displacement, consists in the complete repression of the principal character, the thematic tensions, and the epistolary form itself. In *Pride and Prejudice*, just to give another example, it consists in the foregrounding of romance conventions in order to displace complexities raised by the introduction of realistic social and psychological details. And in *Persuasion* it consists in the double movement whereby the thematic contradictions raised by the problems of individualism and morality are displaced both by the foregrounding of other, apparently equivalent thematic complexities and by the shift of the reader's imaginative engagement to the conflict between the public and the private plots by way of the interest aroused by romantic love.

Austen makes this twin conflict seem as important as the epistemological conundrum it displaces by emphasizing the odds against Anne's happiness. Nearly all of the events of the first part of the public plot reinforce the anxiety we share with Anne that her love for Wentworth will be frustrated a second time. Louisa Musgrove actively pursues Wentworth, circumstances rarely bring the two old lovers together, Wentworth seems determined to misunderstand Anne, and Anne repeatedly retreats from exposure by defining her "duty" as self-effacement. She wants, she says repeatedly, only "to be unobserved" (p. 71), "not to be in the way of any body" (p. 84). Austen further underscores the likelihood that Anne's romantic hopes will be denied by giving us one revealing glimpse into Wentworth's consciousness. This passage constitutes one of the very few departures from the narrative's participation in Anne's point of view; and even though we eventually recognize its defensive tenor, it immediately serves to convince the reader that any struggle between Anne's sense of propriety and her feelings would inevitably lead to frustration and pain. "He had not forgiven Anne Elliot," the narrator tells us. "She had given him up to oblige others. It had been the effect of over-persuasion. It had been weakness and timidity. . . . Her power with him was gone for ever" (p. 61).

The turning point in *Persuasion*—both in Captain Wentworth's feelings and, as a consequence, in the dilemma which is foregrounded for the reader—occurs in the episode at Lyme. Before this episode, Wentworth has insisted that he does not love Anne, and thus the reader—confined, largely, to Anne's subjectivity—has remained engaged in the heroine's attempts to master her still active desire, not so much in the name of some authoritative principle but because circumstances—reality—make such self-discipline necessary. In order for the critical shift in the narrative to take place, two things must happen: Wentworth must realize that he still loves Anne, and this recognition must be conveyed to the reader. Only then will the primary conflict be between the private and the public plots instead of either between selfish and moral desire or between feeling and necessity; for only then will both lovers struggle to make social conventions express and accommodate their feelings. The delicate handling of this series of revelations generates the tension and the power of *Persuasion*.

Two illuminations are necessary for Wentworth to realize that his well-mannered consideration for Anne is actually the stirring of his old love: he must be reminded of Anne's powerful physical attractions, and he must learn to distinguish between simple selfishness in the name of principle and the genuine self-command which Anne can place in the service of others. Wentworth learns each of these lessons at Lyme. His desire for Anne is reawakened by the open admiration of Mr. Elliot, whom Wentworth suddenly sees as a rival. And his appreciation for Anne is given new meaning when Louisa, taking Wentworth's own ideal of "firmness" to its destructive extreme, jumps precipitously from the stile.

Eventually we discover that Anne's selfless and competent attendance upon the stricken Louisa had been instrumental in reanimating Wentworth's love, but we cannot immediately be sure of his feeling for Anne because Austen removes the heroine—and with her the reader—to Bath. But even though we are still basically confined to Anne's perspective, the two episodes immediately preceding Louisa's accident provide the reader with vantage points that materially enhance our appreciation of Anne. In doing so, these episodes settle once and for all any lingering questions about the moral authority of Anne's feelings; and thus they reinforce our hopes (if not our expectations) that her altogether admirable desire will ultimately be rewarded. Each of these episodes means something slightly different to Anne than to the reader. In the first, Wentworth's dialogue with Louisa about the nut, Anne understands only that the man she loves is rejecting her more "persuadable" character for Louisa's greater "firmness." The attentive reader, however, will hear that Wentworth's endorsement of "firmness" actually has a very personal stress. "It is the worst evil of too yielding and indecisive a character," he explains, "that no influence over it can be depended upon" (p. 88). From this statement it is clear that Wentworth does not really want "firmness"; he merely wants to be the one whose "influence" is longest felt. The second episode involves Anne's conversation with Captain Benwick. In his nourished grief Anne sees only a mirror-image of her own lingering sorrow, and in the "allowance of prose" she recommends, she sees only the medicine she has ineffectively administered to herself. But contrasting Anne's public self-command with Benwick's demonstrative and even occasionally eloquent suffering, we recognize how far Anne Elliot really is from indulging the pain she cannot help but feel. These two events reduce Anne to her lowest emotional state, for just as the first convinces her that Wentworth will never love her, the second shows her unequivocally that her love for Wentworth is not yet dead. For the reader, however, they establish the context in which Anne's self-command at Louisa's side can properly be appreciated.

In contrast to the emotional turmoil liberated in Lyme, Bath seems stultifying, claustrophobic. Its occupants and its formalities are artificial and repressive: Mr. Elliot's careful manners are of a piece with the "white glare of Bath," and, significantly, the only truth eventually emanates from Mrs. Smith's "dark bedroom," where Anne finally discovers Mr. Elliot's secret history. Anne's immediate problem in Bath is simply to stifle her feelings once again and to correct her first impression of William Walter Elliot. But Austen makes the month-long "imprisonment" in Bath occupy only three short chapters before she lets Anne know what the reader has already begun to suspect: that Wentworth will not marry Louisa, that he is "unshackled and free." Suddenly, emissaries from the country begin to pour into Bath, and, as Wentworth himself arrives, Austen sets in motion that intricate, almost musical movement through which, point counterpoint, Anne gradually discovers and elicits Wentworth's love.

In order to effect the resolution which will finally bring the private plot into public view, Austen forces Anne to take the initiative, to act upon her own feelings and her intuition of Wentworth's answering desires. Just as her ministrations in Lyme were completely in keeping with the behavior proper to a lady, so Anne's self-assertion is gentle, almost shy: she acts only indirectly, in other words, and only as opportunity allows. "Making yet a little advance," Anne greets Wentworth warmly at the Rooms (p. 181), and she uses their polite conversation to voice heartfelt emotions whose significance only he will fully understand: "One does not love a place the less for having suffered in it," she says, referring to Lyme (p. 184). From Wentworth's response, Anne realizes that "he must love her" (p. 186); and she sets out to dispel the only remaining impediment to their happiness—Wentworth's misinterpretation of her relationship with Mr. Elliot. Fortified by the information Mrs. Smith gives her, Anne resolves to be "more direct" with Mr. Elliot and more assertive with Captain Wentworth. She seizes an "opportunity" to "decidedly" voice her disinclination to accompany Mr. Elliot (p. 229); she openly alludes to her former relationship with Wentworth ("I am not yet so much changed" [p. 225]); and in her conversation with Captain Harville, after she becomes aware that Wentworth is listening, Anne "eagerly" claims the "privilege" for her sex of "loving longest, when existence or when hope is gone" (p. 235).

Even as Anne struggles to make social conventions accommodate and communicate her feelings, Captain Wentworth tries to do the same. Significantly, Austen makes the final reconciliation between Anne and Wentworth depend upon this self-reliant commander's accepting the "penance" and the anguish of the typical feminine situation. Discovering that others assume he is courting Louisa, Wentworth is hemmed in by social conventions, forced to wait passively while circumstances dictate his fate. Even after Louisa's turn to Benwick permits him once more to "exert" himself and follow Anne to Bath, Wentworth is still restricted to the feminine position of helpless onlooker and overhearer, and when he finally takes decisive action he does so indirectly, writing to Anne under the cover of another letter, even as she communicates with him under the cover of her conversation with Harville.

More than any previous Austen novel, *Persuasion* dwells on the reciprocity of love between man and woman. Wentworth's "agitation" is at least as frequently noted as Darcy's, and here this agitation is the counterpart to Anne's agitation, not its illustrative opposite. Perhaps even more important, however, is the fact that in *Persuasion* Austen is more attentive than ever before to the "situation" of women; placing Wentworth in that situation is a means both of making him do "penance" for his unthinking flirtation and of alerting the reader to the frustration such restriction can generate for anyone. Through the character of Mrs. Croft and Anne's conversation with Captain Harville, Austen addresses the implications of woman's social situation more explicitly than in any of her other novels. Recognizing that women are "rational creatures," Austen acknowledges that they are not always treated as such—either because of the patriarchal prerogatives which relegate "all the Marys and Elizabeths" to the single category of "wife" (p. 4) or because of the superficial dictates of propriety which insist that "fine ladies" have "no *right*" to comfortably endure hardships (p. 69), that all women with ruddy faces are "frights," and that the "model of female excellence" should take no initiative and have no desires of her own (p. 159). As Austen depicts them in this novel, women are imprisoned (p. 137), confined (p. 141), "surrounded and shut in" (p. 188), legally and sometimes physically crippled by the actions of men. While the obtrusive artifices of society make such restriction inevitable for every sensitive individual, Austen does not let us forget that women's position is especially cruel. Acknowledging that women love with special force, Anne will *not* grant Captain Harville's point that such fidelity is in woman's "nature." "It is, perhaps, our fate rather than our merit," she explains. "We cannot help ourselves. We live at home, quiet, confined, and our feelings prey upon us. You are forced on exertion. You have always a profession, pursuits, business of some sort or other, to take you back into the world immediately, and continual occupation and change soon weaken impressions" (p. 232). Jane Austen does not sound so very different from Mary Wollstonecraft here;[13] if she does not aggressively agitate for reform, she nevertheless rejects both the determinist argument from nature and the definition of propriety which makes women psychologically and emotionally one-dimensional.

In *Persuasion* Mrs. Smith exists to remind us both how restrictive a woman's situation can be and, no matter how severe that restriction, how resilient a woman's emotions potentially are. "Here was that elasticity of mind," Anne remarks to herself, "that disposition to be comforted, that power of turning readily from evil to good, and of finding employment which carried her out of herself, which was from Nature alone" (p. 154). Significantly, Mrs. Smith's "power" epitomizes female indirection; through Nurse Rooke she learns the secrets of the most private rooms of Bath, and she takes advantage of the momentary incapacities of others to lighten the burden of her own physical affliction. As unsavory as some critics have found her,[14] Mrs. Smith serves as the necessary secret agent of *Persuasion,* analogous to Mrs. Norris in *Mansfield Park* and Miss Bates in *Emma.* Because of Mrs. Smith, the novel's private plot surfaces and finally shatters the complacent round of evening parties and formal concerts. Mrs. Clay and Mr. Elliot are flushed, temporarily, from Sir Walter's home, and more satisfying, the romantic first love of Anne and Wentworth, now proved worthy through endurance and trial, moves the lovers into the prominence they have long held for the reader.

The conclusion of *Persuasion,* as many critics have noted,[15] does not promise general social reform, an authoritative system of values, or even "happiness ever after" for one loving couple. Kellynch will still eventually descend to Mr. Elliot, Mrs. Clay may even preside over the great hall, and the "dread of a future war" is as much Anne's legacy as is domestic affection. For Austen, despite the gratification of romance, Anne's happiness is less complete than was Elizabeth's, Fanny's, or Emma's: "Anne had no Uppercross-hall before her, no landed estate, no headship of a family" (p. 250). And because she will not attain these offices, her society can look forward to no reform from within. Captain Wentworth can restore Mrs. Smith's West Indian property, but he cannot put Anne in her mother's place. For Austen, individual education no longer seems powerful enough to initiate reform; when she celebrates the culminating happiness of Anne Elliot and Frederick Wentworth, it is in the context of the present—and, implicitly, the future—disarray of family and class.

Yet in some respects, because *Persuasion* promises less, it achieves more. As Nina Auerbach has pointed out, *Persuasion* endorses possibilities never before valorized in Austen's novels. Instead of attempting primarily to reform the landed gentry, Austen shows that money—and, along with it, power—is passing from this class to those who actively labor (and, not incidentally, whose labor defends England). Significantly, the naval officers in *Persuasion* are "associated with nature, openness, hospitality, romance,"[16] and as they gain social prominence, Austen lends a new practical power to individual feeling. And because the question of the *moral* authority of feeling is not so pressing as in *Mansfield Park* or even *Emma,* empowering this quality seems to presage general social reform, if only through the gradual erosion of the mannered repression epitomized in William and Elizabeth Elliot. In *Persuasion,* Austen also devotes more attention to those social groups whose absence is so conspicuous—and essential—in her earlier novels. Not only do Mrs. Smith and Nurse Rooke make more than a token appearance here, but at least twice Austen alludes to anonymous groups of workers going about their ordinary business or only briefly interrupted by their social superiors. When Louisa falls, for example, there suddenly appear "workmen and boatmen" who have gathered "to be useful if wanted; at any rate, to enjoy the sight of a dead young lady, nay, two dead young ladies, for it proved twice as fine as the first report" (p. 111). What is startling about this passage is not its proof that Austen was aware of the lower classes but its demonstration, at least momentarily, of the validity of the workmen's point of view ("nay, two dead young ladies"). Near the beginning of the novel, Austen's allusion to the lower classes is more stylized, but again—here as so seldom before—we glimpse a group of people who are not defined by their relation to the upper classes, who are neither agents of the central characters nor even particularly interested in them. Walking from Uppercross to Winthrop, Anne and her friends make the "gradual ascent through large enclosures, where the ploughs at work, and the fresh-made path spoke the farmer, counteracting the sweets of poetical despondence, and meaning to have spring again" (p. 85).

Such brief asides do not, of course, significantly widen the focus of Jane Austen's art, although they do generate that illusion of realistic depth also apparent in *Emma*. But in *Persuasion* these receding depths do not simply expand the sphere of influence of the upper classes. Instead, they are the subtle reminders of the limitations of that influence; in some fundamental sense, the vanity of Sir Walter Elliot is not only foolish but irrelevant, for his preening arrogance no more affects the behavior of his social inferiors than poetic pretensions alter the inexorable rhythms of nature. In *Persuasion* Austen suggests that the landed classes have forfeited their moral authority partly through extravagance and a failure in social responsibility. But their gradual displacement is also partly the consequence of the more general challenge to the stable system of values they ideally represented. This challenge is both political and epistemological; that the lower classes not only exist in their own right but have a distinct point of view provides a social context and content for the epistemological relativity implicit in the very title of *Persuasion*.

But even as it is important to appreciate the direction of Austen's last novel, it is also important to look closely at the inherent contradictions of the resolution she proposes. For even if the conclusion of *Persuasion* promises only temporary peace and limited happiness, its fundamental predication of a private sphere that can accommodate personal desire and yield personal fulfillment perpetuates many of the problems raised by her earlier works. And here we need to remember that these problems are not the stigmata of aesthetic failure but indices of contradictions within ideology itself. Essentially, *Persuasion* advances the argument, proposed as early as *Pride and Prejudice*, that personal feeling can be a moral force within society. Whereas in the earlier novel the way of life eventually ratified by desire was that of the landed gentry, in *Persuasion* feeling is put in the service of—and is gratified by—the much less certain lifestyle of those who earn their social position by ongoing personal effort. And whereas in *Pride and Prejudice* the aggressive energy of Elizabeth Bennet had to be chastened into love by circumstances and Fitzwilliam Darcy, in the later novel Anne Elliot's persistent love prevails, finally triumphing over both the pride of her lover and the institutional inhibitors that would disguise or deny it altogether. But by using individual feeling to inaugurate moral reform and by rewarding that desire with the conventional prizes of bourgeois society—marriage and (implicitly) a family—Austen is finally reproducing an unresolved (and in these terms unresolvable) contradiction inherent in her culture's values. This contradiction centers in the promise which is invariably fused to the demands of propriety; it centers, that is, in the concept of romantic love.

In Austen's society as today, romantic love purports to be completely "outside" ideology. It claims to be an inexplicable, irresistible, and possibly even biological drive which, in choosing its object, flaunts the hierarchy, the priorities, the inequalities of class society. Romantic love seems to defy self-interest and calculation as merrily as it ignores income and rank; as a consequence, if it articulates (or can be educated to do so) an essentially unselfish, generous urge toward another person, it may serve as an agent of moral reform: Louisa Musgrove might become a more serious person through loving Benwick, just as Henry Crawford seems launched on a significant course of moral improvement by his love for Fanny Price. But it is crucial to recognize that the moral regeneration ideally promised by romantic love is as individual and as private as its agent. In fact, the fundamental assumption of romantic love—and the reason it is so compatible with bourgeois society—is that the personal can be kept separate from the social, that one's "self" can be fulfilled in spite of—and in isolation from—the demands of the marketplace. Once one accepts this division of society into separate spheres, it is possible to argue that the gratification of personal desire will inaugurate social reform only if one assumes a social organization which structurally accommodates influence—at the smallest level, the nuclear family or, at a more general level, the patriarchal society modeled upon the family. If this concentric arrangement of "spheres" (which is, of course, actually a hierarchy of power) is disrupted or even seriously challenged—as it was during Jane Austen's lifetime—then the movement from individual fulfillment to social improvement becomes problematic. Ironically, even as the importance of imagining some program for social reform increases, the gap between the private and the public seems to widen and, completing the circle, the more necessary it becomes to believe that at least in the privacy of one's own home, the comfort of one's own family, and the personal gratification of one's own love, there can be deeply felt and hence "substantial" satisfaction.

In her realistic portrayal of the inevitable connections between the public and the private spheres and in her allusions to that complex society beyond the personal interests of her characters, Jane Austen exposes the fallacy of this claim for personal autonomy. Given the fact that living together in society necessarily requires dependence and compromise, the belief that one can withdraw or simply gratify oneself is morally irresponsible and, finally, practically untrue. Even Mrs. Smith has Nurse Rooke to connect her to the public world of Bath, and as Anne's prolonged and problematic courtship of Wentworth proves, even the most adamant personal desire must be defined within other social relations which are also configurations of power.

But in retaining the premises and promises of romantic love even as she makes this point, Jane Austen also perpetuates one of the fundamental myths of bourgeois society. For the model of private gratification which romantic love proposes is able to disguise the inescapable system of economic and political domination only by foregrounding those few relationships which flatter our desire for personal autonomy and power.

But the notion that romantic relationships actually have the kind of social power this emotional prominence suggests is actually an illusion: in the absence of institutions that actually link the private and the public spheres, romantic relationships, by their very nature, cannot materially affect society. And even more distressing, they cannot even provide women more than the kind of temporary, imaginative consolation which serves to defuse criticism of the very institutions that make such consolation necessary. For by focusing on courtship, the myth of romantic love tends to freeze the relationship between a man and a woman at its moment of greatest intensity, when both partners are seen (and see themselves) in the most flattering light and, perhaps most important, when women exercise their greatest power. Romantic love, in other words, seems to promise women in particular ongoing emotional intensity which ideally compensates for all the practical opportunities they are denied. But all it can actually yield is the immediate gratification of believing that this single moment of woman's power will endure, that the fact that a woman seems most desirable when she is most powerful will have an afterlife in marriage and in society. In Jane Austen's society, of course, romantic love did not alter the institutions of marriage or property or female dependence. And even the private gratification available in the domestic sphere could not live up to the intensity and power promised by romantic love, for as a wife and mother, a woman could at best act indirectly, through her children, through sacrifice, through duty. Romantic love, finally, had its most vital, most satisfying existence not in society but in art.

The problems these ideological contradictions generate in Jane Austen's novels are clear in *Persuasion*. In order to give individual feeling moral authority—in order, that is, to place romance in the service of propriety, social reform, and realism—Austen must posit the existence of separate spheres within her fiction. These separate spheres exist at the levels of content and form, and at each level the "private" sphere is theoretically linked to the "public" sphere by the influence bred of contiguity. But these private spheres are actually qualitatively different from the public spheres. Whereas the public spheres activate expectations generated by her readers' actual experiences in class society, whereas they are governed by psychological and social realism and the iron law of cause and effect, the private spheres open out onto romance: they activate and feed off expectations generated by reading other romantic novels; they arouse and satisfy desire. Each of Jane Austen's novels contains these special pockets of romance, not just in their most obtrusive form—those fairy-tale marriages that stop realism dead in its tracks—but in unexpected, out-of-the-way places as well. Thus in *Persuasion* Mrs. Smith remains miraculously, inexplicably cheerful against all the odds her social situation dictates—and even though in the same novel Elizabeth Elliot withers in much less barren soil. And in *Mansfield Park* Fanny and William Price keep domestic affection alive even though we see it atrophy and die in both squalid Portsmouth and immaculate Mansfield Park. At the level of form this division of the fiction into public and private spheres dictates the relegation of all the potentially subversive content to a marginal position or a carefully delimited arena. Paradoxically, the "private," romantic spheres of her novels—Marianne's passion for Willoughby, Darcy's love for Elizabeth, Fanny's yearning for Edmund, Emma's capacity to love, and Anne's fidelity to Wentworth—must all be rigorously contained, whether by the narrative distancing of *Sense and Sensibility,* the circumstantial frustration of *Mansfield Park* and *Persuasion,* or the encrustation of other, less admirable traits, such as we see in *Pride and Prejudice* and *Emma.* This separation is essential to protect romance from the necessarily deflating power of reality. But it is also essential, finally, in order to ensure that the demands of reality will be taken seriously, not merely repressed or imaginatively escaped. For even though the private sphere is the location and source of the greatest fulfillment Austen can imagine, so, too, does this sphere nourish the very subjectivity which is potentially fatal to the claims of other people, to morality, and, implicitly, to society itself.

In the absence of institutional opportunities for power, then, Jane Austen can effect the aesthetic resolution she desires only by *asserting* that the private sphere of domestic relationships can remain autonomous yet retain a unique and powerful moral dimension. Such resolution is only symbolic, of course, and as we have seen, it can be achieved only by repressing or displacing those questions which might jeopardize it. The fact that Jane Austen's novels contain almost no examples of happy marriages despite their inevitable culmination in a happy marriage summarizes both the price of such symbolic resolution and its attractions. For, on the one hand, for Austen to move chronologically, realistically, from the suspended promise of romantic love to a dramatization of the power relations inherent in marriage (dynamics which she portrays elsewhere with such ruthless wit) would be to risk depriving romantic love of its capacity to engage our imaginations by offering us flattering images of socially acceptable (if unavailable) power. And even more damaging, it would be implicitly to call into question both the consoling assumption that the emotional gratification of love makes up for the absence of other forms of self-expression and the enabling belief that the self-denial which society demands can yield the fulfillment that every person desires. But, on the other hand, freezing the narratives precisely at the height of emotional intensity endorses the promises of romantic love and, in so doing, enjoins the reader to imitate the moral love which the hero and heroine promise to bring to fruition in society. And equally important, the model of female power inherent in the premises of romantic love provides Jane Austen the artist a legitimate paradigm for the self-assertion with which she not only expresses her own desires but works in the service of moral reform.

The division of society and morality into separate public and private spheres was a solution particularly attractive to women. Because bourgeois society defined women in terms of their relationships—specifically, their conjugal or familial relationships—because they were granted power within the "proper sphere" of the home, and because the theory of "influence" postulated a model for the dissemination of domestic virtues throughout society, women had a particular investment in conceptualizing their space as special and as containing special moral authority. More generally, however, we should remember that the cultural ideology of which romantic love was but a part had at its heart the same separation of spheres we see in Austen's novel. For bourgeois ideology held out the promise that every individual would have an equal opportunity to work for equal material rewards, a promise which the limitations of natural resources and the inherent inequalities of class society rendered patently false. The existence of a private sphere, replete with the resources of boundless love and uncritical sympathy, essentially promised a compensatory substitute for other kinds of unavailable gratification—for men as well as women. Not incidentally, of course, the home further reinforced bourgeois ideology through this very compensatory gratification, for it provided competitive labor both an end and a means—a goal to defend and, within the patriarchal family, a nursery for the habits of propriety and the promises of romantic love. To the extent that we still defend these goals and seek these promises, we are still anxious to acquiesce in those resolutions which make them seem not only right but possible.

NOTES

1. Some of the most important contributions to our understanding of the role of ideology in Austen's novels include Marilyn Butler, *Jane Austen and the War of Ideas* (Oxford: Clarendon Press, 1975); Lloyd W. Brown, "Jane Austen and the Feminist Tradition," *Nineteenth-Century Fiction*

28 (1973): 321–38; Alistair M. Duckworth, *The Improvement of the Estate: A Study of Jane Austen's Novels* (Baltimore: Johns Hopkins University Press, 1971); Terry Lovell, "Jane Austen and the Gentry: A Study in Literature and Ideology," in *The Sociology of Literature: Applied Studies,* ed. Diana Laurenson (Hanley, England: Wood Mitchell & Co., 1978), pp. 15–37; and Warren Roberts, *Jane Austen and the French Revolution* (New York: St. Martin's Press, 1979).

2. By *ideology,* I do not mean false consciousness but rather the priorities that men and women establish among their needs and desires simply by living together in society and the explanations that they generate to make those priorities seem "natural." Although the prevailing system of values at any given historical moment inevitably serves to protect the interests of a powerful class or social group, ideology is enabling as well as restrictive; it *delimits* responses, in the sense not just of establishing boundaries but also of defining territories. And even though I speak of a "system" of values for the purposes of analysis, ideology is always dynamic, always being refined and revised by the kinds of developments to which I allude in this essay. For pertinent discussions of ideology see Terry Eagleton, *Criticism and Ideology: A Study in Marxist Literary Theory* (London: New Left Books, 1976), pp. 11–63; Fredric Jameson, *The Political Unconscious: Narrative as a Socially Symbolic Act* (Ithaca: Cornell University Press, 1981), pp. 17–23, 58–102; and Raymond Williams, *Marxism and Literature* (Oxford: Oxford University Press, 1977), pp. 55–74.

3. For a discussion of the philosophy and political theory of John Locke in this regard see Elizabeth Fox-Genovese, "Property and Patriarchy in Classical Bourgeois Political Theory," *Radical History Review* 4 (1977): 36–59.

4. One scholar who has so argued is Lawrence Stone, in *The Family, Sex and Marriage in England 1500–1800* (New York: Harper and Row, 1977).

5. Wordsworth to Daniel Stuart, 1817, quoted in Duckworth, *The Improvement,* p. 81.

6. See Isaac Kramnick, "Children's Literature and Bourgeois Ideology: Observations on Culture and Industrial Capitalism in the Later Eighteenth Century," in *Culture and Politics from Puritanism to the Enlightenment,* ed. Perez Zagorin (Berkeley and Los Angeles: University of California Press, 1980), pp. 203–40.

7. See Lovell, "Jane Austen and the Gentry"; and Donald J. Green, "Jane Austen and the Peerage," *PMLA* 68 (1953): 1017–31.

8. For a discussion of the publishing sales of Austen's novels and her

obvious interest in such matters see Jane Aiken Hodge, *Only a Novel: The Double Life of Jane Austen* (New York: Coward, McCann and Geoghegan, 1972), pp. 120–25, 207.

9. Norman Page describes the style of *Persuasion* as a "style in which narrative, comment, dialogue (presented in various ways) and interior monologue very frequently and unobtrusively merge into one another," in *The Language of Jane Austen* (New York: Barnes and Noble, 1972), p. 49.

10. *Persuasion*, in volume 5 of *The Works of Jane Austen*, ed. R. W. Chapman, 2d ed., 6 vols. (London: Oxford University Press, 1923–54), p. 42. Further citations in the text are to page numbers in *Persuasion*.

11. In *Jane Austen and the War of Ideas* Butler argues that Austen presents Wentworth critically, that he is a "well-intentioned but ideologically mistaken hero" whose "personal philosophy approaches revolutionary optimism and individualism" (p. 275). But this interpretation needs to be qualified both by the valorization Austen gives the naval meritocracy in *Persuasion* and by the personal pride she took in her brothers' advancement in the navy.

12. Duckworth also discusses Austen's loss of "faith in manners" (see *The Improvement*, pp. 181-82).

13. See Brown, "Jane Austen and the Feminist Tradition," pp. 321–38; and Nina Auerbach, "O Brave New World: Evolution and Revolution in *Persuasion*," *ELH* 39 (1972): 112-28.

14. See, for example, Duckworth, *The Improvement*, p. 192.

15. See ibid., p. 183.

16. Auerbach, "O Brave New World," p. 117.

The English Institute, 1981

SUPERVISING COMMITTEE

Irene Tayler (1981), Head, Massachusetts Institute of Technology
Leslie Fiedler (1981), State University of New York, Buffalo
Stephen Greenblatt (1981), University of California, Berkeley
James Cox (1982), Dartmouth College
Patricia M. Spacks (1982), Yale University
Charles Davis (1983), Yale University
Carolyn Heilbrun (1983), Columbia University
Murray Krieger (1983), University of California, Irvine and Los Angeles
Kenneth R. Johnston, Secretary, Indiana University, Bloomington

TRUSTEES

Geoffrey Hartman, Yale University
Charles A. Owen, Jr., University of Connecticut
Helen Vendler, Boston University

ARCHIVIST

David V. Erdman, State University of New York, Stony Brook, and New
York Public Library

The Program

Thursday, September 3, through Sunday, September 6, 1981
The Fortieth Meeting of the English Institute
    Thurs. 1:45 P.M.   Welcome: *Irene Tayler, Massachusetts Institute of Technology*
                          Perspective: *Cleanth Brooks, Yale University*

I.   Thomas Hardy
    Directed by J. Hillis Miller, Yale University
    Thurs. 2:15 P.M.   Topography and Tropography in Hardy
                          J. Hillis Miller, Yale University
    Fri. 9:30 A.M.   Historical Development in Hardy's Poetry: The Metrical Consequences of the 1860s
                          Denis Taylor, Boston College
    Fri. 11:00 A.M.   *Jude the Obscure:* Reading and the Spirit of the Law
                          Ramón Saldívar, University of Texas

II.   Literature and Liberty: In Honor of David V. Erdman, State University of New York, Stony Brook
    Directed by Margaret Higonnet, University of Connecticut
    Thurs. 3:45 P.M.   Wordsworth on Man, on Nature, and on Human Life
                          Thomas McFarland, Princeton University
    Fri. 1:45 P.M.   Liberty, Sorority, Misogyny
                          Jane Marcus, University of Texas at Austin
    Fri. 3:15 P.M.   The Representation of Revolution (1789–1815)
                          Ronald Paulson, Yale University

III.   Unreal Cities: Literary Visions of the Urban Landscape
    Directed by Blanche Gelfant, Dartmouth College
    Sat. 9:30 A.M.   From Myth to Mystery: The City of Defoe, Dickens, and Pynchon
                          Richard Lehan, University of California, Los Angeles

Sat. 11:00 A.M.	Torn Space: Joyce and Theories of Spatiality in the City *Philip Fisher, Brandeis University*
Sun. 9:30 A.M.	Illegible Cities: An Urban Tradition for American Writing *Alan Trachtenberg, Yale University*
Sun. 11:00 A.M.	The City in Afro-American Poetry *Michael Harper, Brown University*

IV. Representations of Women in Fiction
Directed by Patricia Spacks, Yale University

Sat. 1:45 P.M.	Female Plot: Women Writers and the Novel *Nancy Miller, Columbia University*
Sat. 3:15 P.M.	Daughters of Adam, Sons of Eve *J. Paul Hunter, University of Rochester*
Sun. 1:45 P.M.	Consensus *Elizabeth Ermarth, University of Maryland, Baltimore*
Sun. 3:15 P.M.	Altered Tales: (Re)production and the *Künstlerroman* *Susan Gubar, Indiana University, Bloomington*

Sponsoring Institutions

Columbia University, Princeton University, Yale University, University of Rochester, Claremont Graduate School, Rutgers University, Michigan State University, Northwestern University, Boston University, University of California at Berkeley, University of Connecticut, Harvard University, University of Pennsylvania, University of Virginia, Amherst College, State University of New York at Stony Brook, City University of New York Graduate Center, Brandeis University, Cornell University, Dartmouth College, New York University, Smith College, The Johns Hopkins University, Washington University, State University of New York at Albany, Temple University, University of Alabama at Birmingham, University of California at San Diego, Boston College, Brigham Young University, University of California at Los Angeles, University of California at Santa Cruz, Massachusetts Institute of Technology, Wellesley College, Stanford University, Indiana University at Bloomington, Tufts University, University of Colorado, Wesleyan University, Fordham University, University of Arizona, State University of New York at Buffalo.

Registrants, 1981

M. H. Abrams, Cornell University; Marianne Adams, The Bunting Institute; Ruth M. Adams, Dartmouth College; Marcia Allentuck, City University of New York; Paul Alpers, University of California at Berkeley; Elizabeth Ammons, Tufts University; Marilyn Arnold, Brigham Young University; Norman Sidney Asbridge, Central Connecticut State College; Nina Auerbach, University of Pennsylvania; James H. Averill, Princeton University

George W, Bahlke, Hamilton College; Teta Banks, University of the District of Columbia; Evelyn Barish, College of Staten Island, City University of New York; J. Leeds Barroll, University of Maryland, Baltimore County; Bertrice Bartlett, Stephens College; James Beaton, Middlesex School; Jerome Beaty, Emory University; John E. Becker, Fairleigh Dickinson University; Nancy M. Bentley, La Jolla Middle School; Sheila Berger, State

University of New York at Albany; Jerry M. Bernhard, Emanuel College; Warner Berthoff, Harvard University; Mae Blanch, Brigham Young University; Charles R. Blyth; Felicia Bonaparte, City University of New York; Carol M. Bove, Virginia Polytechnic Institute and State University; Paul Bove, University of Pittsburgh; Francis Z. Bowers, F.S.C., Manhattan College; Zelda Boyd, California State University; Frank Brady, City University of New York Graduate School; Peter Brand, Buffalo and Erie County Public Library; Leo Braudy, Johns Hopkins University; Pamela Brombery, Simmons College; Cleanth Brooks, Yale University; Gillian Brown, University of California at Berkeley; Judith Gwyn Brown; Maurice F. Brown, Oakland University; Robert M. Browne, Université de Montréal; Peter Brunette, George Mason University; Jane Britton Buchanan, Tufts University; Daniel Burke, F.S.C., La Salle College; Ronald Bush, Harvard University

Ruth A. Cameron, Eastern Nazarene; Barry John Capella, Orange County Community College; Kelly Cherry, University of Wisconsin at Madison; Harriet S. Chessman, Yale University; Martha Chew, Massachusetts College of Pharmacy and Allied Health Sciences; Jerome Christensen, State University of New York at Stony Brook; Jay Clayton, University of Wisconsin; Arlene Colbert, Smith College; Arthur N. Collins, State University of New York at Albany; Mason Cooley, College of Staten Island; James Cox, Dartmouth College; Patricia Craddock, Boston University; G. Armour Craig, Amherst College; Macy A. Creek, Central Piedmont Community; J. V. Cunningham, Brandeis University; William M. Curtin, University of Connecticut

Emily Dalgarno, Boston University; Charles Davis, Yale University; James Y. Dayananda, Lock Haven State College; Leonard F. Dean; Louise DeSalvo, Fairleigh Dickinson University; Andrea Dimino, Stanford University; Evelyn C. Dodge; E. T. Donaldson, Indiana University; Robert A. Donovan, State University of New York at Albany; Deborah Dorfman, State University of New York at Albany

Del Earisman, Upsala College; Martha Winburn England, Queens College, City University of New York; David Erdman, State University of New York at Stony Brook; Elizabeth Ermarth, University of Maryland, Baltimore; Doris Eyges, Wellesley College

Mary L. Fawcett, George Mason University; N. N. Feltes, York University, Toronto; Frances Ferguson, University of California at Berkeley; Mary Anne Ferguson, University of Massachusetts at Boston; Leslie Fiedler, State University of New York at Buffalo; Michael Finney, Youngstown

State University; Philip Fisher, Brandeis University; Angus Fletcher, City University of New York; Marcia M. Folsom, Wheelock College; Carolyn Forrey, Empire State College; John Burt Foster, Jr., Stanford University; Leslie D. Foster, Northern Michigan University; Ethel Frankel, Columbia University; Debra Fried, Cornell University; Michael Fried, Johns Hopkins University; Bettina Friedl, Harvard University; Herwig Friedl, Harvard University; Betty Griedman, Ohio State University; W. M. Frohock, Harvard University

Catherine Gallagher, University of California at Berkeley; Burdett Gardner, Monmouth College; Robert J. Garrity, Saint Joseph's College; Blanche Gelfant, Dartmouth College; Charisse Gendron, University of Connecticut; Julia A. Genster, University of California at Berkeley; Harry Girline, York University, Toronto; Robert F. Gleckner, Duke University; Richard M. Gollin, University of Rochester; Rita K. Gollin, State University of New York at Geneseo; Laura Gooch; Charlotte Goodman, Skidmore College; Terry H. Grabar, Fitchburg State College; Edward Graham, State University of New York–Maritime College; Stephen Greenblatt, University of California at Berkeley; Susan Greenstein, Western Washington University; Susan Gubar, Indiana University

Ann Halbrooks, Davidson County Community College; Violet B. Halpert, Fairleigh Dickinson–Madison; Elizabeth W. Harries, Smith College; Mason Harris, Simon Fraser University; Wendell V. Harris, Pennsylvania State University; Philip Harth, University of Wisconsin at Madison; Geoffrey Hartman, Yale University; Joan E. Hartman, College of Staten Island, City University of New York; Richard Haven, University of Massachusetts at Amherst; Michael Hays, Columbia University; Mary T. Heath; William Heath, Amherst College; Carolyn Heilbrun, Columbia University; Anne Herrmann, Yale University; Margaret R. Higonnet, University of Connecticut; William Bernard Hill, S.J., University of Scranton; Myra Hinman, University of Kansas; Elizabeth J. Hodge, New Jersey Institute of Technology; Daniel Hoffman, University of Pennsylvania; Margaret Homans, Yale University; Benjamin B. Hoover, Brandeis University; Bernard Horn, North Essex Community College; Chaviva Hosek, University of Toronto; Peter Hughes, Universität Zürich; J. Paul Hunter, University of Rochester

Mary Jacobus, Cornell University; Thomas L. Jeffers, Harvard University; Judith L. Johnston, Columbia University; Kenneth R. Johnston, Indiana University; Ben Jones, Carleton University; Iva G. Jones, Morgan State University; Nicholas Jones, Oberlin College; Phyllis Jones, Oberlin College;

Sidney C. Jones, Carroll College; Constance Jordan, Columbia University; Gerhard Joseph, Lehman College, City University of New York

Deborah Kaplan, George Mason University; Judith A. Kates, Harvard University; Norm Katz, Harvard University; Wyn Kelley, Stanford University; Joan T. Kelley, State University of New York at Stony Brook; Romey T. Keys, University of California at Los Angeles; Lawrence Kramer, Fordham University-Lincoln Center; Murray Krieger, University of California, Irvine and Los Angeles; Karen M. Kurt, Smith College

G. R. Lair, Delbarton School; Sonja Lallemand, State University of New York at Stony Brook; Berel Lang, University of Colorado; Richard Lehan, University of California at Los Angeles; Nancy S. Leonard, Bard College; Vivien Leonard, Rensselaer Polytechnic Institute; Herbert Levine, Franklin and Marshall College; Alan Levitan, Brandeis University; Dwight H. Lindley, Hamilton College; Joanna Lipking, Northwestern University; Lawrence Lipking, Northwestern University; Laurence S. Lockridge, New York University; Celeste Loughman, Massachusetts State College at Westfield; Joseph P. Lovering, Canisius College

Heather McClave, Harvard University; Thomas McFarland, Princeton University; Martha J. McGowan, University of Lowell; Michael L. McInturff, Birmingham-Southern College; Patricia McKee, Dartmouth College; Terence McKenzie, U.S. Coast Guard Academy; Cathleen T. McLoughlin, City University of New York Graduate Center; Diane McManus, Temple University; Irving Malin, City College of New York; Bette Mandl, Suffolk University; Darrel Mansell, Dartmouth College; Jane Marcus, University of Texas; Emerson R. Marks, University of Massachusetts; Robert K. Martin, Concordia University; Wendy Martin, Queens College, City University of New York; Leo Marx, Massachusetts Institute of Technology; Donald C. Mell, Jr., University of Delaware; Jay Ronald Meyers, East Strousburg State College; John H. Middendorf, Columbia University; J. Hillis Miller, Yale University; Nancy K. Miller, Barnard College, Columbia University; Michael Millgate, University of Toronto; J. Lawrence Mitchell, University of Minnesota; Kristin Morrison, Boston College; Rose Moss, Wellesley College; Steven Mullaney, Massachusetts Institute of Technology; Elizabeth Muther, University of California at Berkeley

John M. Nesselhof, Wells College; Clare H. Nunes, Princeton University

James Olney, North Carolina Central University; Charles A. Owen, Jr., University of Connecticut

Stanley R. Palombo, George Washington University; Julia DiStefano Pappageorge, New Hampshire College; Patricia A. Parker, University of Toronto; Reeve Parker, Cornell University; Stephen M. Parrish, Cornell University; Coleman Parsons, City University of New York Graduate School; Annabel Patterson, University of Maryland; John Pattinson, New Jersey Institute of Technology; Ronald Paulson, Yale University; Richard Pearce, Wheaton College; Roy Harvey Pearce, University of California, San Diego; Alan Perlis, University of Alabama; Sandy Petrey, State University of New York at Stony Brook; Burton Pike, City University of New York Graduate School; Ellen Pollak, University of Pennsylvania; Roger C. Poole, University of Nottingham; Mary Poovey, Swarthmore College; David Porter, University of Massachusetts at Amherst; Robert O. Preyer, Brandeis University; Wyatt Prunty, Virginia Polytechnic Institute and State University; Elaine Upton Pugh, Ohio State University

David Quint, Princeton University

Phyllis C. Ralph, University of Kansas; Jon R. Ramsey, Skidmore College; Donald H. Reiman, Carl H. Pforzheimer Library; Suzanne Relyea, University of Massachusetts at Boston; James Rieger, University of Rochester; Robin Riggs; Betty Rizzo, City College of New York; Jeffrey C. Robinson, University of Colorado; Ellen Cronan Rose, Massachusetts Institute of Technology; Ruth Rosenberg, Kingsborough, City University of New York; Charles L. Ross, University of Hartford; Phyllis Roth, Skidmore College; Rebecca D. Ruggles, City University of New York; Philip C. Rule, S.J., College of the Holy Cross; Sister M. Paton Ryan, RSM, Marquette University

Elaine B. Safer, University of Delaware; Ramon Saldivar, University of Texas at Austin; Irene Samuel, City University of New York; Sue Weaver Schopf, Harvard University; F. S. Schwarzbach, Washington University, St. Louis; Sayre P. Sheldon, Boston University; R. A. Shoaf, Yale University; Elaine Showalter, Rutgers University; Barbara Herrnstein Smith, University of Pennsylvania; Carol H. Smith, Rutgers University; Mark Trevor Smith, State University of New York at Stony Brook; Olivia A. Smith, Boston University; Thomas R. Smith, Rutgers University; Werner Sollors, Columbia University; George Soule, Carleton College; Ian Sowton, York University; Patricia Meyer Spacks, Yale University; John Daniel Stahl, University of Connecticut; R. M. Staley, State University of New York at Stony Brook; Susan Staves, Brandeis University; Holly Stevens; Catherine B. Stevenson, University of Hartford; Fred Stockholder, University of British Columbia; Albert Stone, Jr., Hellenic College; H. R. Stoneback, State

University of New York at New Paltz; Gary Lee Stonum, Case Western Reserve University; Margaret Storch; R. F. Storch, Tufts University; William W. Stowe, Wesleyan University; Helen Stroupe; Marcia Stubbs, Wellesley College; Stanley Sultan, Clark University

Yosif A. Tarawneh, Yarmouk University; Irene Tayler, Massachusetts Institute of Technology; Dennis Taylor, Boston College; Ruth Z. Temple, City University of New York Graduate School; John J. Tobin, Boston State College; Alan Trachtenberg, Yale University; Lewis A. Turlish, Bates College

Thomas Vargish, Dartmouth College; Helen Vendler, Harvard University and Boston University; Virginia Barrett Villa, Greater Hartford Community College; Andrew Von Hendy, Boston College

Karen L. Wadman, University of Minnesota; Eugene M. Waith, Yale University; Melissa G. Walker, Mercer University; Emily M. Wallace, Curtis Institute of Music; Aileen Ward, New York University; Miriam Weinberg, Fordham University; Sister Mary Anthony Weinig, Rosemont College; Philip M. Weinstein, Swarthmore College; Martha Westwater, Mt. St. Vincent University; Carolyn Williams, Boston University; Judith Wilt, Boston College; Hana Wirth-Nesher, Lafayette College; David Wise; Judith Bryant Wittenberg, Simmons College; Cynthia Griffin Wolff, Massachusetts Institute of Technology; Martha Woodmansee, Northwestern University